Register for Free Membership t

s o l u t i o n s @ s y n g r e

Over the last few years, Syngress has published many best-selling and critically acclaimed books, including Tom Shinder's *Configuring ISA Server 2000*, Brian Caswell and Jay Beale's *Snort 2.0 Intrusion Detection*, and Angela Orebaugh and Gilbert Ramirez's *Ethereal Packet Sniffing*. One of the reasons for the success of these books has been our unique **solutions@syngress.com** program. Through this site, we've been able to provide readers a real time extension to the printed book.

As a registered owner of this book, you will qualify for free access to our members-only solutions@syngress.com program. Once you have registered, you will enjoy several benefits, including:

- Four downloadable e-booklets on topics related to the book. Each booklet is approximately 20-30 pages in Adobe PDF format. They have been selected by our editors from other best-selling Syngress books as providing topic coverage that is directly related to the coverage in this book.

- A comprehensive FAQ page that consolidates all of the key points of this book into an easy to search web page, providing you with the concise, easy to access data you need to perform your job.

- A "From the Author" Forum that allows the authors of this book to post timely updates links to related sites, or additional topic coverage that may have been requested by readers.

Just visit us at **www.syngress.com/solutions** and follow the simple registration process. You will need to have this book with you when you register.

Thank you for giving us the opportunity to serve your needs. And be sure to let us know if there is anything else we can do to make your job easier.

Hacking a
Terror Network

THE SILENT THREAT OF COVERT CHANNELS

Russ Rogers

Matthew G. Devost Technical Editor

KEY	SERIAL NUMBER
001	HJIRTCV764
002	PO9873D5FG
003	829KM8NJH2
004	GHC432N966
005	CVPLQ6WQ23
006	VBP965T5T5
007	HJJJ863WD3E
008	2987GVTWMK
009	629MP5SDJT
010	IMWQ295T6T

PUBLISHED BY
Syngress Publishing, Inc.
800 Hingham Street
Rockland, MA 02370

Hacking a Terror Network: The Silent Threat of Covert Channels

Printed in the United States of America
1 2 3 4 5 6 7 8 9 0
ISBN: 1-928994-98-9

Publisher: Andrew Williams   Page Layout and Art: Patricia Lupien
Acquisitions Editor: Gary Byrne   Copy Editor: Adrienne Rebello
Technical Editor: Matthew G. Devost Cover Designer: Michael Kavish

Distributed by O'Reilly Media, Inc. in the United States and Canada.
For information on rights and translations, contact Matt Pedersen, Director of Sales and Rights, at Syngress Publishing; email matt@syngress.com or fax to 781-681-3585.

Acknowledgments

Syngress would like to acknowledge the following people for their kindness and support in making this book possible.

Syngress books are now distributed in the United States and Canada by O'Reilly Media, Inc. The enthusiasm and work ethic at O'Reilly are incredible, and we would like to thank everyone there for their time and efforts to bring Syngress books to market: Tim O'Reilly, Laura Baldwin, Mark Brokering, Mike Leonard, Donna Selenko, Bonnie Sheehan, Cindy Davis, Grant Kikkert, Opol Matsutaro, Steve Hazelwood, Mark Wilson, Rick Brown, Leslie Becker, Jill Lothrop, Tim Hinton, Kyle Hart, Sara Winge, C. J. Rayhill, Peter Pardo, Leslie Crandell, Valerie Dow, Regina Aggio, Pascal Honscher, Preston Paull, Susan Thompson, Bruce Stewart, Laura Schmier, Sue Willing, Mark Jacobsen, Betsy Waliszewski, Dawn Mann, Kathryn Barrett, John Chodacki, Rob Bullington, and Aileen Berg.

The incredibly hard-working team at Elsevier Science, including Jonathan Bunkell, Ian Seager, Duncan Enright, David Burton, Rosanna Ramacciotti, Robert Fairbrother, Miguel Sanchez, Klaus Beran, Emma Wyatt, Rosie Moss, Chris Hossack, Mark Hunt, and Krista Leppiko, for making certain that our vision remains worldwide in scope.

David Buckland, Marie Chieng, Lucy Chong, Leslie Lim, Audrey Gan, Pang Ai Hua, and Joseph Chan of STP Distributors for the enthusiasm with which they receive our books.

Kwon Sung June at Acorn Publishing for his support.

David Scott, Tricia Wilden, Marilla Burgess, Annette Scott, Andrew Swaffer, Stephen O'Donoghue, Bec Lowe, and Mark Langley of Woodslane for distributing our books throughout Australia, New Zealand, Papua New Guinea, Fiji Tonga, Solomon Islands, and the Cook Islands.

Winston Lim of Global Publishing for his help and support with distribution of Syngress books in the Philippines.

Author

Russ Rogers (CISSP, CISM, IAM, IEM) is a Co-Founder, Chief
Executive Officer, and Principal Security Consultant for Security
Horizon, Inc., a Colorado-based professional security services and
training provider and veteran-owned small business. Russ is a key
contributor to Security Horizon's technology efforts and leads the
technical security practice and the services business development
efforts. Russ is a United States Air Force Veteran and has served in
military and contract support for the National Security Agency and
the Defense Information Systems Agency. He served as a Certified
Arabic Linguist during his time in the military and is also the
editor-in-chief of *The Security Journal* and occasional staff member
for the Black Hat Briefings. Russ holds an associate's degree in
applied communications technology from the Community College
of the Air Force, a bachelor's degree from the University of
Maryland in computer information systems, and a master's degree
from the University of Maryland in computer systems management.
Russ is a member of the Information System Security Association
(ISSA) and the Information System Audit and Control Association
(ISACA). He also serves as the Professor of Network Security at the
University of Advancing Technology (uat.edu) in Tempe, AZ. Russ is
the author of *Hacking a Terror Network: The Silent Threat of Covert
Channels* (Syngress Publishing, ISBN: 1-928994-98-9). He has con-
tributed to many Syngress books, including *Stealing the Network:
How to Own a Continent* (ISBN: 1-931836-05-1), *Security Assessment:
Case Studies for Implementing the NSA IAM* (ISBN 1-932266-96-8),
WarDriving, Drive, Detect, Defend: A Guide to Wireless Security (ISBN:
1-931836-03-5), and *SSCP Study Guide and DVD Training System*
(ISBN: 1-931846-80-9).

Technical Editor

Matthew G. Devost is President and CEO of the Terrorism Research Center, Inc., overseeing all research, analysis, assessment, and training programs. In addition to his duties as President, Matthew also provides strategic consulting services to select international governments and corporations on issues of counter-terrorism, information warfare and security, critical infrastructure protection, and homeland security. He cofounded and serves as Executive Director of Technical Defense, Inc., a highly specialized information security consultancy as well as holds an Adjunct Professor position at Georgetown University. Previously, Matthew was the Director of Operations for Professional Services at Counterpane Internet Security as well as Security Design International, Inc., where he led a team of technical information security consultants providing vulnerability assessments and information security consulting services to international corporations and governments. In addition, he worked as the Director of Intelligence Analysis for iDefense, a Senior INFOSEC Engineer at SAIC, and as a U.S. Customs Inspector.

Matthew has appeared on numerous national and international television programs, as well as dozens of other domestic and international radio and television programs as an expert on terrorism and information warfare and has lectured or published for the National Defense University; the United States Intelligence and Law Enforcement Communities; the Swedish, Australian, Japanese, and New Zealand governments; Georgetown University; American University; George Washington University; and a number of popular press books and magazines, academic journals, and more than 100 international conferences. He is co-author of (Syngress, ISBN: 1-931836-11-6).

He serves on the Defense Science Board Task Force on Critical Homeland Infrastructure Protection. Matthew serves as a Senior Adviser to the Airline Pilots Association National Security Committee, sits on the Board of Directors as a Founding Member of the Cyber Conflict Studies Association, and is an adjunct member of the Los Angeles Terrorism Early Warning Group. He holds a B.A. degree from St. Michael's College and a Master of Arts Degree in Political Science from the University of Vermont.

CD Creator

Michele Fincher (IAM, IEM) is a Security Consultant and trainer for Security Horizon, Inc., a professional security services and training provider and veteran-owned small business. Prior to joining Security Horizon, Michele worked for a research and software development firm and assisted in the development and instruction of its Steganography Investigator Training Course. Michele is a United States Air Force veteran. She served as a Communications Electronics officer and finished her career as an Assistant Professor at the United States Air Force Academy. Michele holds a Bachelor of Science from the United States Air Force Academy and a Master of Science from Auburn University.

About the CD

Could our story actually happen? It's not too difficult to imagine, given the current number and availability of tools that facilitate covert communications and the intentions of criminals and terrorists. The CD-ROM accompanying this book is intended to let you participate as both creator of these hidden messages and as an investigator.

Chapter 1 contains a simple document that provides examples of null ciphers that all result in the same hidden message. Given the message you wish to convey, can you create additional null ciphers that pass for legitimate communication? Chapter 8 is Salah's Web site containing information about the first attack. As a member of the terrorist group, are you able to take the information provided and extract the message? Chapter 15 contains folders from Layla's drive. By using the same scanning tool introduced in the book, what conclusions can you draw about Layla's activities?

Finally, we have provided you with more than 100 tools for creating and detecting covert communications for Windows, UNIX, Macintosh, and DOS. These are just a sample of what is freely available today—how you choose to use them is up to you.

Contents

It was unbearably hot outside. The summers in Ramadi, Iraq seemed to get hotter and hotter with each passing year, and this year, in his city, it was no exception as the mercury pegged out at 42 degrees Celsius. Sweat trickled down his back as he navigated through the dirty side streets of the city—the winding avenues coated with dust and poverty. After turning a final corner, he adjusted the Kufi against his hot, damp head and ducked into a public coffee shop. Choosing a table next to the front window, he set the envelope he was carrying next to a public computer terminal. It wasn't long before a waiter approached his table once he was seated.

He woke up choking on a sob, bathed in sweat. It was late at night (or very early in the morning depending on your perspective) and this time it wasn't the thick heat that had him sweating. Salah had endured many nights like this since his childhood, nights filled with nightmares of his father beating him. He ran his hand across his forehead and pulled back his long hair. Staring out the window, he tried to catch his breath and calm his rapidly beating heart. Father was dead, why couldn't he relax?

Salah unlocked the dead bolt and stepped through the doorway into the barren space beyond. The apartment held no real emotional sway over Salah; it was a quaint dwelling, but only temporary. Walking across the stained brown carpet, he stopped at the window near his bed to look out over the city. The university was only a few blocks away, but even for a single person walking, it was sometimes difficult to navigate the traffic below. He watched silently as the cars on the road below battled to dominate the road, relentlessly working to carry their occupants home.

3: Making Friends 36

"I'm telling you, dude, I've never met a woman who knows so much about networking concepts," Jeremy said. "She's amazing. I could totally use her help. I'm dying here! Have you seen how well she does on those tests?"

4: One Step Closer 43

"Welcome, Jimmy. Won't you please have a seat?" asked the young woman. "Someone will be with you in a moment for your interview. Please let me know if you need anything." Jimmy watched her as she left the room. She was attractive and he was enjoying watching her hips sway as she walked away. "You're not here for the women," he told himself quietly and tried to get his mind back on what he was really here to do—get a job.

5: Over the Line 47

It was already dark outside when he shut the apartment door behind him and locked it again. He had spent more time at school today than intended, but he reminded himself that some things were necessary. Aside from his normal homework, Salah had been doing some research trying to design a better method for covert communication with his team over the Internet.

6: Images of Death 63

It was dark. The clock next to the bed cast an eerie glow across her face as she looked at the time. It was 1:56 a.m. Looking across the small room, she noticed that the small television was still on. She had apparently fallen asleep watching CNN. She was lying awkwardly across the small bed, her clothes still on. The fog in her head was clearing now and she remembered: There had been an attack in the Middle East.

7: The Real Assignment 68

"Jeremy!" A voice shot across the office. Jeremy stood up to look over the cubicle wall and watched as his partner walked across the office toward his cubicle. He was truly enjoying his new life in a real job. His security clearance had been approved about five months earlier, enabling him to start working on actual cases versus sitting in an uncleared facility studying investigation training manuals. When Jeremy had walked into this office for the first time, he found the work already piling up for him, since apparently, the other employees had been anticipating his arrival. But much to his own disappointment, he found all the initial cases to be exercises in futility. The other team members had already grown accustomed to those cases that were likely to be fraudulent and had graciously taught Jeremy his first real lesson on the new job.

8: Creating the Code 85

Salah woke up the next morning with the sky still dark outside and his head pounding. The alarm clock on the nightstand next to his bed seemed to be blaring much louder than normal. As frustrated as he might be, he knew that the clock was set to perpetually ensure that he was up in time for the morning call to prayer and so he took a deep breath and tried to calm his weary mind. His body was exhausted as well. He felt as if he had slept very little during the night.

9: Over the Edge 95

Jimmy woke up to the sound of the small alarm clock going off. Glancing at the clock he noticed that it was 6:30 in the morning. He was due to report to the ship for his next cruise early this afternoon, but until then he would relax. The apartment he lived in was small with very few furnishings because Jimmy had no real intentions of being in this location much longer. In fact, today might very well be the last time he ever slept in this bed. He smiled to himself. The time was almost here.

10: Biding Time 106

Jimmy lay in his bunk staring at the ceiling and pondering the items on his mental to-do list. He was off duty for the day, which meant that he had time for some much-needed reflection. He relished the rare solitude as his roommate was somewhere on the ship, enjoying his day off as well. It had been just over six months since he had started working full-time on the ship, and he was now fully trusted by nearly every crew member on board. He thought to himself about how easy it had been to get hired and become accepted as a part of the team.

11: Covert Channels 129

Jeremy sat up slowly. He had fallen asleep at his desk, and the office was deserted with the exception of the cleaning crew. They must have been especially noisy tonight as they awakened him when they came in the front security door. His coworkers had called him crazy when he mentioned that he would be working this weekend, saying that he had lost his mind and should be out somewhere trying to have some fun. But they apparently just didn't understand. To Jeremy, this was fun.

12: Facing the Truth 164

Layla lay in her bed, crying again. She was desperate; her mind was split down the center into two completely different and conflicting mind-sets, and she was definitely losing it. One side of her had been created years earlier by her father and tormented her day and night. She had a purpose based in hate, excused by religion, and a requirement for her to be cold and uncaring. The other side of her longed to be gentle and tolerant; this side of her wanted to forget the failure of what had been her childhood and develop a new purpose in life. Her youth had been stolen from her, as had her future.

13: Taking Command 175

It can be difficult to sit idly by and wait for the inevitable. The truth can be standing directly in front of you, staring you in the face, and still be invisible when your mind refuses to accept it. Every man is born with some degree of hope and faith, but there's always a limit; the line where the gap has grown too wide for even a leap of faith. Discovering where your own internal limits are can be frustrating and painful. Believing that someone you depend on and trust let you down completely is hard to accept. Our own internal emotional defenses refuse to allow the acceptance of those realities. But in time, the truth becomes impossible to ignore, and that's when the anger sets in.

14: Racing the Clock 201

Jeremy watched silently from a chair across the desk as his partner continued his conversation with the last cruise line company. They had been calling each and every company over the last 90 minutes. He had been surprised to find so many cruise line companies operating in the United States, many of which he had never heard of before. Some went up North to the colder climates to show passengers the whales and icebergs. Others were content with endlessly cruising the tropical climates down South. There were even some companies that took extended cruises to Europe or the Mediterranean.

15: Losing Control 215

"Jesus Christ, Jeremy!" Neil was obviously perturbed. "I need you in the office, and I need you here now."
"Okay, calm down. I'm on my way." Jeremy held the phone closer to his ear. It was difficult to hear Neil's voice above the cars driving by on the street next to him. He stood up from his table on the patio of the small eatery he was at and motioned to the waiter that he would be right back. Opening the door to the inside of the restaurant, he headed to the men's room. "Tell me what's going on. I need to pay my lunch tab, and I'll be right in."

16: Heightened Motivation .238

Jimmy was fuming inside as he sat in the old wooden chair in the rundown restaurant. The food here was awful, but then again, he hadn't found any food in the local establishments that appealed to his Middle Eastern palette. A small but steady stream of locals came and went as he sat at the table looking out the window into the dirty street. They were content enough to eat the food. Perhaps it's just an acquired taste, he thought to himself.

17: Chasing Ghosts 246

Jeremy pressed the small white button just outside the door and waited patiently. He had the clearance required to enter the area, but his badge hadn't been added to the system yet. It just meant that he had to wait until someone came and let him in—not too much of an issue. He heard the sound of the lock click from the inside and the door swung open and the face of a woman appeared. She looked as if she was in her mid-40s and had likely been working in the government for some time. Her clothes were professional, yet casual by most standards. "Yes, can I help you?"

18: Taking Back Control 284

Jimmy sat back in the hard wooden chair and waited as the web browser loaded. He had quickly become a regular at the library in this small town, using the computer several times a day, sometimes for hours at a time. His resolve and motivation had been strengthened when the perfect location for the second phase of attacks had occurred to him. The inability of the local authorities to secure the area, combined with the sheer number of Americans, made the target attractive. He had spent time wondering why this particular idea had never occurred to him or Salah before that moment.

19: Vengeance for Deceit 299

"Sources claim that federal officials have two of the terror suspects currently in custody in the Washington, D.C., area. One of the suspects is said to have been the mastermind of the recent failed attacks on three American cruise ships, and the other was captured while trying to escape."

20: Eliminating False Positives 306

Jeremy flicked his pencil into the air again with his left hand and caught it rather precariously with the two middle fingers on his right hand. His documents were strewn across his desk haphazardly, unorganized piles of information. He had been going over the information repeatedly for what seemed like weeks now. Regardless of how much time he looked at the evidence, it never changed.

21: Gaining a Finger Hold 315

"So how many target images have we actually passed off to the agency now?" Jeremy asked Tyler. The two men were sitting with Neil at a small sandwich shop around the corner from their office. They had been working on finding suspect images for weeks, and he was beginning to feel as if there was simply no way they were going to stop this attack.

22: Compressing Timelines 320

The days were getting cooler, even in this small, dry Mexican town. Jimmy stared out the cracked window of his small hotel room at the night sky. His appearance had changed drastically over the last two months. He had let his black hair grow longer, and it now hung down just above his shoulders. A dark beard now covered his young face. He kept it trim and clean, but it made him look more like the locals.

23: A Plan Comes Together 335

The old junker ground to a halt in front of a small petrol station roughly 150 miles from where Jimmy had started. He had bought the only vehicle available in town, an old pickup truck whose rust-covered surfaced hinted that blue had been the original color. It had been just after midnight when he actually left the small town for good, following the small road out of town for 15 miles until he met with the main highway that ran south.

24: Turning Fiction into Reality 343

The story you've just finished reading was completely fictional. Well, at least the story itself was fictional. The technology was very real and accessible today on the Internet. The unfortunate, and very scary part about all this is that the story fails to touch on the reality of the situation. For years, the Western world has ignored the threat of destructive activities over the Internet. Our perception has been that the technology is neither known nor prevalent in the parts of the world we consider to be dangerous.

Glossary 357

Foreword

From a counterterrorism perspective, discovering terrorist communication networks and methods is extremely important. Terrorists have demonstrated the capability to exchange messages that vary from archaic (using human couriers) to technologically advanced using "virtual dead-drops." The popular press is full of stories regarding terrorists communicating using networks like the Internet, and there is practical evidence to support the stories that have been discovered on terrorists' desktops and laptops from the U.S. to Europe to Pakistan and Afghanistan.

The Internet provides a viable and varied communication forum for terrorists, and the global distributed nature of the Internet makes attribution nearly impossible in many cases. We know that after he was profiled from his first flight, the shoe bomber is alleged to have sent e-mail to superiors asking if he should continue with his attack. We know that bin Laden himself used satellite phones for communication and drafted e-mail messages to coordinate activities with remote cells or to handle administrative matters within Al Qaeda. We know that terrorists have demonstrated an ability to adapt, and it is safe to assume that their communication capabilities will also adapt, enabling them to communicate more securely.

In *Hacking a Terror Network*, Russ Rogers uses a fictional scenario to demonstrate how terrorists may use the Internet to coordinate and launch a new series of terrorist attacks. While the scenario may be fictitious, the techniques and technologies that Russ uses are drawn straight from the computer security world, making this not only an interesting literary read but also a technical manual on how covert channels work and how law enforcement and intelligence organizations can go about discovering and defeating them. This book is packed with real-life examples of how tools work, including screenshots and narrative tutorials. Both amateurs and seasoned security professionals will benefit from reading this book.

Russ's experience within the U.S. Defense Department, as part of the intelligence community, and as an expert in the computer security industry uniquely positions him to make this an interesting and technically viable read. I've often enjoyed my conversations with Russ on a variety of topics at Black Hat and other security industry conferences. He is known for having his finger on the pulse of the industry and for being able to identify trends and emerging issues. The story entertained me, and as a security expert, I can honestly say I learned something from reading this book.

With the arrest of Muhammad Naeem Noor Khan in Pakistan in the summer of 2004, we got a rare glimpse into the logistical and technological effort put forth by Al Qaeda by observing the activities of one of its top technologists. With the Madrid attacks, we saw how terrorist organizations can be self-organizing based on principles that look a lot like scientific theories on emergence. The Internet provides the perfect foundation for another adaptation where cells are self-organizing based solely on interaction over the Internet. What if a lone computer scientist living in the West wanted to join Al Qaeda? To whom would this person turn? How would this person communicate with his or her peers and Al Qaeda leadership? This book provides insights into how such a terrorist connection could be made. Perhaps it is already happening, and failure to give theories and scenarios like those presented in this book appropriate credence could have catastrophic consequences.

Aside from using the Internet as a communication network, terrorists also use it to case potential targets, to manufacture and distribute propaganda, to recruit supporters, and to solicit funds. How much more sophisticated the terrorists become remains to be seen, but *Hacking a Terrorist Network* shows how Internet technology can be used to plan an attack.

—Matthew G. Devost
President and CEO
Terrorism Research Center, Inc.

There is a plot under way to attack American interests. A decade-old grudge against the West comes to fruition as a child follows the path of the father's hatred for America and vows to avenge a brother. The American dream is in danger and can be saved only through the diligence and imagination of one man. An American agent suspects a plot but needs to prove it in order to draw attention to the danger. But how are the terrorists communicating? He needs to break the code to stop the plot that could kill thousands of innocent people.

Prologue

Early 1991

It was unbearably hot outside. The summers in Ramadi, Iraq, seemed to get hotter and hotter with each passing year, and this year, in his city, it was no exception as the mercury pegged out at 42 degrees Celsius. Sweat trickled down his back as he navigated through the dirty side streets of the city—the winding avenues coated with dust and poverty. After turning a final corner, he adjusted the Kufi against his hot, damp head and ducked into a public coffee shop. Choosing a table next to the front window, he set the envelope he was carrying next to a public computer terminal. It wasn't long before a waiter approached his table once he was seated.

"*Ahlan wah sahlan.* What would you like?" asked the waiter.

The young man ordered dark coffee, fresh honey bread called khubs, a hookah with apple tobacco, and some Syrian charcoal. The waiter thanked him with a polite nod and smile before walking to the back of the café to gather his order. He knew the waiter recognized him from being in here regularly for the last couple of months. There weren't many places where he could work on computers outside of the university. Internet cafés were rare, but he had made himself at home here and came often, finding the people in this particular café friendly and quiet. Removing the Kufi from his head, he set it in his lap and turned his attention to the envelope.

He removed a black plastic disk and slid it into the computer drive. As he maneuvered through the login windows, he reflected on how privileged he was to be attending the university. His father was not a rich man, but he had saved diligently to send his son to school. They had chosen Al-Anbar University in Ramadi, Iraq, because it was close to home, had a quality computer program (his collegiate focus), and was affordable for his family.

He was the first from his family ever to attend the university and he had not hesitated in choosing computers as his topic of study. Now in his third year at school, he excelled in his classes, his grades beyond reproach. Once he graduated, he hoped to work on the network of a large successful corporation in Europe, away from the thick heat and turmoil of the Middle East. Not only was his father proud of him and his accomplishments, but his instructors often told him how bright he was. "Some people are just naturals when it comes to computers," his professor had told him. "You have a great future ahead of you. Your family should be proud."

He double-clicked on the icon of the computer and found the necessary files on his floppy disk. There was still a generous amount of research that needed to be done before he could complete his term paper, and the end of the semester was drawing near.

The waiter returned from behind the small counter and set the coffee down next to the computer monitor. The hookah was placed on the floor next to the young man and the tobacco and charcoal was set next to the bread on the other side. Pulling some bills from his pocket, he paid the waiter and thanked him, "*Shukran.*"

Smoke from the hookah filled his lungs and he poured the dark liquid from the steaming pot into his small cup. The coffee was pitch black, like good Arabic coffee should be. As he tore off a piece of the bread he stared out the window, watching people as they passed by. A woman in a black hijab caught his eye.

That reminds me, he thought. *I can't take too long with my school work. It will be time for prayer in another hour.* A piercing whistle drew his eyes to the doorway. *A mortar round?* He thought he heard a woman's scream and a loud explosion before the front of the coffee shop was blown apart. The last thing his eyes saw was a bright ball of fire expanding quickly toward him, filled with shards of glass and wood.

A man sat silently and watched the maddening scene surrounding him. It was enough to drive a father mad; there were men and women from his family tearing at their clothing and screaming in agony as the sun beat down on their bodies. In a matter of just one day it seemed that his world had fallen apart as the dreams for his son were shattered by an uncaring and unseen enemy. Within his mind, the man already found himself taking up arms in the war against this enemy, aiding in their destruction. Over the course of the funeral, a plan was laid out before him in his head, a divine message from a higher power. He stood and walked away from the shabby table he was seated at, through the mourning throngs of people, to his youngest child.

The child turned, hearing a voice from behind. "Allah is truly merciful to have saved me a child to avenge the death of my oldest. You will eventually go to the university, take your brother's place, and learn the technology required to rid the world of the heathens in the West that killed my son. We will win, for Allah wants us to win."

"Yes, *Abi*," was the reply. The path was now laid out for the future. The older brother's place at the university would be filled and his death avenged. The Americans would pay dearly. The young child did not understand the reality of the father's pain; not yet, but in time, that would change.

Chapter 1: The Mind of Terror

Canada, 13 Years Later

He woke up choking on a sob, bathed in sweat. It was late at night (or very early in the morning depending on your perspective) and this time it wasn't the thick heat that had him sweating. Salah had endured many nights like this since his childhood, nights filled with nightmares of his father beating him. He ran his hand across his forehead and pulled back his long hair. Staring out the window, he tried to catch his breath and calm his rapidly beating heart. *Father was dead; why couldn't he relax?*

Salah reached across the small, wooden nightstand and grasped the glass of water sitting under the lamp. The water cooled the heated insides of his body and felt good against the warm skin of his hand. *Salah.* Though born with a different name, he had chosen Salah because of the famous Salah Al-Din, known for establishing the Abbasid dynasty. In 1169, Salah Aldin was a respected Sunni Muslim who fought bravely against the Crusaders to free Jerusalem and Palestine and return it to the Arabs. Salah Al-Din was often compared to his European counterpart and opposition, King Richard the Lion Heart of England—two men cut from the same cloth, but at different ends.

His father had passed on to his youngest child the responsibility of bringing great pain to the American people, avenging his brother who was killed 13 years earlier. And as Salah knew he could not use his real identity in his quest, he had chosen a powerful name and persona to use online, to help motivate *his* followers.

He looked at the small digital clock sitting next to the lamp and saw that it was just 2:34 A.M. Setting the glass of water back down on the nightstand, he pulled the damp sheets off and climbed out of bed. It was early, but he knew that if he closed his eyes again, his father would still be there, waiting, pushing him forward into the lion's den. His destiny was set; the goal would be achieved. The goal *had* to be achieved.

Salah walked across the dark room to the plain wooden desk set against the far wall. The computer monitor blinked to life as Salah pushed the power button. He was still tired, but needed to check on the progress of his plans, and deeply desired a small respite from the image of *him*. Surely the others had checked in by now. There was still plenty of time, but Salah demanded punctuality from his team, and devotion to their cause. The entire team would need to prove their allegiance, technical knowledge, and determination if they hoped to get funding from Al Qaeda leaders. Money was the crucial piece of the plan. Salah had once heard a saying in America that still made him laugh: "Money can't buy happiness." Upon which he had thought to himself, *That may be true, but it can buy everything else, including another man's soul.* From experience, he had come to the conclusion that many Westerners were greedy and would look the other way for the right price. Salah intended to give them what they needed to do just this.

He logged into his Linux box and pulled his damp hair away from his neck. He glanced briefly at the command line prompt and then typed the word *pine*, bringing up his e-mail. Pine was so much easier and safer to use, not to mention its speed compared with other e-mail programs. The threats to the command line e-mail application were few and far between, at least right now, and provided Salah a safer environment from malicious code. It's true that Microsoft had released an operating system that took the world by storm, but in Salah's opinion, it gave people a false sense of security.

Microsoft had given the *normal* people of the world the ability to work within the virtual realm of the Internet without much more knowledge than the simple fact that it existed. These people had no business being on the Internet doing nothing more than checking e-mail or spending money, but it would all work to his advantage in the end. The more people on the Internet, the easier it would be for he and his team to hide within the confusion, unseen.

The added plus for using Pine was that Salah could change the e-mail headers manually, helping hide his identity to an extent. He needed to maintain his identity, or hide it, as the case may be. A strong leader of the people, viewed through a veil of obscurity, like Osama Bin Laden. Salah respected the ability of Osama to lead so many and still remain so anonymous. He would do the same as Osama, only he would do it via the Internet.

Pine afforded a very simple form of this protection. Using the internal configuration options within Pine, Salah had the ability to make his e-mail appear to be from almost anywhere and from almost anyone. Of course, this was a weak form of protection, but it would protect his identity from most prying eyes. But he knew that anyone with an understanding of e-mail would know how to track it back if they wanted to badly enough.

Pine

Salah thought back on the last two years of his life in North America. He had left his home in 2002 to attend school in this strange and far-off land. He had been accepted and granted an all-encompassing scholarship through a foreign-student exchange program, without which he never would have been here. His excitement of exploring a new world was tempered by a fear of the unknown. Before he left, his father had told him that he was walking directly into the pit of vipers. "But fear not, child," he had been told. "They will accept you as one of their own without question. There is no fear in their hearts. Be strong and do not accept their lies as truth." Those were practically his final words—he died of natural causes shortly after Salah arrived at school. There was never a chance to say goodbye, but Salah silently wondered if that was an opportunity that he really wanted; his father had been dead for two years and yet his memories still haunted Salah. He was a child that carried a father's burden. *Will I ever be free of your ghost?* he wondered silently.

He spent his first year at school watching, and waiting. The studies were easy and required very little of his time to maintain good marks. He was genuinely interested in the education and sometimes wished that he could focus on having a life of his own, but the death of his brother was always there, reminding him of his purpose.

At first he kept to himself, interacting with others only when necessary. And though there were plenty of students from Arab nations, he was wary of many of them. Who could he trust? How many could he use? Not all Muslims saw the truth as he and his father saw it. But as he slowly found out, there were some. He met them online, in Internet Relay Chat (IRC) channels and online web forums. They were all as tentative as he was at first. You never knew for certain exactly who could be trusted and who could not. It took time and patience to continually check each person's hostmask, ensuring the identity of each one. In cyberspace, where appearances often were deceiving, the hostmask could be trusted. People often used the same accounts consistently to log in and chat, which meant the hostmask also tended to stay the same.

Salah sat back in his chair thinking about Jimmy, the first person he'd approached to join him on the project. Jimmy was a young man in college who often could be found on IRC chatting with his friends. Salah had chatted with Jimmy plenty of times online, but was always very hesitant to actually approach anyone with his ideas for obvious reasons. As time passed, Salah monitored Jimmy's hostmask consistently, trying to determine if the man was trustworthy.

The hostmask is a unique identifier for every user on IRC. It combines both the username and the user's Internet service provider (ISP) identification. For instance, a user, bobfoley, chatting on IRC with his friends could be logged into Joe's Internet Provider (jip.com). Bob's hostmask on IRC would be a combination of these two things and his computer's unique identifier on the ISP network. The resulting hostmask would be unique to the user bobfoley every time he logged on to IRC. For example, his hostmask might look something like bobfoley@192.168.15.154.sanantonio.jip.com. There were so many freeware IRC clients available on the Internet that anyone with a connection could log themselves into one of the various chat networks on IRC and talk about any topic of interest. The clients under Windows made it very easy to monitor the other users on the network. Salah had set up an alert so that whenever the username Jimmy was used, it was detected logging into the network. The hostmask was always the same. After about six months of watching Jimmy and making sure his login never came from a suspicious entity, Salah had taken a gut-wrenching leap of faith and told the other young man vague details of what he was considering.

IRC Hostmask

Salah straightened in his chair. Now that he thought back on that incident, it seemed almost suicidal, but sometimes you had to take risks in life to make progress. He had read a quote a few years back that said, "A boat in the harbor is safe, but that's not what boats are made for." It was true, he had taken a hefty chance by trusting Jimmy and it had paid off. Hostmasks could be faked or spoofed by someone with relatively moderate technical skills. Many of the applications created for communicating on IRC made the task even easier, by implementing internal servers that would verify whatever hostmask a user configured. Yes, this risk could have been a foolish mistake and potentially lead to disaster, but it didn't and little was gained to think of what could have been.

Over time, Salah and Jimmy became fast friends with various Muslims of similar convictions. They had never met all of them in person, preferring instead to win them over based on who they were inside the web. Salah's convictions were strong and his technical knowledge extensive. By the end of the first year, he and Jimmy had successfully gathered a group of individuals and slowly brought them together under his subtle command. Weeding out the ones who lacked the commitment and vision of the others, the ones who remained would be used for Salah's plan. Not all of them knew about everyone else in the group. He preferred the obscurity provided by anonymity. The time he had spent learning about each individual, evaluating their conviction, testing their resolve, and measuring their hearts had finally paid off. The beginning of the plan was in motion.

By 2.40 A.M., only six of the 27 on his team had checked in via e-mail, but he knew the deadline was technically tomorrow by 7 P.M. (EST). The plan he had crafted to achieve his father's goal was based around operating online. It offered the perfect opportunity for their revenge to be exacted, and it offered stealth and safety. First of all, Americans still mistakenly believed they controlled the Internet, when in fact, they had become an increasingly less important presence. Their overconfidence and arrogance could be used against them. What the Americans saw as the boundary of the Internet was actually a deep shadow that hid threats and dangers, often overlooked. Salah hid in those shadows, working in the dark, hidden from view. "Threats unseen are threats disbelieved," he mumbled to himself. The dark provided cover from the eyes of the Americans who saw things only in the light.

The second reason for operating online was to hide Salah's handicap, one that could threaten the entire project if discovered. It wasn't really a handicap so much as a small obstacle and it meant nothing to him or his father, but to others, it could be cause to abandon faith in the plan. *I was born as I am because Allah wants me this way*, he thought. *I will have faith and succeed in His work.*

His fingers flew across the keys effortlessly as he typed an e-mail to the others. Salah was as familiar with the keyboard of a computer as he was his own face in the mirror. Typing in the dark had never been an issue for him—he had had years of practice, after all.

Soon after the death of his brother, Salah's father had managed to scrape together enough money to bring an old, outdated computer home to Salah, convinced that within his son's former realm of expertise, would be the key to exacting revenge. For his part, Salah was drawn to the computer out of curiosity, as well as a way to appease his driven father. Programming, searching the Internet, learning, and refining his skills, he found that everything in this new technological world came quite naturally to him—and on a computer, *he* was the one in control.

At this point, just a few sentences were needed to ensure that everyone understood their responsibilities and the consequences of failing. Everything had to stay on track, time-wise, or they would all find the entire plan crumbling around them, even if it was only in its preliminary stages. Salah knew quite well that when walls crumbled around you, someone always ended up crushed. The plan would require patience and secrecy to avoid suspicion , and at the right moment, their steps had to be coordinated and timed. The entire group would need to act as a single cohesive entity—one that could act immediately and on instinct.

```
As Salam Alikkum,


Yarhamikum Allah. Days are coming wherein each of us will be required by
Allah to be diligent in our efforts. I pray that each of you is well. Be
strong and remember our cause. We are right to carry out the will of
Allah. Send me an e-mail by tomorrow evening, so that I know you are
online. As a team, we need to be consistent in our communication. I will
send you more later, but right now I need to know that you're all
available on the Internet.


In Allah,
Salah Aldin
```

He pressed the Control and X keys to send the e-mail on its way and sat staring at the screen in front of him. Windows was a luxury he could not afford right now. Sure, it was required for some of the avenues of communication they would be using, but for e-mail and normal use, he could not risk the inherent issues and staggering lack of control that came with that particular operating system. He needed to control all aspects of his network communication in order to remain in those shadows.

Salah closed his e-mail and turned to face the bed. He knew that his father waited there for him when he closed his eyes, but he had to rest if he was to continue his studies at the university. The time was near for graduation and his grades were flawless; there were other things in this life that still need to be taken care of outside of this project. Once he achieved success in this, he knew he would need to have a life outside, in the real world.

Taking a deep breath, he walked back to the nightstand. Staring out the window at the Toronto skyline, he emptied the glass of water with one last swallow. *Soon*, he thought to himself. He opened the window to let in the night air, took a deep breath, and laid back down in bed. "Be with me, Allah," he whispered as he pulled the sheets back up over his head.

The alarm clicked on at 5:30 A.M., waking Salah from slumber. He sat straight up knowing that he had six minutes before it was time for morning prayer, and rose to lay out his prayer mat facing the window. He had chosen this apartment deliberately because it faced the northeast, toward Mecca and toward the Kaaba. He could still recall when he first stepped past the gates of the Grand Mosque and saw the Kaaba.

It had been years since he had made the pilgrimage to Mecca as a child, but still he could feel the holy power there, surrounding the area around the Kaaba. It was called the Hajj, Arabic for *pilgrimage*. The pilgrims counted in the hundreds of thousands and encircled the Kaaba, praying and worshiping Allah. The sacred Kaaba was a cube-shaped sanctuary, believed by Muslims to have been first built by Abraham and his son, Ishmael. The purpose of the Hajj was to not only follow the words of the Prophet but also to walk the same steps the Prophet took. It had been a proud time in Salah's life, and he knew he was indeed lucky to have already made the Hajj. Many faithful Muslims never make it to Mecca for their pilgrimage. These morning prayers and the pilgrimage to Mecca are considered two of the pillars of Islam, the acts that each faithful Muslim must perform. "Allah truly is compassionate and merciful," he said out loud.

At exactly 5:36 A.M., the voice on the radio was replaced by the melodic call to prayer, a voice calling to Muslims across the city to bow down to Allah and pray. This was the *adhan*. The times at which the adhan is called here in North America are calculated by the Islamic Society of North America (ISNA) and used by devout Muslims in most of North America. "Forgive me, Allah, for my transgressions and give me guidance throughout this day, so that I might know what you ask of me."

Praying always made Salah feel stronger in his faith and better about himself. He knew God was keeping a watchful eye on him. "Fight in the cause of God those who fight you, but do not transgress limits, for God loves not transgressors. And slay them wherever ye catch them, and turn them out from where they have turned you out; for tumult and oppression are worse then slaughter..." He liked that verse of the Qur'an: 2:191. His father had taught that to him as a small child. "This is why we fight, my child," his father would tell him. "We must defend the honor of the true God and fight the oppression of Muslims all over the world by the West."

Salah has always understood what his father was trying to convey to him, but had never truly understood why he was chosen by his father; that is, until he had arrived at the university to study. His handicap was power in the West. What Arabs saw as a weakness was viewed differently in America and Canada. He was trusted beyond doubt, and it was that trust that should have been a decisive achievement in his goal that caused him to hesitate. Though he was committed in his heart to the purpose he had set forth, over time his focus seemed to falter. He grew to like many of the people he had sworn to hate, and only the words of his dead father would steel his resolve.

That was when he made the decision to use the name Salah Aldin online. Some would have called it an alter ego, but he had deemed it his reminder, and a base to which he was anchored. It showed power, dedication to Islam and Allah, persistence in the face of overwhelming odds, and intelligent battle with evil. Salah hoped silently that he could live up to the man behind the name. Perhaps, in the future, there would be a place in history where he was listed as also having saved the Arab people from oppression.

When the prayer was over, he rolled up his prayer mat and replaced it gently next to his nightstand. His apartment was humble; he had never been one to collect expensive furniture. The computers in the apartment were hand-built from parts he bought online at discounted prices. The bed was a simple mattress laid on the carpeted floor. Next to the bed was a nightstand that Salah had purchased at a thrift shop. It wasn't much, but he never needed much more than these simple things.

Salah flipped on the computer monitor as he walked past, and headed to the kitchen. The memory of the dreams that woke him last night had become a dull, numb sensation in the back of his mind—amorphous and distant. It was still dark outside, but the sky was slowly turning a dull predawn gray. He needed coffee and breakfast; then he would take a shower and get ready for the day. He flipped the kitchen light switch on and squinted as the sudden brightness burned his eyes.

The kitchen was also simple. The walls were painted a sickly pale yellow, and had a dingy tinge after many years of greasy cooking, children with their crayons, and slow decay. The appliances were old but still in good working condition. Their chocolate brown exteriors were comfortable, but offended Salah's internal senses of taste. A single window over the small sink looked out over the city, facing the northeast. There were cars moving along the Toronto roadways now, carrying people to their jobs.

His coffee pot sat in the sink, where he had left it last night. Turning the water on, he pulled the lid from the pot and poured the remaining coffee into the sink and rinsed the pot. It had become an important part of his everyday existence; it brought him back home. The Turkish coffee he used was delicious and provided the necessary lift, when brewed correctly. He never understood the manner in which people from the West filtered their coffee and stole the flavor from the beans. In the Middle East, the coffee is placed directly into the pot with boiling water where it steeps slowly and deeply, creating a dark, black liquid. He filled the pot with water and set it on the stove, turning the heat up to start the water boiling. Since it would take a few minutes for the water to boil, he turned to walk back to the bedroom and check his e-mail.

Back at the computer, he opened his e-mail. Three more responses had been posted since earlier that morning, *very good*. At this point in the planning, he just wanted to be sure that everyone could be trusted to maintain a consistent connection to the Internet. Soon, he knew, he would need to familiarize them all with the tools they would use to communicate with each other. E-mail was fine for now, but not once the plan was under way, when you know your enemy is out there, somewhere, listening to your conversations.

The years Salah had spent before coming to the university, learning how the Internet worked, and about network protocols and applications, down to the very last details, was what enabled Salah to earn the scholarships he had. Some had deemed him a prodigy for the talents he displayed, which might have been true to a point, but the skills that truly would have earned him this praise were kept secret.

Information on vulnerable systems was freely available around the world, written on web sites, forums, and electronic magazines passed between hackers. He had learned about operating systems and their inherent strengths and flaws. But the most important thing he learned was that information easily can be put up on the Internet for mass consumption but never seen except by the intended recipients: covert channels. It was a powerful lesson when he realized people couldn't see things they've never heard of or what they believe to be nonexistent. Covert channels were the shadows on the Internet, the dark underbelly of global communication.

And during that time of learning and research, he had also laid out his idea, his *grand plan*. He had spent days at a time, planning, thinking, and visualizing how he could carry out his idea. How do you strike down a serpent that watches your every move from eyes hidden everywhere? How do you deal a deadly blow that will never be seen coming? The concept was simple, really. Strike from the shadows before they realize there are shadows at all. He would teach his team to use covert channels of communication to hide their communication and plan their attack.

Salah figured that the key was in how the plan was communicated to the rest of his team. Anything communicated via insecure channels could compromise the entire project and threaten the lives of every person involved. Covert channels of communication could be used to keep their messages secret, hidden from view. His team members were generally very good about going about their normal lives, acting like someone who belonged. They could fit in and not draw attention to themselves. But he had seen enough people in the news that got caught somewhere during the planning stage, when important details were being communicated between the various parts of the whole. If only he could obscure the very fact that any communication was even occurring, he could better protect his plan and the others in the group.

Fortunately, the Internet was ripe with information about techniques and tools created specifically to hide the fact that information was being transmitted. A small subset of hackers on the Internet had uncovered multiple means for sending information between points on the network without detection. Encryption was great for keeping messages private but was a poor solution when you needed to hide the fact that two entities were communicating at all. This was when Salah had decided to implement these types of channels into this plan.

Using these hidden channels of communication during a time of war or conflict was not a new idea. It had been used thousand of years ago when messages were communicated via wax tablets that were inscribed with a wooden stylus. This concept originally was communicated by the ancient Greek historian Herodotus when he referred to how his fellow countrymen would send secret messages back and forth, warning of potential invasion. At some point, the Greeks had discovered that if you melted the wax off the tablet, scratched the message on to the wood underneath, and then reapplied a fresh layer of wax, the message would be hidden and secret. Messengers could be sent, with no knowledge of the hidden message, past the city guards to your accomplice, where the message was received. This was the key to the plan.

Present-day covert channels utilized modern technology, and the network provided a medium for transport. Finding a hidden message on the Internet would be far worse than trying to find the theoretical needle in the haystack. The Internet was much larger than a normal haystack and continued to grow more with each passing day. The technologies were there; they existed today. He just needed to reach out and use them. In some cases, Salah had improved on existing methods of covert communication to further ensure his privacy. Soon, it would be time to share those ideas with his brethren, but first he would start with something simple: null ciphers.

He closed his e-mail and dropped back to a command prompt. Opening a simple text editor called *vi*, Salah typed a short note using null ciphers. *Let's use a simple message that should be easy to guess*, he thought. *Surely someone will get this quick enough. It's best to know now how much more learning we have before the team is ready.* He was anxious to see if anyone realized what the hidden message was inside his e-mail. This would prove to be a simple, yet effective proof of concept to everyone else. Covert channels could and would hide their planning.

```
Dear Sir,

For irresistible glamour, have translucent, iridescent nails. Truly,
having eyes charming and ultra smoky enchants others. Find great outfits;
dress tastefully, having obviously sultry, exotic wardrobes. Hair, often
forgotten, is gloriously highlighted to yield overflowing utopia.
```

Salah silently laughed to himself as he considered the reaction of the others when they received this e-mail. *What will they think of this?* he wondered. The message was certainly simple enough, but the medium wasn't obvious. Unless one of them was fairly analytical, he didn't expect them to understand what he had actually put into the message. He crossed his fingers and saved the file to his directory.

He then opened his e-mail once again and composed a quick note asking all the others to review the attached text file and look for the hidden message within the text. He attached the text file he had just saved containing his null cipher message. The concept behind null ciphers was a simple one. In its simplest form, a null cipher takes each letter of the original message and makes it the first letter of an entire word. Salah had used this same concept to create and hide his message to the others. He hoped at least one of them would pick up on the message.

Now he needed to take a shower and get ready for school. There would be time later today to work on the other forms of communication. Turning off the computer monitor, Salah picked up his coffee cup and walked toward the bathroom. The image reflected in the mirror shot back that image of a person much older than expected. *Allah, please grant me peace*, he thought. *I strive only to do what you ask of me*. With that, he turned on the hot water, stepped into the shower, and silently pondered the networking exam he had later that morning.

Chapter 2: Unseen Planning

March 19, 2004

Salah unlocked the dead bolt and stepped through the doorway into the barren space beyond. The apartment held no real emotional sway over Salah; it was a quaint dwelling, but only temporary. Walking across the stained brown carpet, he stopped at the window near his bed to look out over the city. The university was only a few blocks away, but even for a single person walking, it was sometimes difficult to navigate the traffic below. He watched silently as the cars on the road below battled to dominate the road, relentlessly working to carry their occupants home.

Salah had endured a very long and very detailed networking exam earlier that morning and afterward had gone to the university library to gather more information on steganography, commonly referred to as *stego*. The very name, steganography, meant *covered writing in ancient Greek*, and the concepts held great promise for Salah. Through its use, he and his team would be able to communicate in the open without anyone realizing what was there.

The Relationship between Covert Channels and Steganography

The term steganography comes from two Greek root words. The first, *steganos*, is translated as *covered*. The second part of the word comes from the Greek work *graphie*, meaning *writing*. The two terms together help us describe the idea of hiding information of one type in some medium that normally would be unexpected to the average person. But over time, the term steganography increasingly has been used to describe the hiding of data inside binary files, such as audio files (.wav, .mp3, and .au), digital images (.jpg, .gif, and .bmp), and other binary formats, such as executables.

In contrast, the term *covert channels* often is used to describe the idea of hiding any type of information in any type of medium. For our purposes, this term can be considered to be all encompassing, including steganography. For example, there are other means for hiding informa-

Continued

tion that include everything from obfuscation of the information, appending the data to the carrier file, or including the data in network packets being transmitted across a medium. There are even algorithms that *create* digital information based on the input message supplied by the user. For example, programs exist that will create a music file using nothing more than the original data supplied to it by the end user. Using the term *covert channels* allows us to more adequately include a broader base of information-hiding mechanisms than normally is associated with the term *steganography*, although they are often used interchangeably.

As you read this book, the term steganography is used to denote instances where information is hidden directly within a binary medium, and *covert channels* is used in those instances when obfuscation, appending, or packet modification is concerned.

The creation of steganography within images and the sheer difficulty of detecting legitimate steganography within files found on the Internet captured Salah's imagination. Tremendous information on the topic was available on the Internet. You just had to know what you were looking for and the key words for finding all of it. Salah had researched the topic numerous times over the past year. He had even more recently enjoyed great success toying with some of the applications that help create hidden information freely available on the Internet.

Tools like S-Tools, JP Hide-and-Seek, and Gif-it-up were free and powerful and could be used to hide information in digital images by anyone willing to simply download the software. Images were the perfect medium, at least initially, for communicating with his team. The amount of information that can be hidden in an image with a limited chance of detection is about 25 to 30 percent the size of the carrier file. That would provide enough storage and transmission space in the beginning. A carrier file, simply put, is like a suitcase. You put data inside the suitcase so that you can carry it around protected. The larger the suitcase, the more stuff you can put inside of it.

For example, if you had a 400-kilobyte carrier image within which you wanted to hide information, you would be better off limiting the data to not much more than 100 kilobytes. Any more data hidden within your carrier would start to cause noticeable distortion, and could compromise your hidden communication. His team currently didn't have a need to hide larger amounts of information, but if the need arose in the future, Salah had already decided to utilize audio files instead of images due to their average 5-megabyte file size. Peer-to-peer networking on the Internet had increased the number of audio and music files being exchanged by users all around the world. Programs like Kazaa, Acquisition, and Limewire already were allowing Internet users to search for music files by song name, artist name, and more. This potentially could provide for a more anonymous distribution of information to all the relevant team members. But this was something he would address later, when the need arose.

Corporations around the world had even helped his cause, without knowing it, by standardizing the practice of watermarking the images they posted to the Internet. Watermarks effectively provided the means to let everyone know the image was the corporation's intellectual property. Those images were downloaded by millions of users around the world, every day, littering the world's hard drives. They are, in essence, standardized steganography within images and would aid in hiding his group's activities from prying eyes.

Present-day detection software still has difficulty distinguishing some forms of digital watermarks from legitimate steganography. All of this obscurity should work to his advantage. *It's nearly impossible to find a single and specific fish in the ocean,* he thought to himself. *We are simply a smaller fish in a much larger ocean—the Internet.*

Another standardization within the industry has made his team's work easier as well. This time, through the creation of the standard JPEG (Joint Photographic Experts Group) image format. In the early years of the "popular Internet," as he often referred to the early 1990s, many images on the Internet were GIFs. But the GIF (Graphics Interchange Format) image was littered with copyright and intellectual property issues for any organization that wanted to implement the standard into their own software. Most companies stopped using the GIF for this reason and were more likely use the open JPEG format. This was mostly in an effort to avoid paying royalties to CompuServe, which still owned the patent on the GIF technology. In the end, most companies that deal in digital images preferred to support the JPEG image format.

Nearly all modern, digital cameras on the market created and stored their images in JPEG format as a .jpg file. Digital cameras have been growing more and more popular, partially due to the sheer popularity of computers and the rapid descent of their cost to consumers. JPEG images also can be created using everyday graphics programs available freely on the Internet or in inexpensive commercial versions. Images created by these applications oftentimes were passed off as artwork and posted to various web sites for visitors to admire.

With all of these factors standing solidly behind his efforts, he wondered what could actually stop him. Salah had been working toward a single goal for the last 13 years. His father had made him swear that he would avenge the death of his brother by striking at the heart of America, its people. The concepts were simple, the effect devastating. Using the Internet to communicate would only increase the dismay of the attack because every detail would be passed under the Americans' noses, in public forums. Their miscalculations about the true threat of covert channels would prove deadly.

His team consisted of 27 technologically knowledgeable Muslims who all had one thing in common: they hated the United States. And because of their experience with computers and networking, the days of suicide bombs would be coming to a close. Salah had always thought it seemed a little melodramatic and silly to strap explosive compounds to your body and detonate the bomb, along with your body. In the new world, none of your own people need to die to accomplish your mission. In fact, no one even needs to know you have people or a plan. All activity, all communication, and all your planning could occur without anyone else knowing. There was simply no need for young men to strap explosives to their waists, waltz into a crowded plaza, and blow themselves up along with the target. The new terror attacks could be completely planned, arranged, and organized online.

Inshah Allah, he thought, *the only deaths in this arrangement will be Americans.* It seemed logical to Salah that if his team survived these attacks, they would live to fight another day. Experienced fighters were much more useful than young amateurs willing to die for a cause. Repeated attacks resulting in very little collateral damage were best planned for and waged online. He was proud of his ideas. "Some day soon," he had told his team in a recent e-mail, "we will all organize online. We will have no need to hide in the mountains or the desert in order to avoid capture. Instead, we will hide online. We will appear as no more than wraiths before the eyes of the West. Our normal lives will go on without notice while the bad fruit withers on its vine."

The ease at which JPEG images could be created meant that his team would have the ability to use unique images they created on their own. Using unique images would ensure that no other versions of the digital pictures would be available for comparison with the carrier file. Detection would be much easier for law enforcement if the original image were publicly available on the Internet, because the original image could be compared with the one containing hidden information. This was most commonly done by comparing the hash signatures of both images and looking for clues that could indicate steganography within the image.

Each person on the team had already been told to purchase a digital camera; the higher the resolution the better. "Carry the camera with you at all times," he had told them several months ago in the same e-mail. "Take pictures of everything that attracts your eyes." He was certain that, at the time, it seemed like an odd request, but they trusted Salah's technical knowledge.

"We won't foot the costs of this project for much longer," he told them in his last e-mail. "I have arranged a meeting with the leaders of Al Qaeda where I will tell them of our bold plan. They will likely provide for our needs until this attack is carried out. We will strike terror into the Western heart and show them the powerful hand of Allah in action."

The real key to carrying out this plan was secrecy and anonymity. Salah knew that you could easily find millions of images on the Internet. Different people from all over the world were posting images from their digital cameras on personal web sites. Pages and pages of personal images about family events, vacations, and even bedroom events littered the World Wide Web. Everyone on the Internet felt as if they had a voice, and that surely someone would have an interest in their little piece of the web. Hiding critical plans and information within images such as these was a perfect fit. Even if the American authorities knew he was hiding something, they would have a terribly difficult time locating his images among all the others already on the Internet.

He had decided to start with JPEG images and move to audio files later, if a need arose. He remembered the images and rules he had learned in his research. JPEG images were created much the same way as other digital images, at least initially. If a person takes a picture with a digital camera, the image is stored by software in the camera as a matrix, or grid, of picture elements known as pixels. Generally speaking, the greater the number of pixels in an image, the greater the resolution, or ability to discern detail, is in the image. The number of pixels in a digital image is called *dots per inch (dpi)* or *pixels per inch (ppi)*.

Pixels per Inch

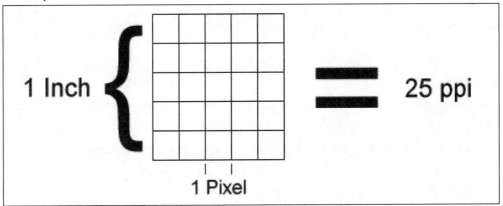

Each pixel within an image is assigned a value that represents the color of that pixel: either black or white or one of 16.7 million possible colors. Each pixel color is represented as a binary number consisting of 1's (ones) and 0's (zeros). These 1's and 0's are referred to as bits. Some images have 8 bits that combine to give a color value to the pixel, whereas others use 24 bits to define the color value for the pixel. When you combine enough pixels, you create an image. Digital cameras actually recreate the image shown in the camera viewfinder as an image consisting of all these colored pixels.

The 16.7 million possible colors refer to the number of colors mathematically possible in a 24-bit image—8 bits by a power of 8. This actually results in exactly 16,777,216 possible colors in a 24-bit palette. An 8-bit image takes 256 of these 16.7 million colors and creates a palette that is used to display the image. So any 8-bit image is created from a maximum of 256 colors. The number stored in each bit of an 8-bit image is actually a pointer to one of the colors in our 256-color palette. An 8-bit image tends to be smaller in size but carries less color detail than 24-bit images because of its restrictive color palettes. This is evident in the math associated with having 8 bits of information that can all be a 1 or a 0. There are 256 different combinations of 1's and 0's in an 8-bit image, thus limiting the color palette of the image to 256 colors.

However, 24-bit images, are created using all 16.7 million colors available mathematically. Since 24-bit images use all the available colors, they don't create a restrictive palette. But unlike 8-bit images, there are actually three sets of 8 bits that define the color for each pixel in a 24-bit image. Each of the primary colors—red, blue, and green—has 8 bits to itself. If we count all 24 bits, we realize 16.7 million different combinations of 1's and 0's are available to define a color. Thus, each pixel can represent one of over 16.7 million different colors. The 24-bit images are called *true color* for just this reason. They are capable of representing every actual red, green, and blue color value available.

8-Bit Image Pixel Color Definition

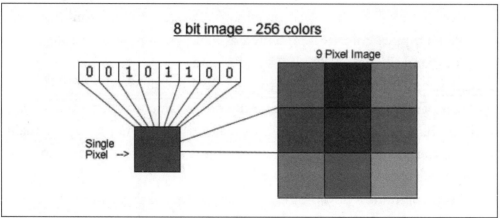

24-Bit Image Pixel Color Definition

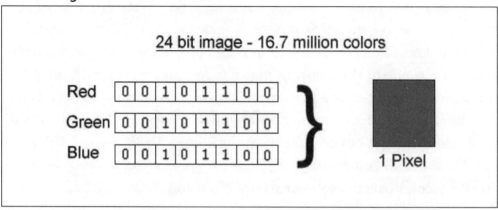

The most popular method for hiding information within an image was called Least Significant Bit (LSB) modification, and is a form of steganography. LSB modification takes the 1's and 0's from the secret message (often referred to as a payload) and inserts those into each pixel, starting at the bit least likely to make a noticeable change to the color of the pixel. Since a 1 or a 0 already exists in that spot, there is only ever a 50% chance that the bit will need to be changed.

Bit Significance

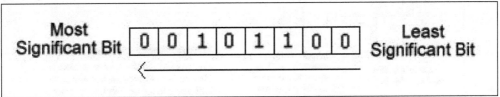

Most steganography applications start at the least significant bits in each pixel and then move down the line toward the more significant bits as data is inserted into the carrier. The more significant bits will make greater changes in color for the pixel when changed. Inserting too much data into a carrier will distort the image to the point that it can be seen with the naked eye. Human eyes are wonderfully designed, with the exception that discrete changes in shades of color or in dark colors in general tend to go undetected.

Example of Data Insertion in an 8-Bit Image

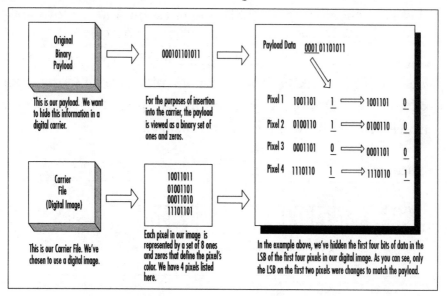

The real problem for the Americans would be when their law enforcement actually tried to get the information out of images they may suspect of having hidden information. Steganography, combined with encryption, would prove their undoing. To top things off, American law enforcement had mostly ignored the issue of hidden information because it was not considered a real problem. In fact, there were even poorly conducted research projects that had come back conclusively indicating that it didn't even exist. Yes, he would use JPEG images and hide the American fate directly under their noses. They would never even notice because there was no such problem.

Salah shifted his weight and realized that he was still staring out the window into the city. He turned and laid his backpack on the floor next to his makeshift bed, where it landed with a *thud*. Walking over to his desk, he turned on the monitor and watched as the screen came to life. He had apparently left his computer on all day. His landlord wasn't overly intrusive, but he chided himself to log off next time.

He glanced briefly at his e-mail to see how many new messages had come in since he had checked last, earlier that morning. Forty-seven new e-mails; it would appear that everyone had responded early at this point. Good. He would read those e-mails shortly, but first things first, some tea and perhaps a small snack.

He walked into the kitchen and filled his pot with tap water. Absently, he wondered if anyone had figured out his null cipher message. *Please Allah*, he thought to himself. *Give me a few leaders among my team. Let them see the value of what we're doing.* He walked over to the stove, lit the flame on one of the front burners, and set the water to boil. The flame on the stove ignited his memory. His brother's frightened face filled his mind as he thought back to that fateful day at the coffee shop. He had relived his brother's death in his own mind for years, recreating the scene as he imagined the pain of it all. He wasn't there when it had happened, but he made up for that every night through his own nightmares of the event.

When his parents and he had first arrived at the site, he was sure there had been a mistake. "There's nothing here but a pile of stone," he recalled saying. But his father had seen him, his brother. At first, it was a disembodied hand sticking straight up out of the rubble. He remembered his father and several other men pulling large chunks of rock out of the pile until his brother's ravaged body was found.

The wet teapot hissed gently as the water still clinging to the outside of the pot sizzled into steam. He shuddered to himself and pushed the morbid details back into the recesses of his mind. His purpose flooded back into his heart and he reflected on his research today at school. One of the papers he had found was written back in the late 1990s and discussed a concept called *stego-noise*. The paper was written by Fabian Hansmann and described a mechanism for writing a benign Internet worm that would search for certain vulnerabilities. When computers were found with the appropriate security vulnerability, they would be compromised, allowing the worm to embed all suitable target files on the drive with steganography. Over time, these *infected* yet benign images would clutter the Internet with images, audio files, and other binary files that had useless steganography, making the detection of legitimate steganographic files extremely difficult. Salah knew that even the most advanced algorithms for detecting steganography today had a surprising number of false positives, making them somewhat unreliable. But this concept could threaten the fragile balance between the creation of steganography and the detection of it.

The premise of the paper had described a benign worm written to take advantage of vulnerabilities on computer systems around the world. As the worm located systems with the vulnerabilities it was looking for, it would infect every image on each system it had access to with a benign form of steganography. The worm was programmed to insert random information into each image, creating useless steganography, or stego-noise, within the image. When law enforcement officials attempted to scan a computer system or the Internet for images with potential hostile or hidden content, eventually they would be inundated with large numbers of images appearing to have steganography within them.

When the paper was originally written, the concept was intriguing to hackers, but largely ignored by the general Internet community, including law enforcement and the military. But in today's networked world, where worms are a daily reminder of the insecurity of the Internet, such a worm could actually generate a tremendous amount of stego-noise in a very short period of time. The Slammer worm was a good indication of how quickly a properly coded worm could spread.

The Slammer worm had taken the computer world by surprise, even though there had been a public announcement of the vulnerability that made the worm possible. The vulnerability was in Microsoft's SQL server, and allowed the worm to spread at an alarming rate. Microsoft had even taken steps to ensure a patch was issued and available before the announcement was made about the vulnerability. When the worm hit on January 25, 2004, it broke all records for the spread of a worm or other virus by doubling in size every 8.5 seconds. The worm eventually infected at least 75,000 hosts around the globe and hit its maximum scanning rate of 55 million scans per second after only three minutes. The scanning slowed after this point due mostly to the inundation of the various network infrastructures in place at the time. He remembered the enormous impact the worm had on the computing world and on the Internet in particular. Stego-noise had the ability to make it look like there were a lot more needles in this haystack then really existed. Salah wondered absently if such a virus already existed and how difficult it might be to develop one from scratch. Perhaps he would consider working on this project another time. The eventual amount of *noise* a worm of this magnitude could cause would be enormous, allowing years of free communication via covert channels. Yes, he would definitely have to think seriously about pursuing this project.

The sharp whistle of the teapot snapped his wandering mind back to the present. And, for a moment, he was just an average college student standing over a teapot, waiting for it to boil. He fought back the brief wish that, for once, he could live a normal life and returned to the task at hand.

The tea was on the top shelf. He wasn't quite sure why he still kept it up there; he had ample cabinet space in his kitchen, but his family had kept it on the top shelf in their kitchen, and he supposed his mind was comforted by small reminders of home. He took a large tablespoon and dumped some of the dark black tea leaves into the boiling water. Picking the pot up off the burner, he placed the pot on a back burner and turned off the flames on the stove.

He was going to need to find out what they already understood. Could he bring a team together under this technology and coordinate an attack? What were his chances of success? He understood that if he expected to get backing from Al Qaeda he would need to demonstrate that his plan was foolproof and would result in a painful wound for the Americans.

Walking back to his computer, he read through the e-mails. He was scanning for a single person from the team, a person who had the most likelihood of having discovered the hidden message—Jimmy. Of course, Jimmy wasn't his real name. Like Salah, he had chosen a pseudonym for use online. "Besides," he had told Salah in a past IRC conversation, "Americans prefer names they can pronounce and understand. I'll fit in better if my name appears to be normal to them." Salah knew Jimmy was right. *Ah, there he is,* Salah thought as he located the e-mail he had known would be in his box.

He and Jimmy had discussed the possibility of using null ciphers in the past. In fact, it had been Jimmy's idea initially. "We'll start with something simple, to get the others comfortable with the concepts," he had told Salah. "Once they understand basic ciphers, we can change the position of the message characters. Eventually, you'll be able to introduce other covert channels of communication, and they'll pick up on those, too."

```
"Fight in the cause of God those who fight you…"
```

```
Jimmy
```

That's all it said. Nothing more would be needed. Hopefully, the others had also read Salah's e-mail and figured out where the message was. *This is going to work*, he thought.

Salah shut down his computer. He still had studying to do tonight, and he couldn't be up late because he had work in the morning. Though Salah had received a scholarship from the university, it wasn't enough to cover his books, food, and housing. After a brief visit to the Student Welfare Office, Salah got a part-time job at the bookstore in the Student Center. The job didn't pay a lot, but it was more than enough to make ends meet. The important thing was that it didn't impact his studies or his side project. Working at the bookstore also provided Salah with some needed discounts on textbooks and supplies; discounts that allowed him to take more classes and graduate early. Shortly after the death of his father, Salah's family had run out of money to pay for school, leaving Salah on his own in a foreign country.

It wasn't Salah's style to worry about things out of his control; he was a survivor, and without hesitation, he willingly added this job to his set of responsibilities. He found that it was even a welcome break from his everyday existence. His routine had grown dull between the constant courses, studying, and his after-hours project. The job provided interaction with other students, many of whom Salah was beginning to consider friends. He had tried hard to distance himself and avoid the insidious emotional connections with the students around him, but he was so young. To many he was an average twenty-something student who needed the social interaction that was available only by having friends on campus, but he soon found himself fighting the internal battle to remain introverted and protected.

Salah walked back into the kitchen and prepared to make some dinner. *I'll get some studying done while I eat*, he thought. *Maybe I'll even watch a little television.* He pulled a frying pan from the drawer hiding at the bottom of the old stove and set it on the burner. Reaching inside the refrigerator, he grabbed a carton of eggs. Dinner would be quick and simple tonight.

Chapter 3: Making Friends

March 22, 2004

"I'm telling you, dude, I've never met a woman who knows so much about networking concepts," Jeremy said. "She's amazing. I could totally use her help. I'm dying here! Have you seen how well she does on those tests?"

"Well, no actually." Kyle replied. "Those grades are supposed to be confidential. Satisfy my curiosity, though, would you? How did you happen to see her grades?" Kyle smirked, satisfied that he had cornered his friend. "Were you hacking the university computers?"

"She sits right next to me, Kyle. It's nearly impossible to miss the constant stream of high marks that pass across her desk when the professor hands back our papers," Jeremy responded. "But I've never run into her outside of class. I wonder if she'd be willing to help me out with my networking project. And no, I didn't hack anything. You know I couldn't hack my way out of a cardboard box with a hatchet."

Kyle smirked again as he looked at his friend. Jeremy was a smart kid, but he could get distracted easily. Jeremy was right about one thing, though: Layla was very smart, but Kyle seldom noticed her brains because she was also a beautiful young woman. She had dark, deep eyes and long black hair, but smiled only occasionally and often seemed to be completely absorbed in her studies. Case in point, he glanced across the student lounge where she was seated. Alone, and completely immersed in a book.

Kyle guessed she was just very shy, but that gave little comfort to his friend. Jeremy stared into his coffee cup lost in thought. He and Layla had been in many of the same classes over the last couple of years, and she apparently was studying computer science with a focus on networking, just like Jeremy was. They obviously had something in common, but he still hadn't built enough nerve to approach her.

Kyle suspected that his friend might have a crush on the girl, but decided not to press the issue. Jeremy was 23, tall, and skinny. All in all, he was basically just a normal, young, run-of-the-mill American boy. He had thick dark hair that often had a mind of its own due in part to the massive curls. Kyle also suspected that part of the problem was because his hair was cut so seldom, but he understood his friend's reluctance. For a college student, getting a haircut was a laborious chore that took time away from more important extracurricular activities, cost too much money, and was easily neglected. This had the unintentional effect of allowing Jeremy to fit in with the current retro 1970s big-hair fad, making him slightly more popular with the girls. Kyle liked to kid Jeremy about looking like Greg Brady on *The Brady Bunch*. But there was no doubt that Jeremy was a good friend who could be counted on.

Kyle and Jeremy had met two years earlier, when Kyle was a new freshman enrolled in the Computer Science College at the University of Eastern Canada. Kyle first met Jeremy at a computer club meeting in the student lounge one night. The club didn't last too long and soon turned into a convenient excuse for a party, but Kyle and Jeremy hit it off after only a few meetings and started hanging out. The two young men had similar personalities, and, as it turned out, backgrounds as well. Kyle had felt overwhelmed by the weight of his new situation at the university and Jeremy understood perfectly well what it was like to come from a small town to a large university for the first time. He had taken Kyle under his wing and the two had become fast friends, hitting the clubs on the weekend, studying together, and hanging out in the student lounge. Kyle was younger than Jeremy by a couple of years, but wasn't the typical freshman. It wasn't unusual to see them hacking away on their laptops in the student lounge trying to get a new piece of open source software to compile so that they could try it out.

For Jeremy's part, he was originally from a small town just south of Oklahoma City, called Moore, and had never really had the opportunity to leave the state, much less the country, prior to college. But when he

had arrived in Toronto the first time, he was surprised to find that it
wasn't at all like a foreign country. The fact of the matter was that
Toronto could have been any American city.

Jeremy was enrolled in this particular university out of sheer financial
necessity and a compelling need to see more of the world. But it wasn't a
bad school at all. In fact, it was one of the best schools north of the
border and the popular Computer Science program was rising through
the ranks of North American universities and colleges in the field.

When he had applied for scholarships, the university had responded
immediately with a full list of grants and waivers. Jeremy jumped at the
opportunity and had started as soon as he graduated high school. Jeremy
wished that the scholarship was due to grades, but it actually was granted
as part of the sports program.

Jeremy was the second-string quarterback for the university's football
team. He had spent a great deal of time in his hometown playing football, but now he was trying to break away from sports and get serious
about starting a career. Sports were fun to watch, but he had no intention
of becoming a professional football player. Instead, his interests were
drawn to the world of computers and networking. With less than a year
left in school, Jeremy had forsaken his former self and moved into the
world of technology. He was first and foremost a computer geek, and
proud of it.

Last semester, Jeremy and his academic advisor began plotting what
his first career move would be. Ahead of the game, Jeremy already knew
his interests involved working for a U.S. federal agency in the computer
or networking field, and he became active in sending out applications. He
liked the idea of working for the government and stability of never really
having to find another job. Sure, he likely could make more money in
the commercial sector, but when it came down to it, he didn't enjoy the
idea of riding the next wave of technology until it came crashing down
around him and left him with no job and worthless stock options. It was
through one of these applications that a response came back, requesting

an interview.

The agency turned out to be the Department of Homeland Security (DHS). The DHS was apparently staffing up with fresh graduates in various technology-related fields. The interviewer gave Jeremy no more information about the job, other than to tell him that he would need a security clearance. The paperwork for the security clearance was both time consuming and long, but once it was done, the process was complete on his end, and an offer letter was received back at his home in Oklahoma.

The job was a great opportunity for Jeremy. The salary was just $30,000 a year, which was much less than what many other graduates at his school were being offered, but the opportunity to work with the federal government was a huge bonus in his mind. The position would be out of Washington, D.C., back in the United States. He was already looking forward to his new job in the big city, but was worried it might all be in jeopardy.

Kyle watched his friend's attention drift and guessed at what he was thinking. Jeremy's grades had always been Dean's List, but had gradually fallen recently. Kyle knew this was driving him crazy. Jeremy was concerned that if his grades slipped at all, the DHS would retract its offer.

The only reason behind the recent drop in his grades was this one class, an accelerated honors class that he was intent on completing. Networking had been relatively easy in the earlier courses, but Jeremy had continued to escalate his learning in the area and now found himself lost at times. Kyle had asked him before whether it was possibly just a case of burnout or whether he was just excited at the prospect of graduating so soon and was distracted. But Jeremy knew, quite honestly, that he was going to need some help in this class if he was going to salvage his grade point average. His answer was sitting across the student lounge at this very moment, engrossed in a networking textbook.

"If she's that good, she might be willing to help you out once in a while. You could ask her to be your tutor," Kyle said. "But I'm not sure

I've ever seen her in a social setting. Are you looking to ask her out or are you strictly looking for help with your school work?"

"No, I'm not looking for a date," Jeremy quickly replied. "Not that I'd say no if it came down to it, but I need to get my grades up, and she knows what's she doing. I'm going to chance it. The worse she can do is say no and I'm prepared for that. Do you mind staying here while I go talk to her? I don't want her to clam up at the sight of two guys walking over to her at once."

"Sure, I'll wait here, dude," Kyle replied with a grin.

With that, Jeremy stood up from his chair and glanced briefly across the student lounge. He wasn't necessarily concerned that Layla would tell him no, but he was a little self-conscious about being rejected; at least the lounge area was relatively clear of inhabitants.

He and Kyle usually spent a couple of hours each day in the Student Union, eating junk food ordered from the university-sponsored student lounge and working on their schoolwork. The lounge was one of the few places that truly felt comfortable to him, but he knew his time at the school was almost over. He was due to graduate in another semester and would be headed back to the States to work for the federal government. But until then, he was still a young man at school and needed help with his schoolwork.

He smoothed his hair back with his hand and sighed to himself as he felt it bounce right back to where it had been. He cursed that he had not gone to get his haircut before he had decided to approach Layla. He glanced over at Kyle, still sitting at the table looking at him expectantly. "No backing out now," he told himself. He steeled himself and walked toward her table.

Layla was sitting alone, as was normal for her. Jeremy wasn't sure if she actually had any friends because he had never seen her sitting with anyone. She was wearing a simple red t-shirt with blue jeans and was studying their advanced networking textbook. Taking a deep breath, he took the final steps necessary toward her. Her table was cluttered with paperwork, most of which appeared too technical and wasn't anything that he had seen in class.

"Hello," Jeremy said meekly, horrified to see that Layla didn't even look up. *What should he do now?* He looked at Kyle with a panicked expression on his face. Kyle just waved him on with his hands. *Ok,* he thought. *She probably didn't hear me; one more try.*

"Hi there, Layla," he said more energetically, to ensure she knew he was speaking to her.

She looked up at him, at first surprised to find someone apparently engaging her in a conversation. But then she smiled at him. "Hello there, Jeremy," she replied. "What's up?" Her accent was beautiful, and she spoke in deep flowing tones that caught him completely off guard.

"You know my name," Jeremy stuttered. It wasn't a question, but a statement made in shock. He hadn't expected this and was equally thrown off by her apparent knowledge of his existence.

"Of course, I do," Layla answered him. "We've been in a number of classes together over the last two years. Besides, we sit right next to each other in networking." She smiled at him. "What's on your mind?"

Jeremy hadn't expected her to be so friendly, but here she was, apparently a very normal person. He pulled out one of the brightly colored chairs across the table from and sat down facing her. "I was hoping you could help me out," he began. "I graduate after next semester, and I could really use some of your help with class. I'm having issues with my grades and need to get them back under control."

"What makes you think I can help you?" she smirked playfully.

Jeremy blushed as he suddenly realized that she had most likely noticed his gawking when her papers were handed back in class. "I'm sorry," he replied. "But it's really difficult to miss all those A's you get. I know I shouldn't look, but I couldn't help it." He paused before continuing. "So could you help me? I'd *really* appreciate it."

Layla laughed quietly. "Sure, I'll help you. We can meet in the library later this afternoon and talk about what exactly you need help with. Can you meet me there at 4:30? I've got Advanced C++ until 4:15."

Jeremy was ecstatic. "Yeah, sure! Great! Okay, I'll meet you just inside the front doors. I really appreciate this," he responded. *Finally*, he could get his grades straight before graduation, and the small potential of flirting with Layla made his stomach flutter.

"Great, see you then," she said.

Jeremy thanked her again before quickly saying goodbye and headed back to his table, with Kyle waiting patiently.

"It's a go, dude," Jeremy grinned, "I'm meeting her at the library later today to figure out what she can help me with."

"Excellent!" Kyle shot back. "She must really like computer geeks, eh?"

Jeremy laughed and took a deep breath. He had someone to help him get through his last months at school. *I might hang on to that job after all,* he told himself.

Chapter 4: One Step Closer

March 23, 2004

"Welcome, Jimmy. Won't you please have a seat?" asked the young woman. "Someone will be with you in a moment for your interview. Please let me know if you need anything." Jimmy watched her as she left the room. She was attractive and he was enjoying watching her hips sway as she walked away. "You're not here for the women," he told himself quietly and tried to get his mind back on what he was really here to do—get a job.

The young woman shut the door behind her quietly, leaving Jimmy alone in the manager's office. The room was neat and orderly. Bookcases lined the far wall, with books titled after exotic foreign lands, and pictures of various cruise ships within the company's fleet decorated the wood-paneled walls, where there was even the obligatory steering wheel from a ship hanging on the far side of the room. Jimmy noticed family pictures on the desk next to the computer and realized that the manager must be a woman since one of the pictures of a small boy was signed in childish handwriting, "For Mommy."

The door opened behind him with a squeak, and Jimmy turned to see a small-framed woman dressed in khaki Dockers and a blue golf shirt. She stood only about 5' 4" tall, but she carried herself with confidence and authority. "Hello, Jimmy, it's nice to meet you," she began. "I'm Lydia Hopkins, and I'll be interviewing you today. How are you?" She extended her hand to which he hesitated before extending his own.

Although he was thrown off by the gender of the manager, he knew he needed to maintain his professionalism. He needed this job, and she was the only one who could give it to him. "I'm well, Ms. Hopkins. I appreciate the opportunity for an interview."

She smiled warmly at him and sat down behind the desk. She opened a drawer to her left, where she pulled out a manila file folder. "Let's see what we have here," she said, glancing through his recent application to the company. "This says you were in college but decided to take a break and see the world. Is that correct?"

"Yes, Ms. Hopkins. I was in the Computer Science program at a school near my home, but I decided last semester that I needed to take a break from my studies. There is a lot of pressure from my family to do well at school and succeed, but the pressure finally wore on me. I decided it was time to take a break and recharge my batteries." Jimmy tried to act excited, but inside he had no interest in traveling on pretentious ships cleaning up after rich passengers. "So I decided to take a year or two off. I'm looking forward to the possibility of seeing so much of the world."

"Well, Jimmy, your application looks good, and you present yourself well. Tropical Cruise Lines is an equal opportunity employer and is ranked No. 1 in the hospitality cruise industry for customer satisfaction and employee benefits. May I ask where you're from, Jimmy? Your accent sounds as if it's from the Middle East?" Ms. Hopkins inquired innocently enough, but he detected a slight tone of hesitation.

"I'm from India," he lied. "My family moved here when I was still young, for my father's work. Our living conditions in India were poorer, and my family realized we needed to move to a land that offered more opportunities. Though some extended members of my family still live there, and we do send money back to them, my family has no intention of leaving our new home, especially since the North American schools and jobs are so much better."

Lydia smiled broadly and nodded, the answer having satisfied any doubt she may have had. *Good*, thought Jimmy. *It's working.*

"The position pays $16 per hour while you're on shift on the vessel. We also provide you with health insurance and room and board while you're on the ship," said Ms. Hopkins. "You'd be working with other members of the cleaning crew aboard the ship, helping keep the ship in top shape for our guests. How does that sound?"

"Yes, it sounds wonderful," replied Jimmy, sugarcoating his every reply with enthusiasm.

"Most of the work is done in shifts, according to when the guests are normally awake or asleep. The shifts are normally static, but most people start with the evening work until they've been on board for a few cruises. Are you okay with starting on the night shift?" asked Ms. Hopkins.

"Yes, I am. I really just want to see the world, ya' know?"

"Oh absolutely," laughed Ms. Hopkins. "I remember when I was your age, I wanted the same thing."

Jimmy smiled back at Ms. Hopkins, knowing that she had bought his story completely. He had every intention of getting this job and gaining her trust. He needed the full confidence of the crew and his management if this was going to work. "What are the normal work weeks like?" he asked politely. "Not that I'm terribly concerned with working every day, but it might be nice to be able to get off the ship at some ports so I can still see the different ports."

Lydia laughed again. "You certainly are excited, aren't you? Well, on the shorter cruises, such as three to five days, you likely will work every day you're on the ship with the guests. But you will still have opportunities to enjoy some of the ports of call. It's all based on a rotating schedule. On the longer seven to ten-day cruises, you'll have several days off to enjoy the ship and some of the places where we stop at along the way."

Lydia scratched her head with a pen and looked at her computer monitor. "It appears that the next available training is next week, starting Monday. If you're willing to take the position now, I'd like to get you into that class so we can get you on the ship and on to your first port of call. Can you attend?" she asked Jimmy.

"Sure! Do I just show up here for the training?"

"Yep. We'll get you straightened out at that point," replied Ms. Hopkins. She reached into her desk again and pulled out another folder. "All right, I just need you to fill out these forms and have them ready when you show up Monday to start work. Congratulations! It's good to have you on the team. You'll be working on the *Ocean Star* initially. Once you learn the ropes, you can put in for a transfer if you like. Welcome aboard!"

"Thank you, Ms. Hopkins," he responded. "I'm really looking forward to this."

After he had been shown back out of the building, Jimmy glanced out over the water. There were no ships at dock right now, but he had seen them here before. Tropical Cruise Lines was one of the biggest and most popular companies in this industry, and Jimmy knew it.

"Time," he thought silently to himself. "All I need is time. They will trust me, and I will fit in with them. I will work hard, and they will never suspect me."

With that, Jimmy stuffed the folder of forms under his arm, stuffed his hands in his pockets, and walked to his car. His part of the plan was in motion, and he needed to let Salah know.

Chapter 5: Over the Line

August 12, 2004

It was already dark outside when he shut the apartment door behind him and locked it again. He had spent more time at school today than intended, but he reminded himself that some things were necessary. Aside from his normal homework, Salah had been doing some research trying to design a better method for covert communication with his team over the Internet.

"But patience will win the war," he remembered his father telling him as a child. "We have all the time in the world to accomplish our mission." That's really what it had all come down to for the team. In order to get all the team members into the right place and with the correct level of responsibility and privilege, it would take time. It had already been six months since Salah had officially initiated his plans. It seemed like only yesterday that he had sent out the first null cipher to the team to unravel. Their minds were sharp, and they picked up on the cipher quickly. Now they were all employed in strategic locations around North America, allowing him to manipulate events in the future; events that would shake the nation.

And over these same six months, Salah had worked diligently to improve his plans and make each one of them foolproof. No detail was overlooked. Salah knew that the devil was in the details and the slightest mistake or miscalculation could cost him the project and his life. Each person on the team was now completely immersed in the project. No one was willing to back out at this point, and it made Salah proud to have such a great team. He thanked Allah aloud as he set his backpack down next to the desk.

Salah walked from his room to the kitchen. His day had been long, and he had somehow managed to miss lunch. There was normally more time to stop in at the student lounge and grab something during the day, but his research today had consumed the day.

Opening the old refrigerator released a stale odor into the air. He quickly grabbed a can of juice and shut the door again. There was a box of Cheez-Its on the counter that didn't appear too old, so he picked those up as well and walked back to the bedroom. At his desk, he pushed a pile of papers aside to make room for his snack, pulled out his chair, and took up temporary residence. The room and the desk had slowly slipped into a state of controlled chaos as the piles of papers, diagrams, and newspapers piled up over the course of these months. Seemingly unorganized, each pile served a purpose and Salah knew what each one was.

The color monitor flicked on as Salah pressed the power button on the front of the case. Some of his equipment was older now, but it was still capable of performing the simple tasks he required of them. Most of his time now was spent organizing and preparing for the next stage of his plan, ensuring that the team was properly entrenched and had the money they needed for their expenses. The funding was the hard part, as Salah had suspected it would be; there were supplies that were required for this work that he could never have obtained on his own.

For these reasons, Salah had resolved to contact the world's richest and most wide-reaching organization for these types of projects against the West: Al Qaeda. There were several associates of the group known to be residing overseas in various locations, but he really had no idea how to contact them initially. Any information he had about them or their locations was generally very vague and not helpful. Their secrecy and clandestine movements that he so admired now became an annoyance.

Obviously, there wasn't a lot of information available online about where to find them either. In desperation, he had finally asked some of his friends online discrete questions about whether they knew anyone and how to contact them because he was working on a project they might be interested in. But everyone he had asked said nothing. No one there seemed to have any information. If they did, they certainly knew better than to say anything, which left Salah wondering whether he really would be able to make this work.

Just when he was beginning to think there was no way, a strange e-mail had arrived from a person he did not know. The original e-mail headers were fake, and any response back resulted in a bounce reply from his server. He knew enough about networks to suspect the headers when he first saw them, but faith had again overwhelmed him and he had replied anyway.

The message was simple:

```
Salah Aldin,


We have heard of your cause. Your faith will be rewarded in time. Stay
true.
```

That was it. No contact information was given. No mention of how they had heard of him. His initial e-mail reply was all he had left to try, but after his message had bounced back he had almost become disheartened. But today, the past was in the past, and things had progressed much better than even Salah had hoped.

Salah continued to go to school during the day and work on the project at night. He still spent his time in IRC chatting to friends on the channel. There was a thin line of conversation that could be carried concerning the project, but he maintained his opinions in the channel.

About a month after the first e-mail, he had received another one. This e-mail was different, but still not valid.

```
Salah Aldin,


We have been watching you for some time. The West had laden our path with
traps and tricks, trying to find us and hunt us down. But Allah is
gracious and gives us speed and stealth. Your words have rung true for
two years now. I personally have watched you. I want to hear more, but
not via this channel. You will find a personal ad in the Toronto Star
newspaper within the next few days. You will know the ad because it will
```

```
appeal to you. Use the number to Secure Shell into the server. You have
an account, and your IP has been added to our access list. Check Pine.
```

```
G0dCh1ld
```

Salah's initial thought was that it could be a trap; it was too bizarre a situation. How would he know if it was real? How could they have added his IP address to their access control list (acl)? There were so many questions swirling dizzily around inside his head that needed answers, and he wanted them now. It occurred to him that perhaps they had used the same mechanism for determining his IP address as he had used to verify the identity of Jimmy and the others on the team. He had logged into IRC again and performed a *WHO* command on his own username. The answer had been right there in front of him as the output appeared in the chat window.

Output of WHOIS Command Showing Hostmask

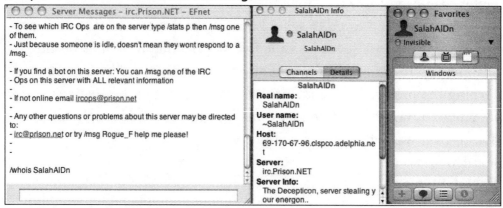

Staring at his hostmask on the screen in front of him, how could he have forgotten? For over a year, Salah had used a static IP address through his ISP, enabling him to access his boxes remotely should he need to. This one configuration setting had standardized his hostmask. It was the same every time he logged IRC. It had provided the person on the other end of that e-mail with a mechanism for determining Salah's true network address. Verifying the fact that the address belonged to a consumer ISP was easy. Adding that address to an acl would be simple for someone with a technical background.

Then, for four days in a row, Salah had gone by the student bookstore on campus and purchased the Toronto Star. He would then walk to the student lounge and carefully go through each of the ads posted there. The personals were sickening to him, but he read every one of them. That entire section of the newspaper seemed to be full of people longing for what they deemed *love* or *respect*.

But he refused to miss the message among the hundreds of personal ads; men looking for men for casual encounters, women looking for men, and men looking for women. There were even ads for "purchasing a foreign wife" aimed at the lonely man. After days of fruitless searching, Salah found his initial excitement waning and was about to give up when his eyes passed a particularly curious ad, one that seemed very out of place when compared with all the others he had read.

```
Woman seeks a God-fearing man
to create a beautiful future with.
Must understand the sacrifices
required for that special relationship.
Strong beliefs required, material wealth
not needed as our reward will be in heaven.


(213)23-11-138
```

The ad had struck Salah as odd simply because it didn't follow the same format as the other personal ads he had been reading for days. In fact, it was the single ad he had read in the entire four days that had not offended him in one way or another. And there was an apparent typo with the ad that resulted in an extra dash in the listed phone number.

This was the only ad he had found possessing the potential to be what he was looking for. *That looks like an IP address*, he thought. He quickly jotted down the phone number, replacing the parenthesis and dashes with periods to see if it fit within the standard for network addresses.

```
213.23.11.138
```

A quick check on that particular IP address showed that the entire network range was assigned to RIPE Network Coordination Centre out of Amsterdam in the Netherlands. *Perfect.* The laws in that part of the world were more flexible and allowed for fewer eyes scrutinizing your every move. It made sense to him. He also found it slightly ironic that the range was only one octet from the U.S. Department of Defense networks at the 214.0.0.0 address range. Mistyping the first octet potentially could lead to curious eyes peering in your direction.

Output from ARIN WHOIS

A quick Nmap port scan of the suspect IP address resulted in finding a single service open on the box, SSH.

Nmap Port Scan Results

```
arting nmap 3.50 ( http://www.insecure.org/nmap/ ) at 2004-08-12 19:21 MDT
st dsl-213-023-011-128.arcor-ip.net (213.23.11.128) appears to be up ... good.
itiating Connect() Scan against dsl-213-023-011-128.arcor-ip.net (213.23.11.12
 at 19:21
ding open port 22/tcp
e Connect() Scan took 0 seconds to scan 1659 ports.
teresting ports on localhost (127.0.0.1):
he 1653 ports scanned but not shown below are in state: closed)
RT    STATE SERVICE
/tcp  open  ssh

ap run completed -- 1 IP address (1 host up) scanned in 0.439 seconds
ocalhost :~$ []
```

Secure Shell (SSH)

The secure shell (SSH) service is a more secure option to the legacy clear text protocols that traditionally have been used to connect with remote servers or transmit files. The SSH service uses encryption to protect the information being transmitted across the network. In the past, services such as Telnet and FTP were used, but provided very little security, as any information transmitted by these mechanisms was sent in clear text and easily could be intercepted and viewed by anyone within the path of communication.

Although Telnet and FTP are still widely used on the Internet today, SSH is considered a secure alternative to these older services. Both commercial and freeware versions of this software are available and easy to install.

Salah sat back in his chair for a moment and smiled to himself, continuing to munch on the Cheez-Its. Those same sensations came flooding back to him as he reflected on the first time he had SSH'd into the foreign box. Until he actually had attempted to log in to the address, he had never even wondered what his login and password might be. But once he had that initial login prompt in front of him, he had panicked. *What should I use,* he wondered.

In the end, he tried using *salah* as his username, since that was what he used everywhere else online. Since no one had met him in person (nor would they have a chance if he had it his way), his handicap was still a safely guarded secret, and his nickname online still valid. The e-mail had told him to check Pine once he logged in, telling him that it was indeed a UNIX box. Usernames on UNIX hosts normally consist of all lower-case characters, so as not to confuse the users. But even knowing his user-name didn't provide any clues as to what his password might be to the system.

He had tried multiple words that might make sense. *Salah. Aldin. Password. Allah. Islam.* All of them had failed, leaving Salah curious and a little frustrated. He had even tried each individual word in the ad, just to see if he may be missing something. That was when the epiphany had come. In desperation, Salah had gone back to the e-mail, looking for clues, when a word caught his eye. The e-mail had been signed at the bottom by someone with the name of *G0dCh1ld.* He wondered briefly what the chances were that this was really a person, versus his own password.

Salah knew from his own research into the most basic of covert chan-nels that some of the most dangerous and important information could be planted right in front of your nose and still never be seen. Information could be made public, but the meaning obscured simply by the apparent contextual use of the information. It made sense to him, but he won-dered if it was really the case or not. The only course of action had been to try because he had no other clues at the time.

It had indeed worked. The password had been placed in the e-mail as a signature to obscure its real use. He had been proud to have come so far. There had been an e-mail waiting for him, a simple e-mail that simply said *Tell Me.* Salah had put his faith on the line at that point and laid out the entire plan.

He explained everything in vivid detail. His entire project was defined in a single, long-winded e-mail to a complete stranger on a strange system. Of course, he had been fearful that it could have been a trap, but the precautions apparently taken by the person on the other end had reassured him that it was indeed safe. There was also the matter of having made appropriate escape plans in the event something went terribly wrong during the project. He didn't want to have to flee, but he didn't want to lose what was potentially the only opportunity he would get for guidance and funding. Or, for that matter, to miss the only chance he had at having a somewhat *normal* life.

Returning to the present, Salah brushed the orange crumbs from his fingers and flipped the switch on his Keyboard-Video-Mouse (KVM) sitting near the backside of the monitor and watched as the Linux command prompt disappeared and a Microsoft Windows screen flickered to life in its place. He needed to do a review of the project again, looking for flaws in his plan. As much as he might abhor using Windows, it was a necessity. By making its operating system so easy to use for the rest of the world, Microsoft had inadvertently created a user-friendly environment for individuals wanting to hide data from others.

He clicked on his Start button and scrolled through his Program Files until he found the shortcut for Visio. Once the program opened completely, he scrolled through the recent files until he found the diagram containing the entire layout of the various cruise ships his team was on by now. The first ship was the largest and belonged to Tropical Cruise Lines. Jimmy was working there and had been an employee for six months.

There were three different cruise lines in total; one of Salah's men placed within each company. The time and patience Salah had worked so hard to master had paid off. "We need to gain their trust and trust takes time," he had told his team. "Each of you will occupy a position of trust in both your work and personal lives on those ships. You will be called *friend*."

It was true. There were three key men doing nothing but working on cruise ships full time; working alongside other people who considered them friends. However, there were other team members whose job it was to assist these three individuals in their duty. The most vital positions involved team members who worked in the security agency that monitored the baggage belonging to the crew and passengers.

There were actually two phases to the plan that Salah and Jimmy had devised, and the cruise ships were only the first. The two key team members on two other cruise ships would begin their work several days before Jimmy. Then, when their efforts were finally coming to the headlines, Jimmy would strike on the third cruise ship, causing mass panic.

They had chosen cruise ships for the first phase because of the lax security and their severe isolation when on a long extended cruise. They also knew that a cruise normally carried a great number of people and would be unprepared for a serious disaster at sea. In fact, the National Transportation Safety Board (NTSB) in the United States had noticed the lax safety and security precautions taken. The idea to use cruise ships was actually the result of a press release from the NTSB detailing a fire in the laundry room of one cruise ship due to improper safety precautions, a story that Salah had bookmarked and referred his team to, at www.ntsb.gov/Pressrel/2001/010514.htm. The smoke from the fire had spread throughout the ship, making many of the passengers and crew ill, but there had been very little damage from the actual fire. That had provided Salah with an idea. There was a way to cause a great deal of terror and panic on the ships without jeopardizing the lives of his team members. There would be no suicide attacks this time.

They planned to use the ships' isolation and lack of concern as a tool against the Americans. If everything went according to plan, the team members would be long gone before the actual attack was recognized. All three ships would be on 10-day cruises when the attacks occurred and help would not be near enough to save all of the victims. The best part about this plan is that the group was using publicly availably information about the ships, along with planted personnel to complete the attack. Salah had systematically gone through the complete deck plans of all the most popular ships, which are conveniently located on web sites created to provide cruise information for potential passengers. There were useful cruise portals, especially for Salah. Ships just like he had just pulled up on his desktop.

Cruise Ship Floor Plan

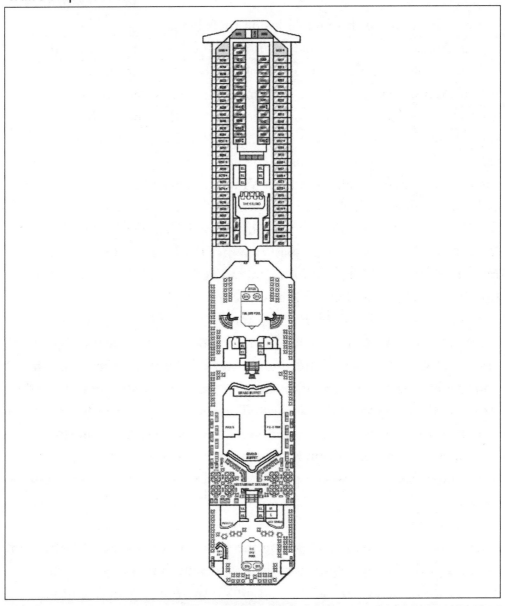

But Salah recalled with satisfaction how this was really only the first phase of their plan. Another much larger target had been chosen and would be hit shortly after these attacks. Just a few people among the thousands crammed into a small area. The death toll would number the thousands before it was complete, but the sheer fear and panic it would cause the American people was the greatest victory. And it would all be done without one of his people losing their lives.

Al Qaeda had been thrilled at his ingenuity. His plan required precise placement of each team member. Each person on the team would work for an extended period of time to generate the trust required to have access to sensitive information and areas. When the day finally arrived, those individuals could escape unharmed. With luck, they would be considered one of the poor victims of the attack and would not be searched for or sought after. Salah closed out Visio and clicked back on his Start button. Scrolling back through his Program Files he came upon the icon for CompuPic. CompuPic helped him maintain his free webspace on Yahoo! and Geocities. For the past five months, Salah had taken various random pictures that he and his team had collected and created two web sites, one at Yahoo! and another at Geocities.

Each web site contained nothing more than 10 pictures of apparent vacations and trips around the globe that had been taken with digital cameras. CompuPic was an inexpensive tool for creating these web sites and would take a directory of images and create the entire HTML code structure that supported the web site. The tool could be had for free from a number of web sites that allowed users to download key generators for the software. Salah never purchased legitimate licenses of the software he used simply because it would provide another mechanism for tracking his movements.

He had used this same technique for months to get the remaining folks in the group used to checking the web site for updates. At this point in time, all they were required to do was to send him an e-mail when they noticed changes to the site and pulled the null cipher from the intended image. But this time, Salah needed to add something real to these web sites. Real data would be inserted into the images this time; key information that Salah needed to start passing to the other team members via these public web sites.

He opened the application by clicking on the CompuPic icon on the menu. Using the Folders menu on the left frame on the user interface, Salah navigated to the Web Pics folder on his D: drive. This is where he kept all his images for the web sites he maintained now and more that he would post at a later date.

Salah's D: Drive

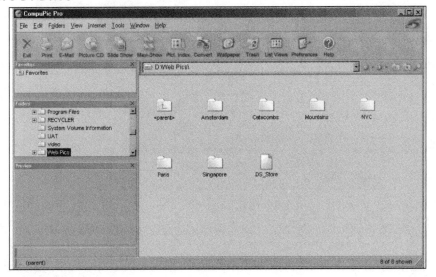

Salah took a moment and reflected on the process he had started. If this was to succeed, he would need everyone on the team to pay attention and do their part. He began by selecting a folder of images for his web site. He would need the aid of the software to create a quick and easy web site, with thumbnails, links, and backgrounds. Once this was complete, he could worry about inserting the data into the various images.

The first thing to do was to select the automatic web page generator option from the Internet menu. This would allow Salah to create web pages with the appropriate image thumbnails to make browsing easier for people on the Internet. He had chosen to use the pictures of Amsterdam in the Netherlands for this web site.

Web Page Generator

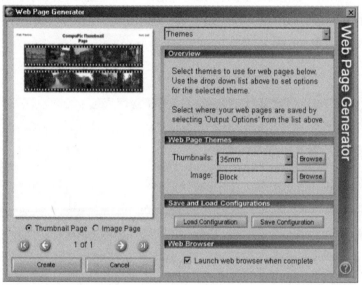

The next thing he needed to do was to select the appropriate options from the drop-down menu in the upper left hand corner of the Web Page Generator window. This would allow him to customize the look of the final web page, including background images, themes used on the page, size of the final thumbnails, directory locations, and even the color and size of the fonts used. The actual creative styling of the web page wasn't nearly as important as the content would be, but at the same time it needed to look like a personal web site. If the page looked as though it were created by an amateur, it could more easily be overlooked.

Once he had selected all the options he wanted for this version of his site, he exported the files to a directory by clicking the Create button at the bottom of the window. The program brought up Microsoft's Internet Explorer, allowing Salah to verify that the images had converted correctly and that the links all worked as he expected. This was the easy part. Technology allowed even the most inexperienced techno-phobe to create a decent web page and post it for the entire world to see. Once everything was configured the way he wanted, it was time to call it a night and get some rest. There would be plenty of time tomorrow to hide his data and upload the new site to one of his sites. Salah closed the Compupic software and shut down the computer. He pressed the monitor's power button to turn the monitor off and reached carefully across the piles of paper on his desk to turn the small lamp off.

My Vacation to Amsterdam

Walking back to his bed, Salah grabbed the small remote control and clicked on the television. He needed a break from the planning. Although he couldn't afford cable television, there were still plenty of channels available on the public airwaves to provide an escape for a while. He kicked off his shoes and sat on the bed. As the images flashed across the small screen, his mind began to relax its grip on reality and Salah began to breathe more evenly.

Chapter 6: Images of Death

August 13, 2004

It was dark. The clock next to the bed cast an eerie glow across her face as she looked at the time. It was 1:56 A.M. Looking across the small room, she noticed that the small television was still on. She had apparently fallen asleep watching CNN. She was lying awkwardly across the small bed, her clothes still on. The fog in her head was clearing now and she remembered: *There had been an attack in the Middle East.*

The news was on nearly all the television and cable networks; they all gratuitously showed blood in the broadcasts, splattered across the broken concrete, bricks, and splintered wood laying in haphazard piles. The bombing had occurred earlier that day in the Iraqi town of Najaf. The world press had jumped on the story hoping to play on the tragedy, recognizing the audience loved death and destruction, as long as it was far from home.

The inadvertent victims of the attack this time were children; their small, innocent bodies lying in the road, covered with blankets as their mothers and fathers sobbed as they kneeled beside them. CNN was rattling off useless statistics about body counts and the number of injured while live pictures of the fatal incident flicked across the screen in an endless stream. The scene made Layla cry. Although she tried to be strong and make her heart cold inside, there was a hurt inside of her; memories of her past tormented her. She could recall her own experience within that violence, losing someone she loved to what they had called an "unfortunate accident." *Unfortunate*, she thought viciously.

As she watched the horrible images on the screen, her mind drifted off, oblivious to the tears that fell slowly from her face, wetting the front of her shirt and blurring her vision. *There was too much death in the world.* Watching these children cry in terror was nearly more than she could bear. The children who had died were now safe, having escaped from the pain. Those who had survived were destined to bear this pain for years, until their own death. Something inside told her to change the channel, to run away from the images, but she couldn't, not yet.

The local authorities in Najaf were reporting that the intended target actually may have been a British government building on the neighboring block. The British army had been using a local building as a command point, but that location was still safe, untouched. There had been an error in the attack. A young man, roughly 17 to 18 years old and of Middle Eastern descent, was seen walking into the building wearing a red backpack just moments before the explosion. No one even questioned him. "He wasn't a foreigner, what was there to fear from our own people?" No one tried to find out why he was there. Perhaps they thought he was someone's brother.

Layla imagined in her mind what it would take to convince a young man that killing so many people was worth ending his own life. What power held sway over his mind, causing him to believe this one act could possibly be the right thing to do? She prayed silently to Allah for some guidance. She desperately needed to understand. Why would He allow someone doing His bidding to wander into a school full of young children? The boy had likely been confused since he had walked into a clearly marked grade school. That one point kept eating at Layla's insides. He hadn't really wanted to do it. He was just as innocent as the other children who died today.

Layla imagined the young man's thoughts as he watched the explosives stuffed into his bag earlier that day by the men controlling his mind and his actions. Did he have the same thoughts she was having? Was there a genuine fear of dying in his eyes? Had he considered the implications of taking other human lives through his own actions, or had he blindly followed where the religious zealots had led him? She wondered whether he had realized at that last moment the mistake he had just made.

Wherever he had started that morning, there were older men behind this, hateful men who had used the boy to achieve their goals. But in the end it was the boy that had died, along with a lot of other innocent children. There had been a misfire in their war. Instead of inflicting harm on the enemy, it had created a tremendous amount of pain for their own people. Their own children had died. It was Arab blood that coated the surrounding sidewalks and roadways.

Religious zealots, regardless of their god, were experts at bending the truth, manipulating words and intentions to fit their own goals. It was easier with children. Kids knew less about life and death. They had fewer life experiences with which to gauge their thoughts and actions. Over the course of history, religions around the world had and still were used by their leaders to make people do terrible things. Layla imagined the words that filled the boys ears while he was being prepared to die for their cause. She could almost hear their voices in her own ears, "This is the will of Allah. You will have a great reward for your actions."

The actions of terrorists reminded her of the Crusades. When a people decided collectively that something was either wrong or right, even in ignorance, the results were devastating. How many people had died in the Crusades because they would not agree to the demands of the religiously zealous? How many of her own people must die before this religious war also came to an end?

A voice in the back of her head urged Layla to ignore the images and concentrate on the reality of the situation. But she was finding it increasingly difficult to concentrate on what she had to do. Her grades were dropping, and she was losing serious sleep due to bad dreams. She had put all of her energy into her work, but she was starting to realize that she had missed that precious balance between what was really important and those things that were just idealistic shadows; shadows placed in her mind by someone else. She missed having friends, having a social life. Inside her mind, she wondered where her youth had gone. Where was the fun in life? She had started taking courses during the summer semester in an effort to graduate a little quicker, but she was starting to wonder if that was part of the reason she was so emotionally strung out lately.

A British correspondent on the screen was trying desperately to talk over the chaos in the background. Men and women crowded the site digging through the rubble, looking for signs of life. Western military forces from the U.S., Britain, Germany, and France scoured the area looking for clues and trying to maintain the peace. The news anchor tried as best she could to appear sympathetic to the chaos and pain surrounding her. Layla had always wanted children. She had always wanted a family. *What would her husband be like? Would he play with the kids in the backyard? Would they have a backyard?*

The real trouble in her mind had started when she had really taken the time to examine the words within the Qur'an on her own. In the past, voices had told her that Allah commanded diligence in the fight against the West. They used a verse in the Qur'an to defend their position. She could almost hear men telling the young man responsible for tragedy on the screen the same things, filling his mind with confusion so that he would be more likely to act in faith.

> *And slay them wherever ye catch them, and turn them out from where they have Turned you out; for tumult and oppression are worse than slaughter; but fight them not at the Sacred Mosque, unless they (first) fight you there; but if they fight you, slay them. Such is the reward of those who suppress faith.* Qur'an 2:191

She had believed her entire life was in her control, but found herself being controlled by ghosts, figures from the past. The truth in the words of the Qur'an had been distorted and half-spoken. These battles were only to be fought when you were attacked first. Her young heart had followed along faithfully, as a child should. But now she was an adult with her own mind. Layla was fighting desperately to free herself from her past. Human life was worth treasuring and protecting.

The clock read 2:13 A.M. when she finally broke down and turned the television off. She laid back down on the bed, quietly crying to herself. The soft, warm sheets cradled her and held her close. There seemed to be no easy way out. She trembled with fear and the cold feeling of let down. She had been betrayed by her family and friends. Whom could she turn to now? Jeremy was the closest thing she had to a real friend. The two had become close when they had started studying together. He offered no malice or pretensions, just a friendly smile and affinity to make her laugh.

The two had enjoyed speaking to each other, but no pretense was ever made at evolving the relationship beyond a simple friendship. They had spent many days and nights studying their schoolwork, trying to bring Jeremy's grades up before he graduated. She was proud to have helped him achieve his goals. They were comfortable with that arrangement, and neither seemed bent on changing their situation. But Jeremy had graduated months ago and now she felt utterly alone at school. She had his new phone number and thought that perhaps she would feel better if she called him. It had been a couple of weeks since they last spoke.

He was now working back in the United States, for some organization in Washington, D.C. Although they didn't see each other much anymore, there was always time for a quick phone call or an e-mail. Perhaps she would call him tomorrow and check on him. E-mail was always convenient, but she really needed the warm touch of a friend's voice on the other end of the phone.

Her head started to drift into the darkness. Jeremy's face flashed before her mind's eye just before she lost all contact with conscious world.

Chapter 7: The Real Assignment

September 23, 2004

"Jeremy!" A voice shot across the office. Jeremy stood up to look over the cubicle wall and watched as his partner walked across the office toward his cubicle. He was truly enjoying his new life in a real job. His security clearance had been approved about five months earlier, enabling him to start working on actual cases versus sitting in an uncleared facility studying investigation training manuals. When Jeremy had walked into this office for the first time, he found the work already piling up for him, since apparently, the other employees had been anticipating his arrival. But much to his own disappointment, he found all the initial cases to be exercises in futility. The other team members had already grown accustomed to those cases that were likely to be fraudulent and had graciously taught Jeremy his first real lesson on the new job.

The voice currently bellowing his name from across the room was his partner, Neil Hanson. Neil was a nice guy and had worked in the intelligence community for over 20 years, but had not adapted very well to the change of working environment that came hand-in-hand with the creation of the Department of Homeland Security. Neil's position had been absorbed into the new agency because his job duties were believed to fall into that gray, confusing, nebulous realm of responsibility given to the new DHS. Unfortunately, Neil's technical knowledge was dated. In short, it had simply been too many years since he had worked in the technical weeds. Jeremy originally was concerned that he may have landed the *partner no one else wanted*, but over time he realized that being partnered with Neil allowed him to play with the technology while Neil handled the paperwork and politics—things that Jeremy found boring and monotonous.

Jeremy's string of bad cases certainly didn't reflect the organization as a whole. The department was just starting to get really organized, and the intelligence coming from the field was filtering in, more every day. The latest wave of advisories had warned, almost incoherently, of identified terrorist groups communicating and planning across the Internet. Some of the older colleagues considered the idea far-fetched and never gave it much more thought. But Jeremy had already decided that he believed the reports. He knew there were some methods of communicating securely across the Internet without anyone really knowing it was happening.

Neil's short, squat body came fumbling haphazardly toward Jeremy with a folder in his hands. Neil was about 5 feet 2 inches tall and slightly rounded around his middle. His hair was a mix of blonde and gray. Although he was still only in his early 40s, Neil looked older than that. Jeremy suspected this was because Neil had gone through two very painful divorces during the last 10 years. There was also the issue of Neil's diet, which was typically littered with processed cheese sauces, fried meats, and few vegetables and fruits. But Neil's attitude was eternally optimistic, and Jeremy genuinely enjoyed working with the man. The difference in their age had very little effect on their relationship, and they quickly became close friends.

"Jeremy! I think we actually may have gotten something legit this time around. Look at the documents in this folder and tell me what you see here."

Neil panted at Jeremy with a broad smile on his face. Jeremy smiled back, knowing that this is how every one of their cases began. Neil would get excited at the prospects of the *case of a lifetime,* but it would most likely lead to a dead end. He extended his arm across the space between them and took the envelope from Neil's hands. It looked like all the other envelopes he had opened in the past five months to find nothing but a wild goose chase hidden inside. There was a Top Secret cover sheet on the outside indicating that the information potentially could cause extremely grave damage to the country if it fell into the wrong hands. His heart sank slightly as he internally readjusted his expectations.

Opening the envelope, he pulled out a standard manila folder and opened it across his hands so that he could look at the contents. The document on top was typed in an Arabic font. "Hmmm, it looks like a captured transmission in Arabic to me. But you know, I can't read any of this," Jeremy said as he surveyed the material.

"I know that, dude," Neil responded with a grin. "The translation is in there, as well. It would appear that there is a terrorist project under way that's using the Internet as a communications medium. The analysts believe the two people speaking here are members of Al Qaeda."

"Al Qaeda? Are you sure about that, Neil?" Jeremy asked. "That's a pretty big claim. The analysts are certain about this?"

"Well, that's what they say. I asked them point blank about how certain they are about this information, and they simply said that without giving up the actual source of the tap, they're fairly confident." Neil responded. "You know how they are about revealing their sources. Plus, we aren't cleared for that type of information."

"Oh, yeah, I understand that. Sorry, I didn't mean to come off like that. But honestly, terrorists have been using the Internet for a long time now. It's common knowledge. Heck, I studied transcripts of Internet communication between known terrorists when I first got here. But everything we've seen in the past has always been irrelevant e-mails, right? They've never sent anything significantly useful before, at least that I know of." Jeremy was confused by the involvement of Al Qaeda officials in the transcript. This wasn't the normal style of Al Qaeda. They preferred the appeal of mass media to sending low-key messages. Jeremy always thought it had something to do with the fact that terrorists like to scare as many folks as possible at the same time.

"Neil, why would Al Qaeda chance a transmission about using the Internet to move sensitive information about an attack when they know we have the ability to monitor that? It seems odd and out of character for them."

"I don't know, Jer. That's one of the issues that has me stumped. But the transcript was sent back to the analysts twice for retranslation, just to be certain. Each time a different analyst translated the transcript from Arabic to English the results were nearly identical. They're planning on using the Internet to coordinate the attack."

"It's almost as if they're taunting us. You can almost hear them say, 'Just try to find us.'" Jeremy wasn't comfortable with the message at all. "So there were three translations total? Do we know the targets yet?"

"No other information was given. Man, I know what you mean; it's almost as if they want us to know they're planning something. Jeremy, my instincts tell me that this is either really big or a complete load of bull."

Jeremy was a little caught off guard, but wanted to look through the entire transcript again. It didn't make sense to him. His first thought was that someone had probably just gotten overly excited by the transcript and had misread something, somewhere. "I can't tell which way to take this either. Why don't I go over the transcript and see what I can come up with? Then we can meet back here or in your office over lunch and discuss our options. Is that okay with you?"

"Sure, have at it. I need to get some paperwork finished up before I can devote all my attention to this anyway. Why don't we have lunch in my office so that we can shut the door? I'll have Stephanie order for us."

"That sounds good to me," replied Jeremy. "I'll see you then."

With that, Neil turned on his heels and walked back toward the other side of the office. It really didn't make sense to Jeremy. Al Qaeda knew the Americans had the ability to monitor their activities on the Internet. Most of their communications on the Internet took place in locations where traffic was routed through a US location eventually anyway. So why would they give away their intentions so blatantly? The only real answer seemed to be a deliberate misdirection on their part. *Maybe they're trying to send us off on a wild goose chase so that an attack against a legitimate target goes undetected until it's too late*, he thought to himself.

He cleared a space on his desk for the folder and set it down in front of him. The folder had only about 10 pages in it, including the three analysts' translations and the original text in Arabic script. The documents in native format simply looked liked a bunch of gibberish to Jeremy. The writing looked graceful enough and Jeremy found it slightly ironic that such a beautifully written document could contain information about the intentional attack on innocent individuals. Jeremy noticed the tracking information on the cover of the folder, showing the document's traversal through the U.S. intelligence channels to be verified and reverified.

Shuffling through the documents, Jeremy pulled the initial translation, done by the first analyst, from the pile. He had decided that it was probably best to read them in order. The analysts worked at another agency and underwent consistent training and retraining in language skills to ensure that they could perform in their jobs effectively. They had been trained for situations like this one. But the analysts were still human beings, and human beings make mistakes often. Jeremy was told early on that this was the precise reason that transcripts were sometimes sent back to the originating agency for verification. The fact that real intelligence data was even flowing between the different federal and military departments in the United States was a testament to the fact that the people in charge really *were* interested in making the Department of Homeland Security a success.

This was one of those times when the information needed to be verified. The American government had already received bad press for poor translations and errors in interpretation. Someone else must have thought this communication important or it would have never been sent back for the second verification. Jeremy placed the first translation on top of the remaining documents and turned on the florescent lamp sitting at the back of his desk. He took a pencil and followed along with its tip as he read each line.

Date: 20 August 2004

Analyst: jks4513-c54

Source: FSY67901-00871

<Male 1> 4567 to 9856

<Male 2> 9856 to 4567. You are clear.

<Male 1> Good morning, brother. God bless and protect you.

<Male 2> God bless and protect you as well. What news do you have?

<Male 1> God is surely with us. We are vigilant as always. The training continues and we see new recruits every new day.

<Male 2> That is wonderful. We are meant to perform great duties. He is aware of the good things you're doing and agrees that you have a talent for bringing in strong young men to follow in our footsteps.

<Male 1> Thank you. I am truly grateful. He honors me.

<Male 2> Are your supplies current? Do you need food or weapons to continue the training?

<Male 1> I sent a request yesterday for new supplies and expect them to arrive within the week. Thank you. We conserve what we have, but still we need more because the number of new soldiers grows with each passing day. They migrate to us just like the birds in the sky.

<Male 2> This is great news surely. I have news to pass on to your students. This information will light the fire in their souls and keep them passionate.

<Male 1> Excellent! What news do you have for me?

<Male 2> We have uncovered a new plan that will cause the Americans great pain and suffering. This plan was not born of our family, but rather another who holds true to the same cause. The plan is bold and will strike directly under the American nose, like an asp in tall weeds.

<Male 1> That is good news! How did you come to know this?

<Male 2> I cannot say. I do not know. But the Americans can look to their front and look to their back and never see these attacks coming. We should be proud.

<Male 1> I will definitely pass this news on to the soldiers. You are right. It will excite them further.

<Male 2> Goodbye, brother. With peace until next time.

<Male 1> Peace to you until next time.

The idea of so many men, young and old, flocking to these training camps looking for an opportunity to take down America sent a shiver through Jeremy's spine. *It's creepy*, he thought to himself. *So many hate me but don't know I exist.* After a brief moment of reflection, he set aside the initial translation and moved on to the first verification. Aside from a few differences in the choice of vocabulary used by the translator, the overall gist of the two documents was the same. Al Qaeda had uncovered a plan to attack US interests within the country and would be utilizing the public Internet to communicate the plans and monitor progress. But it still didn't make sense to Jeremy. They had to suspect by now that the Americans had the ability to monitor most of their Internet traffic, so why would they use public channels to communicate plans they intended to be successful. He set the document down on top of the other and moved on to the second verification.

The format of the translations was standard. It identified the date the traffic was collected, provided the identification of the analyst, and gave a source code that meant absolutely nothing at all to Jeremy. He had speculated a few times on what that alphanumeric code really meant, but finally resigned himself to the fact that he would likely never know. It was the content that really mattered anyway and what this message was saying seemed clear, but Jeremy wasn't so sure. Each version of translation mirrored the others, with only minor differences in the choice of vocabulary chosen by the analyst.

It seemed to Jeremy as if the two men communicating in the transcript either didn't have a clue about what was really happening or they were attempting to divert the United States government's attention away from another, more legitimate attack likely being coordinated and carried out elsewhere. The only other option was that they were simply taunting the American forces in order to watch them jump. Jeremy wasn't sure which one of these things it actually was, and the doubt left him feeling disconcerted and wary.

As he considered the ramifications of what might be happening, another question popped into his mind. How had Al Qaeda "uncovered" the plan in question? There were any number of different terrorist groups around the world, including Hamas, that could be in on the action. All these groups would jump at the chance to cause pain and suffering for thousands of American citizens. But who, specifically, had developed the plan? And how did this plan come to the attention of the most influential and feared terrorist group on the planet? Jeremy's mind brought up an image of the movie *Wizard of Oz*. Who is the little man behind the curtain? he wondered to himself.

He sat at his desk for another hour analyzing the documents and trying to make some sense of what he was reading. Meandering around in his investigations like a child lost in the park was not his style. But despite the current lack of clarity in the case, Jeremy realized that all this speculation wasn't getting him any closer to solving the case. And regardless of the real intent behind the communiqué, Homeland Security would want to know what it meant. In reality, he and Neil were likely to spend the next two weeks chasing ghosts. But he couldn't gamble the lives of hundreds, possibly thousands of Americans on his reluctance to waste his time. The truth was that this could all be real.

In those cases where there was a suspected mistranslation in a document, the various U.S. departments would send the original transcripts to one of their agents who was also a native speaker, someone who knew the language inside and out and could more easily discern the connotations hidden in the message. But Jeremy knew these were in high demand and that their time would be difficult to obtain. Looking at his watch, he noticed that it was almost time for his lunch appointment with Neil.

He quickly placed the documents back into the folder, replaced the cover sheet denoting the classification of the contents, and closed the clasp on the end. Looking back at the tracking sheet on the front, he noted silently that Neil had been the last to sign for the documents. He double-checked the other documents lying on his desk, reassuring himself that no classified information had been left out for prying eyes. Verifying that his computer screen had been locked and would require his password to log back in, he picked up the envelope and walked out of his cubical toward Neil's office across the workspace. "Just once I hope this isn't another wild goose chase," he thought to himself. "Maybe I'll feel better after I get some food in my stomach."

"Did you find anything useful?" Neil asked as Jeremy walked into his office.

"Nothing really," he responded as he quietly shut the door behind him. "And I'm not really sure where we should start with this one."

Jeremy glanced over at the small conference table in the corner of Neil's office and noticed that lunch had already been delivered. The piles of documents and manuals that once occupied the space on the surface of the conference table had been carefully placed in piles against the wall, behind the table. Neil had his own methods of organization that Jeremy never really could grasp, but he knew that if he needed something, Neil knew right where it would be. He heard his stomach growl softly and found himself hoping that they had remembered to order him pastrami on rye with mayo, his favorite.

"I'm a little confused about why they would give so much information out via a channel that they have to suspect is compromised," he continued. "They have more secure channels of communication. Do you think that maybe they're trying to send us off the trail to what's really going on?"

"I really don't know, Jer. I have to admit that I have some of those same suspicions. It might be nice to have a real case this time. I think we've been tortured enough by your training, at this point." Neil had a way of occasionally mimicking the thoughts in Jeremy's head. Sometimes it proved to be a good thing and other times it was simply annoying. This time, however, Jeremy just smiled back at Neil, knowing full well that it was good-natured ribbing.

"Did you get your paperwork done, yet? I want to get this case started so that we can get on with our lives," Jeremy said as he smiled. He knew that Neil likely rushed right back to his office and already would have completed his reports and hand delivered them up the chain. Neil enjoyed starting new cases, but rhythm of the changing case load kept the job interesting for both of them.

"Of course I got the paperwork completed and filed it about 45 minutes ago for final review with the department head." With that, Neil stood up and walked around his desk, heading for the boxes on the conference table holding their lunch. "Time for lunch. We can talk more while we eat. I'm starving to death here!"

"Well, I'm trying to be excited about this one, Neil, but it just seems as if we get all the least popular jobs. When you told me that I wouldn't get a real case for a while, I was hoping you were just giving me a hard time." This fact had annoyed Jeremy since he started this job. He knew deep down that it was a simple fact of life that the newest members of the team were assigned the cases least likely to be legitimate. In fact, it might even be a great training program for new agents, but everyday he hoped his dues would be paid, and he'd be rewarded with something a little more interesting.

"You know how it works by now. Besides, be glad that we're not on some heavy job. Do you know how many times I missed a good home-cooked meal so that I could stay at work and follow through on something that was considered critical?"

Jeremy suspected Neil was right, as was normal in situations where his inexperience needed to be checked. But he hadn't had a real case yet and he suspected deep down that this one would be no different. "Fine. But I don't have to like it, you know. You called it on-the-job training; I call it boring."

Neil laughed out loud, causing Jeremy to realize that Neil had sat down at the table and was already opening one of the boxes, marked *Turkey* on top with a big black marker. Jeremy walked over to the table and pulled out the chair across from Neil. Reaching to the center of the table, he grabbed the other box and smiled to himself when he saw the word *Pastrami* written across the top in the same black ink. Stephanie, their office manager, already had him pegged and took just as good care of him as she did the other agents. "You won't be a rookie forever, Jeremy," she had told him just last week. But he still wasn't completely convinced yet.

"Well, buddy, all I can really tell you is to hang in there. You've got good analytical skills, so I'd imagine that it won't be much longer before you're in over your head like the rest of the teams." Neil pulled the toothpick with the skewered pickle and olive off the top of his sandwich and set it to the side. "Besides, who's to say that this assignment isn't the real thing? You never know for sure."

"I suppose you're right," Jeremy responded as he watched Neil take the first bite of his sandwich. "You never really answered my question, though. Doesn't it seem odd for Al Qaeda to try and bait us like this? In all your years doing this type of work, have you ever seen something so seemingly obvious?" he asked before leaning over to take the first bite of his sandwich.

"No case is ever the same," Neil began. "But to tell you the truth, all the new technology has really changed the way I view the world, and this job. We can't afford to overlook even the most obvious of clues. When I first started this job, it was easier to spot the planted evidence and rule it out. The simple fact that almost anyone can afford a computer and a connection to the Internet has me believing that most things I used to think were impossible or foolishness are now quite possible or realistic. It's a scary thought"

Neil grabbed a chip out of his open box and popped it in his mouth. He was watching Jeremy chew. "What is it about this particular case that has you all wrapped around the axle like this, Jeremy? Is it the actual documents themselves, or are you just getting burned out on getting run around with the crap cases?"

"Well, sure, I'm tired of not having a real case, but it's really the way the two subjects in the message talk about the attacks. One guy basically lays it out there that there is this great new plan to kill Americans but that they didn't create the plan themselves. Then he uses the word *uncover* to describe how they initially got involved. On top of everything else, he doesn't give any details about the plan beyond the fact that someone out there has the same agenda as Al Qaeda. It's so general and vague that it's disconcerting for me. I'm not even sure that they actually *know* any of the details." Jeremy popped open the can of soda next to his lunch box and took a sip.

"True, that is definitely an interesting choice of vocabulary," Neil answered. "I don't think we should get caught up in a single word, but it does raise the question of why another group would approach Al Qaeda with a plan they devised on their own. Most of the terrorist groups out there seem to want the spotlight for themselves."

"Money, maybe? If you're a terrorist, have a great idea, but no means for carrying it out, would you share the spotlight with someone else in order to achieve your agenda?" Jeremy had been required to take a two-week terrorist psychology course as part of his training for the new job. Most terrorist organizations preferred to take credit for actions they performed in the name of Allah. The agent was left to his or her own devices to wonder why, but Jeremy had decided somewhere along the way that it was basically for bragging rights. *I'll have a greater reward in heaven than you will.*

"That certainly provides us with a motive for the planning party to alert Al Qaeda. And heck, it even makes sense, at that." Neil chuckled to himself as Jeremy frowned at the joke. "But we still don't have an idea who did the planning in the first place and whether they're still controlling the operation. On top of everything else looming over our heads at the moment, we don't even know *what* the plan is at this point."

Jeremy had to concede that point, even to himself. "After lunch I think I'll go check out the normal terror-based web sites and see if I can figure something out. Should I just go through all the normal steps for this one and see if we can locate any corroborating information?"

"Actually," Neil began, "that's a very good place to start. If we run out of leads, we'll delve a little deeper on this one. While you're doing that, I'll go have a talk with some of the other agents and see if they have anything that could be connected."

"When are we due to give our initial thoughts on the case?" Jeremy asked.

Neil grimaced slightly, realizing that he hadn't passed on that bit of important news to Jeremy. "It's due tomorrow afternoon before we leave for the weekend."

Jeremy glanced up at Neil. "That's a really short deadline, Neil. Maybe this *is* the real deal." He had already started to get his hopes up about this case. "All right, I'm going to get back to work." He stuffed the remaining sandwich back in the box and closed the lid. Grabbing the box, the folder, and his drink, Jeremy walked toward the office door.

"I'll check in with you in an hour or so and see how you're faring. Gotta finish lunch first, ya know?" Neil responded. "And let me know if you come across anything interesting so that I can follow up while you continue doing your research."

"Sure thing." Neil balanced his soda can on top of the box lunch, turned the doorknob, and left Neil's office. "*Gawd*, I hope this is a real case."

Neil watched as the door closed quietly behind Jeremy. Once the coast was clear, he got up from his chair and grabbed the phone on his desk, quickly dialing an internal number. "He's starting off great on this one. I told you he was ready."

"Hey, Layla! It's great to hear your voice. How are you doing?" Jeremy was genuinely excited to hear from his friend. It had been several weeks since they had last spoken, and he suddenly remembered that he was supposed to call her next. Flushing with embarrassment, he realized that work had absorbed his attention. "I'm sorry I haven't called. A new project fell into my lap, and I've been totally swamped."

"It's okay. It's good to hear your voice, too," came the reply from the other end. "Things are a lot more boring without you here." Layla laughed softly. It made Jeremy smile, listening to her laugh always made him smile. "I'm getting closer to my own graduation now and find I'm going to have to leave the safety of college soon. Were you scared when you were looking at being out in the real world?"

"Sure, I was scared, but I was also really excited." He paused—she sounded distant and distracted. "Just think of all the cool stuff you get to do once you get out! With your grades and knowledge, you should be able to get a job anywhere you like. And I have to say, getting that paycheck every couple of weeks is still a good feeling. One of the guys I work with, Neil, tells me the newness will wear off soon, but I'm having the time of my life. Have you considered where you want to work yet?"

There was a beat of silence on the other end of the line before Layla answered. "Jeremy, I've been so scared to leave the school that I haven't even gone to speak to a counselor yet. I really don't know what I want to do. I guess I've been in school so long that I can't imagine a life outside the university." Layla laughed again, this time nervously before quickly changing the subject, "How's your job going now, or is it too top secret to talk about?"

"It's getting better. I was really starting to get bored until this last project popped up. One thing I've learned is that it's considered normal practice to torment new people in the office by giving them all the nasty projects. But it looks like things are turning around now," Jeremy answered, but he refused to have the conversation shift to him, he was concerned about his friend. "You really should go talk to a counselor and apply for some jobs, Layla. Do you need any help or advice from me? Remember, I've already been down this road, so maybe I can help quell some of your fears."

"Oh, I'll go soon. I guess I've just been putting off the inevitable." Layla drew in a deep breath. "Jeremy, do you think I'd have an issue getting a job, a good job?"

"That's a pretty silly question coming from you. You're not going to have any issues getting a job." Jeremy sighed quietly to himself and lowered his voice, "What's got you all wound up, Layla? Seriously, you're the smartest person at the university in this field. Why are you so worried? Is something wrong?"

"I'm not totally sure what it is," came the reply. "I suppose at some level it has to do with the role of women in my culture. Women aren't exactly considered prominent members of Middle Eastern society, at least in most Arabic countries." Layla paused, trying to collect her thoughts. On the other end of the phone, Jeremy waited, allowing Layla the opportunity to continue as she needed.

"Jeremy, I really am scared of the quote-unquote real world. I know it sounds cliché, but it's hard for Middle Eastern women who have walked this path to be accepted back home. To be honest, I guess I've never really considered what it is I want to do for the rest of my life. There has always been something else out there distracting me and helping me avoid the fact that eventually I'm going to have to be a member of the working class."

Jeremy could understand at least part of her concern. He had desperately avoided making any decisions about what he was going to do. But in the last year that he and Layla had been friends, it had never occurred to him that she had unusual obstacles that he hadn't experienced. "Layla, I had never really considered what you're up against. That's probably a lot of pressure for you. But let me assure you that you have what it takes to be a success. There is a very bright future ahead of you, all you have to do is reach out for it."

"I suppose you're right," she answered. "I need to figure out a few other details in my life before I graduate, but I'll definitely make plans to see a counselor in the next week or so." She sounded more hopeful now, and it made Jeremy smile.

"If you need any help, just let me know," Jeremy replied. "I mean that. I want to help you with this."

"Thanks, I'll take you up on that. Well, I better let you get back to what you were doing. Can I call you next week once I start making some progress on this? I'll likely need another one of your motivational talks." Layla laughed.

"That sounds great, Layla. If I don't hear from you by the following weekend, I'll give you a call myself. Hang in there. You're a smart young woman, and everything is going to work out fine."

"You're a good friend, Jeremy," she replied. "Take care of yourself, and I'll call you later."

"Bye, Layla. I'll talk to you soon."

Layla hung up the phone quietly and sat in her apartment staring at it sitting on her nightstand. Jeremy had faith in her abilities; he had been there to support her without ever asking for anything but her friendship in return. And, that's what she really wanted, to be accepted, and a chance to be normal. Her entire life had been spent trying to live up to other's expectations and not her own. Every day, now, was spent fighting an internal battle about what was right and what was wrong. Did she really have an opportunity to be something more? The real question was whether she had the ability to clear her mind of those built-in misconceptions and take those steps toward her own future, a future she had dreamed of often enough.

She was tired of fighting herself. The battle inside her was nearly over, and her past was losing. She breathed a sigh of relief at the thought of being free. Hundreds of years of cultural beliefs had consumed her since birth, but she envisioned herself as the phoenix rising from the ashes. It was time to tell Jeremy the truth. She needed serious help with this.

Chapter 8: Creating the Code

September 24, 2004

Salah woke up the next morning with the sky still dark outside and his head pounding. The alarm clock on the nightstand next to his bed seemed to be blaring much louder than normal. As frustrated as he might be, he knew that the clock was set to perpetually ensure that he was up in time for the morning call to prayer and so he took a deep breath and tried to calm his weary mind. His body was exhausted as well. He felt as if he had slept very little during the night.

The truth of the matter was that his sleep had been restless, at best. His father's image has become an even more frequent occurrence. The lack of sufficient rest was clouding his mind, sometimes making it difficult for him to concentrate. But today was Saturday, and it would take him only a couple of hours to get his work done this morning, then he could relax. Basically, he really just needed the break.

He climbed out of bed and pulled the sheets back up. There were a few minutes left before the prayer, so he headed to the bathroom. Today would be a good day. He had some very important things to attend to, then he would be free. Yes, today would be a great day.

After the morning prayer, he started his coffee and took a quick shower to wake himself up. Salah walked out of the bathroom wrapped in a towel, feeling a little more refreshed. After drying off he made his way to the small closet on the far wall of his bedroom, looking for some clothes to put on. A T-shirt and blue jeans should work; he could change later if he decided to go out once the work was completed. If the web site wasn't updated today, there would be questions from the group. The last thing he needed were questions from the others about where he had disappeared to or why he had stopped responding.

When Salah finished getting dressed, he decided it was time to pour himself a steaming cup of coffee, grab some breakfast, and finish up the web site with the hidden content for the other group members. Walking into the kitchen, he turned the heat off on the stove and poured the dark, steamy liquid into a clean cup. Salah set the pot back on one of the back burners and looked in the fridge for food. He grabbed a small block of cheese from the fridge and set it on a plate. Reaching across the counter, he grabbed a loaf of French bread, tore off a piece, and set it on the plate next to the cheese. The finishing touch to his breakfast was a red apple, cut into slices.

Once he had his breakfast in hand, he walked back to his computer desk and set the plate precariously on a pile of papers next to his monitor. The coffee was set down on a coaster conveniently placed in the only clear spot that still existed on the desktop. Salah admonished himself for failing to keep his work area clean and made a mental note to get that done before he left for the day. It wouldn't take much longer, and it wasn't his style to be sloppy. *It must be because I'm so tired and distracted*, he thought to himself. *I'll take care of this in a little while.*

Salah sat down in his computer chair and turned on the computer. Last night he had managed to at least get a web site created inside CompuPic before he simply could not do any more work. All 10 images were integrated into a full set of hypertext files and thumbnail images that could simply be uploaded to his server. Today, he needed to hide his first real message in the images. He wanted the information to be freely available on the Internet, but not be noticed. In order to accomplish this, he had come up with a creative scheme for hiding the information by utilizing all 10 images. Even if someone managed to detect the information in one or more of the images, which was unlikely considering how much information he was hiding, they would find it very difficult to find out how to get the information back out again.

Salah had decided to use 10 images on each web site he created for planning. Only one of these images contained the actual message he intended the members of his group to read. The other nine images would act as both a diversion and a single step in the process. He had imagined the nine images as a disassembled staircase, lying on the floor in front of the tenth image. But the stairs could not just be put together randomly; they would need to be in a particular order or they would all fall apart.

Each of the nine images would contain a single word message that somehow gave a clue to the user about how to get the information from the tenth image. He had created a path of competence that each user would have to traverse in order to obtain the final message. Not even the members of the group could get to the real message until the rest of the puzzle was unraveled.

Hiding the Message

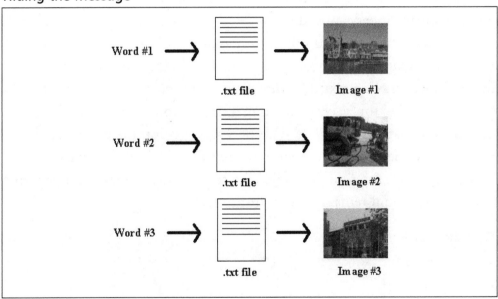

The only information his team would receive was a string of numbers. Nine digits in random order that would provide the right mind the key to the hidden information. There was no chance that someone would accidentally stumble across the information. Even if someone happened to capture the information as it traversed the Internet, it would look like some random string of numbers. No other associated data would be sent. But the next step for Salah was to create nine text files with one key word each.

Salah logged into his Windows box and brought up the Notepad application. Notepad was easy to use and created very simple text files with no extra format information. A lot of data was contained in binary document formats, like Microsoft Word, that could dramatically increase the size of your text file. Salah understood that, as more information was hidden in a file, the chance of detection would increase as well. Notepad would create a text document containing the information he needed to communicate without adding unnecessary bytes of superfluous binary data to the file that would inherently threaten to compromise his plan. He wanted the information to be out on the Internet, but he did not intend to make it easy to find.

The application popped up on his desktop with an empty document. He began typing the first word that would be hidden in the first image in his sequence. Nine text documents were created and saved into a folder on his desktop, each containing a single word. Every time he needed to update the web site with new information for the group as a whole, he would have to recreate new text files for insertion into the 10 new images. But the time it would take to do this was worth the fact that the message would remain hidden from view.

Example Text Payload

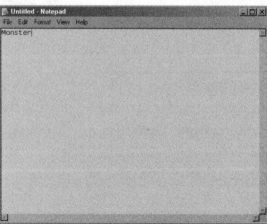

When all nine files were created and saved to a folder on his desktop, Salah opened the JPHS (JP Hide and Seek) software. This would serve as his tool of choice for creating the hidden information on his web site. There were some bright men in the group who easily could have learned to use a more difficult tool, but Salah understood that there were also some others that wavered right on the edge of understanding the entire process. He had what Allah had given him to work with, and he would not turn away someone willing to put his or her life on the line for this project. Pushing a more difficult tool on the group at this stage could have unexpected and possibly unpleasant results in the short term. Plus, the tool was freely available on a number of web sites, including the Stego Archive at www.stegoarchive.com, making it very easy for the team members to download on their own. The other positive aspect about using this particular tool was that it could be used under the Windows operating system. Not everyone on the team had experience with Linux, so it made sense to stick with the Windows-based tools.

The first dialogue to pop up was a disclaimer written by the author of the tool. Salah found it slightly humorous that a disclaimer was written into an application like JPHS. It seemed obvious what the use of the application was intended to be when it was created. He clicked the button at the bottom of the dialogue, indicating that he agreed not to try to pass the work off as his own or to export it to dangerous lands.

JPHS Disclaimer

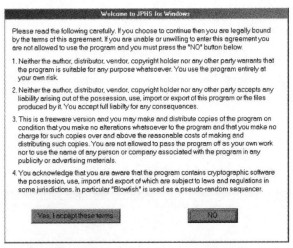

Salah was immediately met with the main JPHS window.

Main JPHS Window

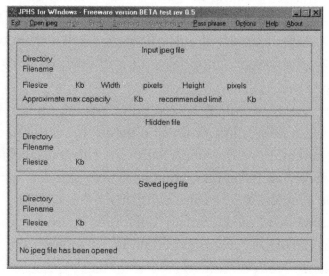

Salah looked at the open JPHS window on his desktop and noted the four distinct sections in the window. The program was written to be easy to use. The first section gave information about the JPEG image that was loaded under JPHS. This was the carrier file. The second section gave information about the file being hidden, also known as the payload. The third section would give the user information about the file once it was saved back to the disk. The last section, section four, would provide a status on the process of hiding information. He took note that the program showed that no image file had been opened yet, which was the first step in hiding information under JPHS.

He needed to open a JPEG image file. JP Hide and Seek works the same way whether you're hiding data or pulling hidden data back out of the image. The image has to be opened first. Salah clicked on the Open Jpeg option on the menu bar at the top. JPHS brought up a file directory dialog so that Salah could pick the carrier file from his hard drive. He chose the first image in his Amsterdam directory and clicked Open.

Open...

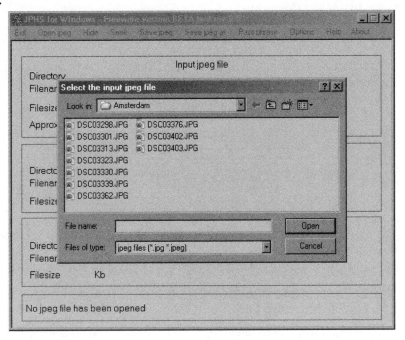

Salah could see that the image was indeed loaded and ready for him to hide his data. He clicked the Hide option on the menu bar at the top of the window and was immediately prompted with a file selection window to pick the file he wanted to hide. Salah navigated to the directory containing the nine text files and chose the one that would be hidden in this image and clicked Open. The software prompted him for a pass phrase that would be used to hide the text file in this image. Without this pass phrase, no one would be able to pull the text file back out of the image. Salah entered the pass phrase twice, as prompted by the software. Clicking OK, he watched as the software returned to the main window.

Returning to the Main Window

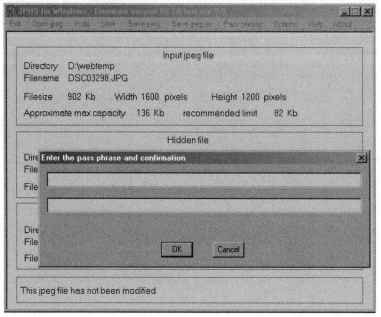

Once Salah had clicked OK, the program brought up another file directory dialog box, prompting Salah to pick the payload file. Salah navigated to the first of the text files he had just created with Window Notepad and clicked Open on the dialog box. The ease of using these free tools always amazed Salah. Their creators built these applications and posted them for public access. Some of the best tools for this type of work never required a payment from the user.

Salah looked at the screen and smiled to himself. He had to admit that there were still bugs in the software that caused him to occasionally grunt in irritation. Sometimes the application would just hang, doing nothing at all. At other times, the entire operating system would freeze up, requiring the user to cold boot the computer. Still, the software was free to use and was powerful enough to do what Salah needed. He easily could live with a few known bugs. Besides, the software didn't crash *that* often when you really sat and thought about it.

Picking the Payload File

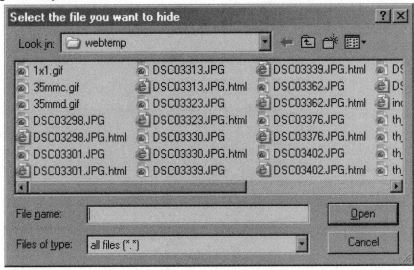

Salah smiled at himself as he considered again how easy it was to hide information like this. The mechanism itself was simple enough, but the plan behind the technology would make the planning a success. He intentionally had chosen a simple process with a complex plan. The plan would cover for the ease of the technical side of the project. When the file was selected, the software returned to the main window again, waiting for Salah's next command. Looking at the bottom of the JPHS window, Salah noted to himself that the image and the payload file had been selected, but the jpeg image had not yet been saved to a new file on the disk. He clicked on the *Save jpeg as* option to save the image with a new filename. A new window popped up, prompting Salah for a directory and a new filename for the new image.

New Directory and Filename

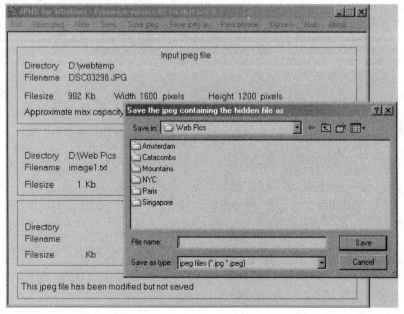

With the first file complete, Salah began work on the next eight images. The work took only about an hour before his web site was complete. When he had uploaded the site, he checked his work and then shut down the computer. Now it was time to clean this mess of a desk and get out of the apartment for a while for a well-deserved break.

Chapter 9: Over the Edge

September 29, 2004

Jimmy woke up to the sound of the small alarm clock going off. Glancing at the clock he noticed that it was 6:30 in the morning. He was due to report to the ship for his next cruise early this afternoon, but until then he would relax. The apartment he lived in was small with very few furnishings because Jimmy had no real intentions of being in this location much longer. In fact, today might very well be the last time he ever slept in this bed. He smiled to himself. The time was almost here.

Rolling over in bed, he reached across his pillow to the nightstand and grabbed the remote to the small television that sat on an old milk crate against the far wall. The small box flashed on as he pressed the power button. Scrolling through the channels, he stopped momentarily on Headline News Network, watching intently as the anchorwoman went over the details of the chaos in Iraq. On his screen were the images of Iraqi men and women standing in the street protesting the presence of the United States' military forces in their country. Jimmy began to feel that warm electricity flow through his veins as his anger started to flare.

The scenes on the old set streamed across his vision in a torrent, feeding the intense white flames that burned inside his heart. *These bastards should not be there*, he thought to himself angrily. *There is no justification for what they've done.* Jimmy suddenly was filled with a burning desire to spit on the putrid American soil upon which he had been living. But living here was a necessity. There was no other option. *They will pay for their interference. We will teach them to stay out of our business, even if every last American must die in the process.*

On the screen, angry Iraqis of all shapes and sizes bounced up and down, faces flush with hatred. The American forces had occupied the Middle Eastern country on the premise that the leader, Saddam Hussein, was housing potentially lethal weapons of mass destruction (WMD). The president repeatedly had stated his concern that the leader was sharing dangerous weapons with terrorists around the world. *As well he should,* thought Jimmy. *If I had the ability, I would certainly give the righteous men, called to fight the West by Allah, anything they needed to be successful.*

In the background of the images on the television stood American soldiers, many of them young and armed with large automatic weapons designed to mow down the helpless. They watched the crowd warily; silently hoping things did not get out of hand. They looked like the kids in Jimmy's high school. They had that same arrogant look. Men and women alike stood there, in the space outside the demonstration, absolutely positive they belonged there; that their mission was just and meaningful. But Jimmy could not fight them there. Devout Muslims were already fighting that battle, inflicting the pain on the invading armies. But Salah and Jimmy had discussed this exact point earlier, and Salah had pointed out to Jimmy that the American army was like an anthill. They would keep coming and coming, their numbers seemingly endless. And as the battle raged there, more Arab men, women, and children would be the real victims. *Let's take the fight to their own homeland,* he remembered Salah saying once. *We will burn their houses for a change. They will sleep restlessly, fearing what might happen in the night, just as our people do now.* Jimmy liked that about Salah. Something inside him hoped that the young man was just distracted. *Regardless,* he thought, *I will continue what I began.*

The same thing happened every morning. Jimmy would switch on the television set and watch as the American media fed dose after dose of the Iraqi drama to the violence-hungry Americans. Fox News, Cable News Network, NBC, and CBS. They all were whoring out the suffering of the Arab people. *Pimps for violence and death,* he reflected. *We'll see how much they like it when the blood stains their own soil for a change. Let them watch their own children die in front of their eyes.*

Unable to contain the energy that had already built up inside his furious mind, Jimmy jumped out of bed and started pacing in front of the television. It was a ritual, almost religious in nature. The morning newscasts provided the fuel his anger needed to stay alive, much the same way the morning meal fed his body and kept him strong. It motivated him and kept his mind focused like a laser on his goal.

The most frustrating aspect of all this was that Salah had quit communicating with the team. Jimmy originally had believed the man to be as motivated as he himself was. But where had he gone? Now was not the time for the man to back down. In just a few days they would face the dragon and bring it to its knees. Hesitation was a sign of weakness and Jimmy would not accept failure as an option. The only end result would be the death of as many Americans as possible. He would make sure of it. Jimmy decided that it was time to write another e-mail to Salah and remind him of the importance of their task. Allah had set them on this road. The Americans would die. It was justified.

Jimmy walked back across the small room and sat back down on his bed, next to a small table set next to the bed. He pushed the power button on the small monitor on the desk and watched as the Windows desktop came to life. The computer was old, the operating system struggling to stay alive under the pressure of having so few resources to work with. But it was enough. He had never had a desire for one of those new powerful computers that packed in the memory and the hard drive space. The processor in the box was a couple of years old, but sufficient to run the simple applications that Jimmy needed at home. He double-clicked the icon for the Netscape browser and waited as the room filled with the sound of the old hard drive spinning, trying desperately to load the application into memory. When the web browser had loaded, he typed in the address to hotmail.com and logged into his e-mail. No new messages. *That's not good*, he thought. He clicked on the link to compose a new e-mail and typed Salah's e-mail address.

Salah,

I am concerned that you may be losing your resolve in this project. You have not communicated with the team for some time. Allah has set us on a difficult road, but he never puts us into a situation that we cannot handle. This will be my last attempt to contact you.

I have just finished watching the news from Iraq. Have you seen the way the people there, faithful Muslim Arabs, fight against the American invaders? Have you seen their angry faces, screaming at the Western military forces. Many good people in the Middle East have died needlessly due to the American interference. The West is motivated by greed. You know this is not the first time that they have caused so much death and chaos in the area. If we do not step up, it will not be the last time either.

The day is approaching when we will start the war against the Americans on their own soil. In just a few days we will initiate our own first strike. Americans will be the ones to die this time, choking painfully on the fumes of our vengeance. With that in mind, I've been considering the next phase of attacks. I want to hurt them badly and cause the pain to linger on for generations, a constant reminder that when you play with snakes, you get bitten.

Think about it, Salah! We can strike them where it really hurts. We can crush their children while they sit in school, studying diligently. There will be no refuge, no place for them to hide. We will blow up the elementary schools, where the children are very young and treasured by their parents. High schools around the country will be brought down from their very foundations, crushing the young people who held so much promise in their parents' eyes just moments before.

In case you have lost your strength in this, remember how your brother felt as his body was blown apart, his blood painting the sun-hardened streets. He was not the only Arab to die at the hands of the West, Salah. Remember the small baby you told me about, and how his precious life was taken. They will not be the last to die until *we* put an end to it. Americans must understand the full consequences of killing innocent Arabic people. Allah has set us on this path.

I hope, for your sake, that you have not run from this, not now. But I promise you that we can do this. And I promise you that I will not stop

until I succeed. Stay steadfast to those plans we created so long ago.
Remember the pain you've lived with for so long. Write me back so we can
finish what we've started.

Jimmy

Jimmy clicked the Send button and watched as the web browser
refreshed after sending the e-mail. He could give the young man only a
few more days. The two had worked so hard and so long to get to where
they were, and Jimmy was dedicated to what they were doing.

He wasn't angry at Salah, not at all. In fact, his young friend had
demonstrated an innate ability to distance himself from his enemies
emotionally. Their conversations online had shown Jimmy a side of Salah
that was both cruel and relentless. These were both characteristics that
Jimmy valued. He knew what they were doing was difficult, probably
more difficult than anything they had ever done in their short lives. Only
their faith in Allah and their incessant hatred of the West could carry them
through. He preferred to channel his energy toward his enemy instead of
waste it worrying about whether the other man had the backbone to do
what was required of him. So he carefully kept his emotions in check,
using them to his advantage and thoughtfully avoiding traps that could
eventually drain his power.

It wasn't always so easy to control his anger, however. In his youth, his
hatred for the Western world had burned intensely, and often out of control. Young boys in their teen years can have erratic reactions to emotionally charged situations, and Jimmy understood very well that he had been
no different.

Going to high school as an Arabic student in America only increased
his hatred of the country and its inhabitants. He wasn't the same as they
were, and what he considered a blessing, they saw as reason to ridicule
him. American children were brutal and malicious in their torment. They
had been vicious and unremitting in their verbal abuse, calling Jimmy out

publicly using derogatory terms. *Towel head, camel kisser, and sand flea* were used daily to reference him as he would walk down the halls, study in the library, and simply sit in class waiting to go home. The teachers, supposedly in place to both teach and protect the students, had conveniently ignored the young man's plight, preferring instead to live vicariously through their own students' displays of ignorance and brutality. Jimmy had learned, early on, that the teachers felt the same things as the students, but were afraid to voice their opinions so openly. Instead, they consistently turned a blind eye to the situation. It didn't matter. He would have hated them anyway. Like maggots squirming on a dead carcass, the young of America would eventually grow wings, replacing their predecessors as they moved across the face of the planet, feeding on others. It disgusted him.

The young man stood up and straightened his bed idly, ensuring that the sheets were pulled up neatly. He looked around the room, wondering why he even bothered to clean up. He wouldn't be coming back, not from this particular trip. Walking into the tiny bathroom, he stripped off his nightclothes and left them in a pile on the floor. After turning on the hot water in the shower, he stood in front of the sink and began shaving, his mind drifting back to his past. These attacks were not the first he had carried out.

Jimmy was proud of his ability to hide and control his emotions, channeling them toward more productive ends. But it hadn't always been this way. There was a point in high school when Jimmy had endured more abuse than he could take and began acting out silently against his adversaries. Initially, they were small acts of defiance, actions that would likely get him beaten up by the bullies on the football team or suspended from school for a week if he ever got caught by one of the teachers. He had slashed tires and broken the windows of those responsible for the constant barrage of abusive behavior. But some of the kids wouldn't stop. They never did—until Jimmy stopped them permanently.

Two kids in particular had attracted Jimmy's ire during his third year in high school. They were both boys in his grade, jocks by day and closet potheads at night. Physical education was a requirement for graduation at the school, and Jimmy was not particularly athletic. He could still remember several incidents where the two had caused him issues. They had done everything from putting medicated menthol rub in underwear to tying his shoelaces together. When he had complained to the principal, the acts of these two boys were referred to as *harmless pranks*. "Why don't you try to get along with them better?" the principal had asked him.

He absently smeared lathery shaving cream on his face, preparing to shave, as he thought back. Then, one day, in the middle of the school hallway, he passed them, one on each side. He watched them closely as they approached, but they seemed completely absorbed in their conversation, so he ignored them and continued walking. Looking back now, he realized that that had been his mistake. He had underestimated his enemy for the last time. When he almost had made it past the two boys, they both stuck their feet out, tripping him and laughing as he hit the hard-coated concrete floor face first. His nose had been broken that day, and he could still taste the blood in his sinuses.

He finished his shaving and rinsed his face. After quickly dabbing on aftershave lotion, he stepped into the steamy shower. The two boys had been suspended for a single day because of that incident. Jimmy had needed a trip to the emergency room and several stitches. That day was the day he snapped. Americans had to be dealt with, and he was now willing to do it.

As he scrubbed his dark flesh with a soapy washcloth, he thought about how long ago that was now. It didn't seem real—more like remembering a movie he had seen at the time versus reality. He had followed them for weeks, learning their schedules, knowing their hangouts and their interests. Despite how important they made themselves appear, they were actually quite simple creatures with extremely repetitive habits. Their Friday nights were spent at the local burger joint near the school where they would talk about cars and try hitting on girls. Around 11 P.M. every Friday, they would realize suddenly that they weren't going to get *lucky*, as they called it, and would head back home.

The two boys lived in the same neighborhood. Jimmy still remembered the streetlights and how all the homes looked the same. There was even a reservoir near the neighborhood where the boys would both head to smoke pot. It had become a ritual, and they thought no one knew. But Jimmy knew. He knew them very well.

They always went to the same spot, just below the base of the dam where the water would come pouring from the other side. They would sit on the sharp gray rocks overlooking the base of the damn and smoke two joints. It never took them long to get so high that they were barely cognizant of the real world. Jimmy had thrown rocks down into the water in front of them once and they had barely stirred. That was when he came up with the idea: push them into the water, and they'd never survive the rolling currents and the sharp rocks downstream, especially in their current state.

Their faded blue jeans and bright white sneakers had been easy to spot, thrashing around in the water as they were washed away in the moonlight. The two boys hadn't even screamed when they found themselves in the churning water. Jimmy stood there several minutes, watching them from the darkness as they made the journey from living to dead.

He turned off the water, grabbed a towel from the towel bar, and stepped from the shower. It really did seem like a long time ago. When the bodies were discovered two days later, they were waterlogged and in bad shape. One boy's body had been caught on a sharp rock along the shore about a mile downstream from the dam. The other had been caught up in a dead tree that had fallen into the river below. One of them also had been found with marijuana in the front pocket of his blue jeans. The police had ruled it an accident, saying that the teens had apparently gotten high and been goofing off near the damn when they fell into the water and were carried downstream.

A memorial was held at the school for all the students. Pictures of the boys were enlarged and placed on easels on the stage of the auditorium so that every student could see their faces and remember their smiles. Jimmy had controlled his emotions back then as well, only it wasn't anger. He was proud. He was happy. He had managed to solve his own problem. Things were better for him the rest of the year as most of the remaining student population never quite recovered emotionally from the event before summer break.

Jimmy slipped into his underwear and then pulled his pants up, fastening the button above the zipper before slipping on his shirt. He had never told a single soul what had happened that day, but Allah knew; He had seen it. Jimmy had never been the same. And it was that same passion and fire that he had seen in Salah. But not everyone is strong enough emotionally to do what it takes to get rid of a problem. Even small annoyances are ignored in the hopes they'll go away eventually. Jimmy remembered that one ant often meant that hundreds more were nearby. One ant might not mean anything, but when that one gets back to the others, you'll have hundreds of them crawling all around you. Jimmy knew that if they could just start stepping on the Americans, they would learn to avoid the Middle East. The Arabs would have their lands back.

Salah sat at his computer staring at the e-mail that had just arrived. The words of the e-mail bounced around inside his head, repeating themselves, haunting him. He had lost count already of how many days he had been avoiding the rest of the team. His inbox had been overflowing with e-mails from the various members of the project asking where he was and what they should do next. But the e-mails had started to dissipate, and the others started to understand he was gone now and had no plans to return. Some of the e-mails he had received were patient, concerned. Others were simply angry and frustrated. Their words were filled with vague threats, frustrated rage, and promises to seek out Salah in order *to ask him personally.*

He wasn't overly concerned about them ever finding him. The experience level of most team members on the project simply wasn't good enough to find someone they didn't know personally. But Jimmy was a different story entirely. His technical skills were on the same level as Salah's. The only reason Jimmy agreed to follow Salah was that Salah had the ability to manage and lead. But, based on this last e-mail, it looked as if Jimmy was about to step up and take over the project. That scared Salah. He knew that Jimmy had the potential to be a very angry young man and was likely to up the ante. Things had not become easier for Salah, as he might have hoped. Instead, it appeared that the situation just might have intensified.

Instead of hitting the Reply button like one of the voices in his head was shouting at him to do, he closed his e-mail program and sat back in his computer chair, staring at the screen quietly. His mind was looping all the conversations he had had with Jimmy back through his mind, over and over. Salah was now forced to admit to himself that through his own foggy thoughts he had never really comprehended the true nature of Jimmy's desire and motivation. Whereas his own mind teetered precariously on the edge of sanity and logic, Jimmy had volunteered his own mind in an effort to make this project successful. The words of the e-mail were burning inside his mind; *I promise you I will not stop until I succeed.*

Salah was worried. *What do I do now?* he thought to himself. *If I walk away and disappear forever, I'm going to be haunted by every person who dies in these attacks.* He had been trying to figure out how to deal with the situation for several weeks. He didn't want this anymore; it wasn't *his* goal to kill Americans. But there didn't seem to be a clear way out for him.

Jimmy really *would* go until he was successful. *Either that or until he's caught,* Salah suddenly heard in his head. A woman's voice was breaking through the din of the other voices in his head. Who's voice was it? It wasn't his mother's. He sat silently, listening, hoping for a solution. *The only way to stop this is to help catch Jimmy. It's the only way for you to escape.*

Catch Jimmy, he thought to himself incredulously. It seemed a ridiculous idea, just another fanciful lie from the voices in his head. Salah sat straight up in his chair and threw his shoulders back, breathing steadily. The only way he had learned to rid himself of the voices was to relax and clear his mind. After just a few minutes, the room was silent. He could hear the cars in the street down below as they passed his apartment unknowingly. A deep sigh escaped his lungs as his body finally relaxed in the chair.

But he was still left with his initial problem. Jimmy was taking over the group in order to keep the project alive. People were assuredly going to die before this was all finished. On one hand, Salah understood that he had started the wheels of this project in motion, but in the end he was only one person. There seemed to be no one whom he could call, no one whom he could trust. He didn't want anyone else to die, but there was also the prospect of being held in an American prison for his part in the project, even if he did confess.

He booted down the computer, turning it off completely before turning off the monitor. *And what about Al Qaeda?* he wondered. *What will they do now?* Salah didn't know if they would try to find him, or even if they could, but he *did* know they had the resources. They had proven it several times at this point, sending him large sums of money. He needed time to think. He also needed answers, and he knew of only one sure way to get them.

Standing up from his computer chair, he grabbed his prayer mat from beside the window and nightstand and laid it out in front of the window. It wasn't time for the call to prayer yet, but he needed help. He removed his shoes and knelt on the mat. Looking one last time out the window, he silently asked Allah to hear his prayers today. With that, he bent forward on the mat as far as he could go and began to pray.

Chapter 10: Biding Time

October 1, 2004

Jimmy lay in his bunk staring at the ceiling and pondering the items on his mental to-do list. He was off duty for the day, which meant that he had time for some much-needed reflection. He relished the rare solitude as his roommate was somewhere on the ship, enjoying his day off as well. It had been just over six months since he had started working full-time on the ship, and he was now fully trusted by nearly every crew member on board. He thought to himself about how easy it had been to get hired and become accepted as a part of the team. Considering the security ramifications of hiring the wrong person, American businesses were still very trusting. Rudimentary background checks were run on potential hires, but not much else beyond that was ever done. The concept of *innocent until proven guilty* was definitely working in his favor. Although, even if they did dig a bit further than usual, he didn't have anything in his background that would raise a red flag to authorities.

He always had practiced caution since he arrived in the United States. Aside from that one incident back in high school, he had nothing in his background to fuel suspicions, and the event was ruled an accident. Murder had never even been considered as an option. Even online, he had been careful not to announce his beliefs too loudly or overtly, even taking the precaution of using a computer from his local library when he did. In the outside world, his opinions were his own secret, and he would protect those at all costs. It was dangerous believing what he did, but total silence provided adequate protection.

The only time anyone on the ship was even slightly leery of Jimmy was when he was still new on board. No one was ever really sure how any of the new folks would adjust to the ship. Nobody knew who would cause trouble or who would make life more difficult for the rest of them, but now he had friends who trusted him. He had complete access to nearly every corner of the cruise ship. Of course, there were restrictions on where even normal personnel could come and go. He still wasn't allowed near the bridge or the maintenance deck, although he had managed to make some friends in the engine room, near the rear of the ship.

When he initially had met Salah online a couple of years ago, he never would have thought that he would be in his current position, working aboard an American cruise ship. Salah never asked for Jimmy's real name, and he doubted if "Salah" was legitimate either. Jimmy was normally a suspicious person, so when he had first heard Salah speaking in the IRC channel he was surprised that he hadn't avoided the man completely out of paranoia. Like Jimmy, Salah never had been overt in his anti-West rantings, but he often drew very close to crossing that dangerous line of saying too much. Unlike Salah, his reasons for wanting to attack America were purely personal. Jimmy had never been a religious person, even if he was a Muslim by birth.

Jimmy had been even more nervous when Salah had reached out to him. Hesitant at first, Jimmy just listened to Salah, feeding back very little information into the conversations they had. But Salah was consistent and never withdrew when Jimmy refused to say too much. In time, Jimmy began slowly to believe in Salah and in the deep pain behind his words. Salah had a noble and justified reason to strike at the Americans, whether it was based on religious principles or not. But still, something in Jimmy made him pray to Allah, asking Him to clarify whether Salah was a person whom he should trust.

Over time, the two had developed a relationship that could best be referred to as friends, and Jimmy had trusted Salah more. Allah was never so obvious with His answers that he would simply tell Jimmy that Salah was safe, but Jimmy decided to trust that emotional and gut feedback he associated with Allah's answers. Jimmy had worked closely with Salah on the plans Salah had created, and Jimmy had provided valuable feedback to help offset the possibility that Salah might have missed some crucial point. The one thing the two men had never shared up front was infor-

mation about their personal lives, beyond their reasons for their mutual
hated of the West, although Salah shared with Jimmy what quite possibly
could have been the most important moment in his life, the death of his
brother.

Jimmy had scoured the Internet, hoping to validate Salah's story of a
mortar round attack in the Iraqi town that had claimed his brother's life.
Finally, after weeks of searching news archives, a small article had confirmed the attack on the coffee shop, even mentioning the shop by name.
Though Salah's brother's name was never mentioned in the article, Jimmy
had been pleased to see that Salah's words were relatively true. After that,
Jimmy had truly bonded with Salah as a friend. He recounted the story of
how his uncle and father had been caught in the crossfire of the first war
in Iraq, years ago. His father had survived, but his uncle had not. The stories his father had told of innocent children shot dead during these battles
in the desert had served to stoke the flames of rancor in Jimmy's heart.

His uncle and father were volunteers for the Red Crescent, an organization very similar to America's own Red Cross. They had been trans-
porting food and supplies across the desert to some smaller towns that
needed aid when the fight between the Iraqi Royal Guard and the
Western military units had started. Although both military sides were
cognizant of the role Red Crescent played, Jimmy's uncle had been killed
by a stray bullet that had penetrated his brain, killing him instantly. His
father believed that the Americans had no business forcing their politics
into the Middle East. When things weren't going in the direction they
wanted, the Americans fell back to the one thing that could change the
course of world politics, their army. Jimmy now carried this belief as well.
And now, it was time to take the war from his home to the American
home front. Let the American people mourn their losses for once, he
thought to himself.

The hatred that brewed in some men's hearts was hot enough to burn
cinder block, but that fire was often misguided and stoked by errors in
their understanding. Jimmy had spoken to many different men in the past

years of his life; each one of them had a story. Some of the men could tell stories of pain that were real, based on real life. Others, however, were doing what they had been programmed to do. There was no history inside their hearts for the burning desire to injure the Western world. Jimmy refused to follow these weaker, dependent-minded soldiers who blindly followed whatever fanatic led them. But with Salah it was different; Salah had a verified reason to hate the Americans. He had an understanding that many Arab people would never have.

Jimmy finally was won over completely when Salah had revealed his idea of planning attacks on American interests using their own beloved creation, the Internet. The irony of the plan didn't escape Jimmy's quick mind; the potential undoing of the American people would be through one of their own great inventions. The Americans had often taken full credit for the creation of the Internet. It was probably justified to some degree, he thought, since the DARPA project had been initiated within American interests, leading to the eventual creation of the Internet as it is known today. Now, however, the Internet belonged to the world, including Jimmy, Salah, and their team. People around the globe knew of the Internet and were using it every day to advance their own interests, whether those interests were commercial, military, or personal.

America had created the means for its own demise. Jimmy knew that the idea held sufficient merit and could work. The actual legwork would still need to be handled by individuals, but the planning and communication easily could be handled across the Internet. He knew that some people were trying to coordinate attacks across the Internet on Western information assets, but the actual feasibility of carrying out such plans was still too remote for Jimmy to jump on board. This eventually led to Jimmy's helping Salah recruit the remaining team members from other individuals on the Internet, as well as some he already knew.

The team, for the most part, consisted of other men whom Jimmy and Salah had met online, with only a few having ever met before in person by Jimmy. It made sense at the time to maintain the sense of anonymity that everyone needed to be safe. All the members of the team were men. The dominant cultural attitudes in the Middle East were very focused on men and their abilities, as compared with the envisioned role of women in their society. Women were caretakers of the family unit and were not designed to carry out acts of war against an enemy.

There had also been a conscious decision up front not to let everyone else know how many other team members there were or how to contact anyone else on the team. In the event someone was caught, questioned, or arrested, they wouldn't be able to compromise the entire network. The only two people who know all the team members were Jimmy and Salah.

At the beginning of the project, Salah had sent Jimmy an e-mail containing a quote that summed up everything he was thinking. It showed that time provided a mechanism for stealth when it wasn't available through any other means. He had printed out that quote and kept it with him, to motivate him through the difficult times, and there had already been plenty of those.

> A nation can survive its fools, and even the ambitious. But it cannot survive treason from within. An enemy at the gates is less formidable, for he is known and carries his banner openly. But the traitor moves amongst those within the gate freely, his sly whispers rustling through all the alleys, heard in the very halls of government itself.
>
> For the traitor appears not a traitor; he speaks in accents familiar to his victims, and he wears their face and their arguments, he appeals to the baseness that lies deep in the hearts of all men. He rots the soul of a nation, he works secretly and unknown in the night to undermine the pillars of the city, he infects the body politic so that it can no longer resist. A murderer is less to fear.
> —Marcus Tullius Cicero, 42 B.C.

Though the quote had been written from an opposite perspective, there was truth inherent in the words. If the team could simply take the time to obtain the trust and faith of their victims, the amount of damage and pain they could inflict would increase tenfold. Time was all they needed to earn that precious trust. The fear each victim experienced on the final day would escalate beyond anything they had ever encountered. Doubt and paranoia would be everywhere, anyone could be working against them, trying to hurt them, and so fear would then become the way of life. Living in fear and doubt was something his people had suffered for so long, and now the West would suffer. And so, Salah had struck upon a very important concept in this war with the West. If you want to really hurt another human being, make them love you before you hurt them. Love and trust spring eternally from longevity and understanding.

Then the incredible had happened; Salah had employed the help of representatives from Al Qaeda. According to Salah, just as Salah had scouted out Jimmy and his interactions on the Internet, they had scouted Salah; representatives from the famous terror group had kept tabs on their conversations on IRC. After Salah had introduced Jimmy as his second in command, the man who would follow in Salah's footsteps should anything happen to the young man, Jimmy had been made privy to various conversations between Salah and their contact. But things had been quiet lately, no communication from either end with no apparent explanation.

Jimmy sat up in his bunk and smoothed back his dark hair with his hands. His small cabin was getting warm and his fingers gleamed from the sweat on his scalp. The work on the ship was mindless, allowing him time to think and plan. His job was to clean the open spaces on the ship, areas where passengers gathered and activities were held. Each of the guest rooms was cleaned by another team on the ship, although he also knew many of them at this point. However, the access granted to Jimmy was greater than that given to a crew member on the guest room detail because he needed access to some of the operational areas of ship.

He had already done a good deal of research on how he was going to get to the more secure areas within the ship, the places he might need to be for the plan to work. His ability to access the various parts of the ship was paramount. The goal of this phase of the overall plan was to incite fear and confusion among the passengers. People who survive a terrifying experience remember it in distorted colors as opposed to the black and white reality that it was, and it was these stories they were counting on to be told and retold through media outlets around the globe, further spreading the fear. Tales of masked predators lurking in dark corners of the ship would fill the heads of the Western world as obviously distraught and terrorized men and women told how they caught a quick glimpse of the perpetrators. The weaknesses in human short-term memory would help the fear grow into something much bigger than the reality. There would be, of course, some deaths as a result, but not many. That wasn't the goal here. The real death would be dealt out in the second phase; but for now, the team would spread a feeling of vulnerability and insecurity.

He was getting excited by the idea. An American motion picture turned into real life, fiction made true. He was the producer and director of a major event in human history that would demonstrate the eventual fate of the Western world and their interference in the Middle East. Another chapter of lessons learned by America and Great Britain.

Jimmy stood up and pulled a map of the ship out of his footlocker beneath his bed. The map was given to all new employees and listed all the areas on the ship, including those areas considered off limits unless special permission was given. The creases on the map were worn from the constant use by Jimmy; he would have to tape it up soon if he wanted it to last much longer. The area of most interest for Jimmy was the rear of the ship, near the water's edge. The hull of the ship was too thick to use explosives from the inside. Instead, the plan was to place detonators along with a payload of chemicals, easily found in the ship's supplies, to create toxic black smoke that would be carried through the ventilation system to the various rooms and common areas. Jimmy had already imagined how the thick cloud would drift behind the ship, in a long, wide trail. The panic among the passengers and crew would feed upon itself, growing, as people ran around frantically looking for their loved ones and their children. *Was anyone hurt? Was my husband killed? Oh my God! Where is my daughter? What has happened?*

There were so many questions that would be asked by the frenzied passengers, and Jimmy knew that not a single one of them would be answered easily. Each answer would take time. It seemed that time was a player in everything. Time could win you a battle you had no hope of winning. Time could destroy your mind, burying you in despair, given the chance, or it could open up opportunities you only ever hoped for. And it was time that was providing the team with an open doorway into the American dream for their opportunity.

The biggest concern for Jimmy right now was how the team members were going to get the correct mix of chemicals on board the ship in the first place. Most cruise ship terminals were designed to mimic airport terminals in that they employed standard security screening processes to ensure the safety of the passengers and crew. Having their own team members on board the target ships as trusted crew members would relieve some of the restrictive security procedures, but not to the point that any one of them could bring potentially dangerous substances onto their ships.

The first phase of security was normally an identification check before being allowed to check in to board the ship. In most cases, these checks were fairly rigorous, requiring the appropriate documentation before letting you board the vessel. Each passenger and crew member was required to provide a valid passport or American identification in order to move into the next stage of security. Failure to provide appropriate documentation would result in that individual being declined entry to the ship. But in most cases, this process wouldn't cause much of an issue for the team because each team member possessed his or her own identification documents. The question of whether the documents were legitimate or not was never asked, since they would have needed the real thing in order to get the job on the ship to begin with.

The next phase of the security process was sure to catch anyone trying to sneak harmful substances on the ship. Each passenger would be required to pass through a room with large stainless steel tables, metal detectors, and baggage screeners. The room actually reminded Jimmy of a hospital, not so much in the arrangement of the room as the actual contents. The security area possessed a very medicinal feel with its white tiled floors, stainless steel equipment, and Transportation Security Agency (TSA) personnel running around in white shirts waving electronic equipment. Even the ceilings and walls were painted a flat white. The final touch was the recessed florescent lights in the ceiling, shining a sterile light across the room below.

The cold, impersonal feeling of the security room always left Jimmy with a queasy stomach. Even though he had not done anything illegal, he still found himself nervous around the American officials. The ritual was always the same. He walked through the room without saying much to anyone, just a polite smile on his face. He was careful to make sure that his bags were clean and that they didn't contain any questionable objects before he entered the room. Each bag was opened and screened on a stainless steel table by officials wearing latex gloves. The one good thing Jimmy could say about the security screeners is that they genuinely enjoyed their jobs and tried to be friendly to all the crew and passengers.

As each bag finished the screening process, it was passed through a large freight door behind the counter to the ship. The freight doors were really nothing more than large garage doors made out of steel, allowing the doors to be opened and shut easily using a hand control hanging on a large black cord from the ceiling. The smaller bags that were being hand-carried on board by each passenger were combed through by TSA personnel. The larger bags were put through industrial-sized x-ray machines where TSA agents stared at monitors looking for potentially dangerous objects being brought on board. Even employees were subject to these procedures. However, any larger bags that were owned by the passengers eventually were brought to the individual guest rooms by the bell staff on the ship, whereas the employees had to carry their own bags to their quarters.

Jimmy had tested the security screening process a few different times with various innocuous items he could afford to have confiscated while not really drawing any serious attention to himself as a potential threat. He needed to know if it would be possible to slip something by undetected. In both instances, the agents had found the items hidden on his person or in his bags. He never used anything overtly dangerous, just a pair of small sewing scissors, a small, very blunt pocketknife, or some small electronics from a kit at Radio Shack. The electronics were easier to get onboard a cruise ship without much hassle, but there were the occasional random checks that might pop up. The crew often was allowed a bit more leniency when it came to bringing items on board, but he needed to know where those lines were before he tried something that could get him in trouble.

In the end, Jimmy suggested to Salah that the team member who had been planted on each of the three ships start looking for suitable items that could be assembled, on board, and placed without notice of the TSA agents. That's how Jimmy ended up with his current quest: how to build a device to generate a toxic cloud by using materials that were already located on the ship. Several different options existed that were commonly known and available on the Internet. Chlorine, vegetable oil, ammonia, and sodium chloride were all useful components for explosives and toxic smoke bombs, and other materials were easily available on the cruise ship. The various recipes were all options, and Jimmy had passed each one of them along to the other team members via Salah.

Looking at his watch, Jimmy realized he needed to check his e-mail and the web site to see if there was any new information posted for the team.. Each crew member was given access to the Internet via a small room in the crew lounge. Ten computers were set aside for the crew, and each person could reserve a time slot to check e-mail and surf the Internet. He had reserved a slot 45 minutes from now, but hoped he would be able to sneak in there sooner if possible. If not, he'd grab a bite for lunch first.

He put the map and his other personal belongings back into his locker, grabbed his USB key drive to bring with him, and locked it. He walked to the door, clicked off the light switch, and closed the door to the cabin behind him.

Jimmy strolled into the Crew Lounge, checking to see if there was anyone he knew. He had some acquaintances on the ship though he refused to believe he genuinely liked them. It was a difficult choice when he first started, but he knew that he would never back down, and would never truly care for those he considered the enemy. The hatred that burned inside him was so much stronger than the friendships he had made in a mere six months. They were all guilty. Even if they didn't pull the trigger or press the button to launch a missile, their ignorance and apathy for the pain his family and world suffered were just as accountable.

Across the room he saw a few crewmen playing pool near the windows. He knew who they were but the relationship wasn't much deeper than that. One of the men in the game looked much like one of the boys in his high school who had met an untimely demise. Jimmy shuddered as he silently considered the possibility that ghosts really do exist. It's probably better if I eat alone, he thought. He walked into the small crew eating room, which housed a walk-up counter with menu boards hung overhead, and stood there looking at the menu. The company kept the crew very well fed and the selection on the menu reflected this fact with several dozen items available for crew members at no charge. Everything from sandwiches, burgers, chicken, salads, and more filled the menu. Preferring his usual, the chicken sandwich, he walked up to the young man at the register and placed his order, being sure to approach him with his adopted upbeat and friendly demeanor he used for all interaction with others on the ship.

"Hey, Tony, can I get the chicken sandwich with lettuce, tomato, and mayo?"

"Sure thing. Do you want some chips, fries, onion rings, or anything else with that?" Tony replied, with a polite smile on his face.

"No, thanks. But I'd like an apple juice if you got one."

"Okay. Your order's in and should only take a few minutes." Tony finished writing down the order, preparing to take it toward the kitchen. "Apple juice is over there, in the bin, and you're welcome to wait here or if you would rather head over to the game room, I can call your name over the intercom when it's done."

"Actually, do you know if there's a free terminal in the computer room?" Jimmy asked. "I'd love to get in a few extra minutes before my time comes up. The family freaks out if I don't e-mail them regularly, and I was hoping to surf for a while." The excuse sounded lame to his own ears, but he had heard the same one used many times from other young crew members on the ship. It was a phrase they all understood and could associate with.

"I know what you mean. My family does the same thing," Tony laughed. "You'd think we were on some military ship or something with how concerned people get sometimes. But we're only on a cruise ship, ya know? My mom is terrified we're going to sink. She was a handful after she saw that Titanic movie a couple of years ago. The only real risk we have out here is gaining too much weight!" Tony laughed again and handed Jimmy his order receipt.

Jimmy smiled but didn't say anything else. He had still not gotten his answer, and didn't want to get too far off-topic by encouraging Tony to talk more about his mother. Tony was a nice guy, but the long hours sitting in the crew mess, taking orders, made him more talkative than most.

"Anyway," the young man began again. "I haven't seen anyone come in for over an hour, so I'd imagine the room is probably empty. Go on in, and I'll holler when your food is up."

"Great, thanks man!" With that Jimmy, walked over to the soda cooler standing next to the wall, pulled out an apple juice, and headed back to the computer room.

Even though food was free for the crew, the order process was in place for inventory purposes. The company liked to track what was actually consumed by the crew during each excursion. In the long run it made everything better for the crew since the company understood precisely what food and drink items were most popular.

Jimmy walked next door to the computer room and happily found it empty, just as Tony had said. He took his place at a computer in the back corner of the room where there would be less chance of someone watching over his shoulder. Losing the confidentiality of this project because of a stupid mistake could be as serious as the death penalty. Best to play it safe and sit with his back to the wall.

He set his bottle of apple juice on the desk next to the computer monitor. The ship had purchased the computers from one of the massive online dealerships along with the small computer workstation desks and chairs. The computers were small black desktops that had been attached to the side bar of the computer desk using custom brackets from the dealer. Jimmy had been surprised to find the computers had a decent processor and sufficient memory to run all the steganography applications he needed to run. But then again, most computers were probably sufficient; it just would have been a much slower process to create the hidden data files.

Jimmy pulled out the small computer chair and sat down in front of the small desk. The computers were almost always left running with the monitors turned off. The ship had crews that worked at various hours of each day, so there was a constant stream of candidates who might want to use the computers. He pushed the found button on the monitor and moved the mouse on the mouse pad, waiting for the screen to show him the login prompt to the operating system. While the monitor was coming up, Jimmy leaned down and plugged his USB key drive into the USB slot on the front of the computer. Many of the users on the ship used the USB drives to store information they wanted to keep from their online use. Jimmy had seen some of the other crew members working on online degree programs and saving homework or project papers to their drives. Others simply saved pictures sent to them from family members or to store pictures to share with family members from their own digital cameras. Jimmy used his key for much the same reason, but he doubted the overall intent was the same.

Cruise lines had very little in the way of information technology and hadn't hired a large network administration team to keep the network in order. Instead, the work was handled by one or two crew members who worked only during the day shift. Users did not have their own usernames or passwords; instead, they shared a common desktop and operating environment. This did not provide a lot of privacy for users, unless they knew what to clean up at the end of their sessions. Jimmy had browsed through the computers several times to see what other sites the others were surfing. He was never surprised to find the standard fare of cheap porn, get-rich-quick business schemes, or religious web sites. The predictability of these people was almost boring and only further proved to him that they had nothing to offer. By the time he finally logged into the computer and brought up a web browser, Tony came walking into the computer room with his order.

"Here ya go, dude," Tony said as he sat the food down on the desk next to Jimmy. "There's no one in there right now so I thought I'd just bring it to you. It's totally dead down here today, must be some sort of tournament up on deck or something."

"Yeah, you're probably right. Thanks for the food." Jimmy knew that Tony was likely looking to have a conversation. "I really appreciate you bringing this out, dude. I'm up to my eyeballs in school work right now and probably wouldn't have heard you call over the intercom. You're a lifesaver."

Tony smiled. "Hey, no problem. I didn't realize you were taking classes this semester. I had better let you go for now. But if you're interested in getting together to play pool sometime, let me know, okay?"

"No problem. Sounds like fun. Talk to you later."

"Later."

Jimmy watched from the corner of his eye as Tony left the room. Once he was again alone in the room, he turned his attention back to the computer. He really should send an e-mail to his folks back home, but they didn't really ever check their e-mail. Jimmy had set them up with an account at a local Internet service provider, but they were never really comfortable enough to get on the computer without him standing there beside them. But his mother had surprised him once before and written back a response to one of his e-mails, so he held out hope that she would do it again soon. He was doing this for them, after all, and reaching out to them eased his mind.

He took a bite of his chicken sandwich, which was still steaming from the grill. He typed a secure web address into the location bar at the top of the web browser and waited until the page came up. He preferred to check his e-mail via web mail because he was never quite sure who else on the crew was combing through the common files on the computers when no one was looking. At least with web mail he could go in and erase the cookies and all the files in the web cache. He was always sure to clean up the computer after his every use, just in case. Even the history of the web browser that contained the last web sites visited on that computer was deleted once Jimmy was done working for the day. It took only a few minutes to clean up, but it could protect him from prying eyes.

Hmmm, no e-mails tonight. He was concerned about Salah's lack of activity. Jimmy had found that recently he was doing more and more of the management of the group. Salah had started communicating less not only with him but also with the group as a whole and the attitude in his e-mails to Jimmy seemed to reflect a lack of focus and commitment. It wasn't like Salah was outright neglecting his duty, but the excitement had apparently faded, replaced with some other unknown variable.

He had tried to ignore the situation, preferring instead to think that perhaps Salah was just sidelined with issues within his day-to-day life. But perhaps it was time to try and track Salah down and have a conversation face to face; they had come too far already to fail. Unfortunately, that would need to wait until he was back on dry land. One thing he wouldn't do was leave potential clues on the hard drives of publicly accessible computers. He wanted the project to stay on track, but they still had a couple of months left, so waiting a few more days would be okay.

Jimmy took another bite of his sandwich and leaned back in his chair. Looking at his watch he noticed that it still wasn't even time for him to be on the computer, but the room was still empty. The team had come so far in such a short period of time. When you're standing at the beginning of an extended period of time, it can be overwhelming. But now they were nearing the end of the first phase and would soon be starting the second phase. Jimmy had been considering a new method of communication with the team, one that wasn't as complex as the web page. Salah had taken a relatively simple concept and made it much more difficult to understand. He still wasn't certain that all the others were really able to pull the messages back out of the carrier file. The entire 10-image scheme, although secure, was probably more overkill than required. The truth of the matter was that it was unlikely anyone would discover their plans anyway, even if they were less secure. Out of the millions of web sites on the Internet, no one was likely to accidentally stumble across the page and notice anything out of the ordinary.

Jimmy's concept was simple. He wanted to use the USENET newsgroups on the Internet to swap information with the remaining team members. There were some newsgroups that generated a tremendous number of messages every day. A few extra messages in the group each day would hardly be noticed. If he could talk Salah into using this method, then all the team members would be able to post images along with their messages to the newsgroups for everyone else to download. Once the images were pulled out, the stego could be removed, revealing the message.

It might even be simpler just to tell the remaining team members what username to look for in the newsgroup. Whenever they saw messages from that username, they would download the attached image. But what newsgroup should they use? It would certainly help if Salah would start answering e-mails consistently again. In a few more days, he thought to himself. Then I'll be able to get in touch with Salah.

Jimmy decided to take the opportunity to double-check the last message Salah had posted on the web site. He logged out of his e-mail in the web browser and entered the address to the web site containing the various vacation pictures. The site contained original photographs, certainly, but the true reason behind the site was to communicate and post information on the project for the team members to read. Once the web site came up, Jimmy downloaded the entire site, including the linked full-size images, to his USB key drive. These would need to be deleted immediately once he was finished, but he needed the images on a device that at least could be removed from the system. Using the hard drive inside the computer would have been a mistake.

The site was still using the same images that Salah had posted a week ago and no new e-mail had been sent out giving information on a new password or web site update. The e-mail with the number was the only thing that Jimmy ever left on the key drive, just in case he needed it later. But the headers had been removed, leaving only a string of digits in the seemingly benign text file. Jimmy double-clicked on the text file and watched as it came up in a window above the desktop. This number is what he'd need to retrieve the password and open the final image.

Magic Number

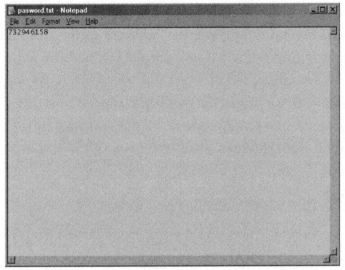

The text file was named password.txt and simply contained the string of numbers that Salah had e-mailed all the group members. To any normal person, the numbers would appear meaningless, but to the group the number was the key to a hidden lock. Jimmy left the notepad window open, but minimized it long enough to open the Jpeg Hide and Seek software on his USB drive.

JPHS Software Window

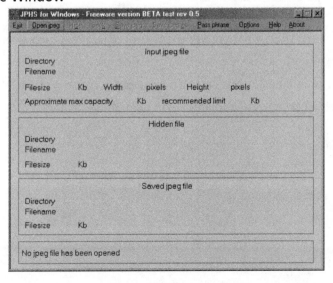

Once he had the JPHS software open on his desktop, he clicked the Open Jpeg option on the menu bar at the top and was prompted to select an image from one of the drives attached to the computer. The first image in the password sequence was image 7, so he browsed to the D:\ drive, his USB key drive, and selected that image from the web site archive that he had just saved. The software showed him that the image was loaded into memory and ready to be manipulated, so Jimmy selected the Seek option from the menu bar at the top of the screen.

Seek Option

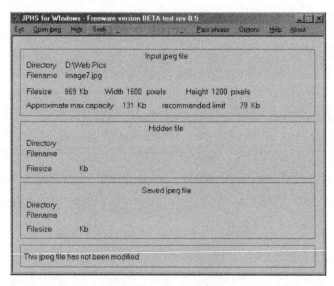

The software then prompted Jimmy for the password used to originally hide the payload inside the image. The password used was the number that Salah had e-mailed the group, so Jimmy entered the password in both entry fields and clicked the OK button.

Password and Login

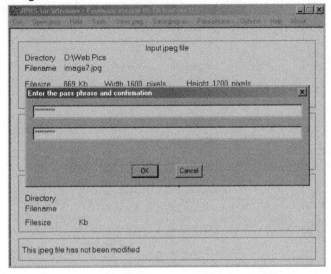

When the password had been entered twice, the program prompted Jimmy for a filename and directory to save the hidden content to. The trick with JPHS was that it wouldn't tell you if you had entered the wrong password. Someone could try over and over to brute force the password manually. But the software would never reveal whether you had the password correct or not. In fact, Jimmy had discovered early on that the software wouldn't even tell you if there was really anything hidden in the file to begin with. He had been run around by this software once before when he was inadvertently trying to pull data out of the wrong image file. It was frustrating trying to fight the software, especially when it was your own mistake that had you running in circles. JPHS didn't care what the file was; it knew where information was normally hidden and would pull out whatever was there, whether there was anything useful in that space or not.

Saving the Hidden File

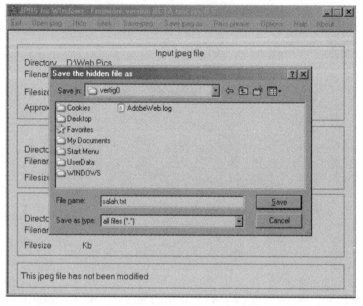

Jimmy browsed to a directory on his USB key drive that was set up to mimic a user's home directory structure under Windows and saved the file as salah.txt. Once this was completed, he moved on to the next image in the web site, image number 3. Jimmy repeated this process over and over until the last of the nine images had been processed and all the information had been saved to his drive.

In the end, he had saved nine text files to his drive. He knew at this point that he needed to go through them in order and copy the words to the text document containing the password. Each text file contained a single word that, when put in order with its counterparts, created a sentence. The sentence itself was not the message, but contained the password to open the final image. Jimmy carefully copied the words from each text file, in the order specified by the password, into the password.txt file. When he had finished, he carefully looked at the results to make sure the sentence made sense. The sentence made sense to him, but the topics Salah used in his messages were curious, to say the least.

Salah's Sentence

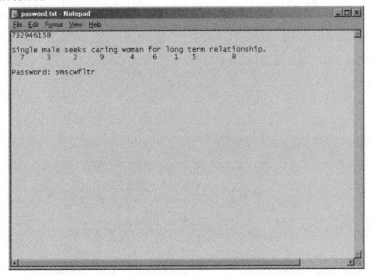

Assuming the process had worked correctly, Jimmy knew that taking the first letter of each word in the sentence would create the password for the final image with the actual hidden information that Salah had sent to the team. The use of null ciphers was a great method for concealing information, but the overall process still seemed too complex to Jimmy. He sighed to himself as he remembered that Salah had been irritatingly out of contact for nearly a week now.

Jimmy walked through the process once more with the final image. But this time, he used the new password instead of the original numeric sequence. When the Save File As prompt popped up on his screen, he browsed to his USB key drive one last time and saved the output as a text file. The final message provided no clues to the strange behavior of Salah or his recent silence online. Salah gave an update, as was his style, including information on when everyone would receive their next payment for the operation. The payment was arranged by Salah with Al Qaeda and was set up so that no one on the team got a lump sum of money all at once. When large amounts of money suddenly show up in your bank account, people tend to ask questions, and no one on the team wanted that. But the money was intended to help cover the incidental costs associated with the project. Each person in the group had their own worries concerning the project and the money required to accomplish their piece of the puzzle. But aside from the normal traffic, Salah gave no indication that he was going to be out of touch.

Salah's Message

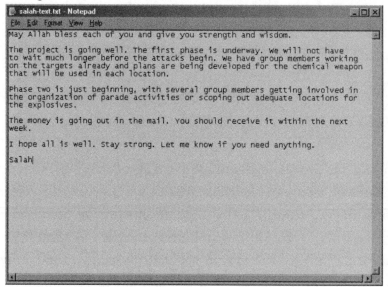

Jimmy was growing worried. It wasn't like his friend to be silent so long, at least not silent to Jimmy. With his sandwich and business finished, he decided it was time to go. He cleared the cache on the browser, deleted the web history that was stored in the browser, removed the remnants of the web page from his USB drive, and turned off the computer. Reaching down to remove the USB key drive from its connection, Jimmy reminded himself that one week really wasn't that long and he should worry less. Salah had things completely under control.

Chapter 11: Covert Channels

October 2, 2004

Jeremy sat up slowly. He had fallen asleep at his desk, and the office was deserted with the exception of the cleaning crew. They must have been especially noisy tonight as they awakened him when they came in the front security door. His coworkers had called him crazy when he mentioned that he would be working this weekend, saying that he had lost his mind and should be out somewhere trying to have some fun. But they apparently just didn't understand. To Jeremy, this *was* fun. He hadn't spent so many years in college studying networking and learning advanced programming techniques just to ignore the opportunity to expand his skill set. In fact, one of the managers who had interviewed Jeremy inadvertently had admitted to him that one of the primary reasons he was given an interview was because he had included a senior course project that had impressed one of the senior technical folks in the department.

Jeremy leaned back in his chair, aching. His neck was sore from having been stretched at such an odd angle. He raised his arms above his head, stretching his back muscles and letting the blood return to his limbs. Glancing at his watch, he saw that it was already 9:13 P.M. It had been hours since everyone else in the office had left for the day. Neil had stopped by Jeremy's desk to see how his research was coming along, but he had been overwhelmed and couldn't even really remember what he had muttered in response to Neil. After some small talk, Neil had eventually meandered away, wishing Jeremy luck on his work.

Two weeks ago, Jeremy had run across an article on the Internet that discussed the possibilities of using covert channels to communicate between two points, undetected. Initially, he had been excited to have a potential clue. The concept of covert channels was foreign to him though, and once he really got into researching the topic, he realized that there were dozens of possible means of communicating without being noticed. There were cases of text manipulation, where individuals used e-mail or text documents to communicate. He had found information on using network packets themselves to hide dates within and communicate across a network in near real time, without detection. There were even instances where data was hidden inside digital images or audio files. Apparently, he still had a lot to learn on the subject.

But now it was two weeks later, and though Jeremy had spent nearly every day researching covert channels, he was no closer to knowing which ones might be in use. In fact, if he didn't come up with something soon, he would just ask Neil to pass it up the chain that there were dozens of possible methods out there. Hopefully someone would have some idea of what to do from here. But he wasn't giving up yet. In fact, he found the idea of covert channels very intriguing. He absently wondered to himself how many other individuals inside DHS knew there was such a thing and whether anyone considered them a real threat.

Reaching across the table, Jeremy grabbed what had been the leftovers from his dinner, but was now cold and inedible. There was a small cafeteria downstairs that was open 24 hours a day to accommodate the employees that happened to be there after hours. Normally, he didn't really care much for the food in the cafeteria, but he seemed to be eating there quite a bit over the last two weeks. He threw the trash into the round, dark gray waste can to the left of his desk. His mind had been completely absorbed in his research lately, so even the little things that normally nagged at him, like eating enough, went ignored a lot of times.

The computer screen displayed the standard DHS screensaver, so Jeremy clicked on his mouse to bring up the login prompt to the system. DHS recently had implemented a required password-protected screensaver function that activated after only a few minutes of inactivity on the system. According to the time, Jeremy estimated that his had been running for about 25 minutes. When the login prompt appeared, he logged in normally and was greeted by his most recent research project, S-tools 4.

S-tools 4

S-tools was a freeware program available on the Internet that would allow a user to hide data in a variety of different binary files, including bitmap files (BMP), Graphic Interchange Format (GIF), and standard wave audio files (WAV). The tool hadn't been maintained in nearly a decade and was one of hundreds Jeremy had found on the Internet. His first search on the Internet had yielded several different archive sites dedicated to storing applications that allowed users to create their own hidden data. The sheer number of programs available had shocked him at first. There were applications available for many different platforms as well, including Windows, DOS, OS/2, Amiga, Java, Linux, and BSD. That was the point at which Jeremy had realized how widespread this concept of hidden communication really was. Some of the tools created different forms of steganography, which allowed the hiding of information in many different binary file formats. Other tools listed would allow a user to create hidden messages inside text documents or inside network traffic. The S-tools 4 application was used to create steganography.

List of Tools

Invisible Secrets v4.0 (2.9 mb) *Shareware $99.95*

Lookout Steganos, there's a new kid on the block! Invisible Secrets encrypts and hides files in JPEG, PNG, BMP, HTML and WAV. Loaded with new features, it provides strong encryption (Blowfish, Twofish, RC4, Cast128, and GOST), shredder, password manager and generator, self-decrypting archives, internet trace destroyer, IP-to-IP password transfer, and application locker. Interfacing nicely with Windows Explorer via right-click context-sensitive menus, this low cost shareware program is definitely worth checking out!

Camera/Shy v0.2.23.1 (1.4 mb) *Freeware*

Camera/Shy is the only steganographic tool that automatically scans for and delivers decrypted content straight from the Web. It is a stand-alone, Internet Explorer-based browser that leaves no trace on the user's system and has enhanced security. As a safety feature Camera/Shy also includes security switches for protection against malicious HTML. Picture that. Spanish, German, and Chinese versions also available.

Cameleon (374k) *Freeware*

French language GIF-based stego with strong (256bit AES) encryption.

CryptArkan (471k) *Shareware $29.99*

Hides *data* files and directories inside one or more *container* files, such as sound/music (WAV) and images (BMP). Hidden data can be directly read off an Audio CD. Strong encryption and plugins for added features.

Stego-Lame (2.3mb) *Freeware*

An alpha-version program in Windows C source code which hides data in various audio streams (MP3, Ogg Vorbis, MPEG 2/4 AAC, G.72x). No precompiled binaries yet.

Gifshuffle v2.0 (33k) *Freeware*

Gifshuffle is a command-line-only program for windows which conceals messages in GIF images by shuffling the colourmap. The picture remains visibly intact, only the order of color within the palette is changed. It works with all GIF images, including those with transparency and animation, and in addition provides compression and encryption of the concealed message.

Stegdetect (XSteg) (2.3 mb) *Freeware*

Stegdetect is an automated tool for detecting steganographic content in images. It is capable of detecting several different steganographic methods to embed hidden information in JPEG images. Currently, the detectable schemes are jsteg, jphide (unix and windows), invisible secrets, outguess 01.3b, F5, appendX, and camouflage.

JPegX (18 kb) *Freeware*

JPegX is an encryption program that hides your important information inside standard JPEG image files. The image is left visually unchanged and messages are encrypted and password protected. To decrypt the message, you need to open the JPEG file that holds it and enter the password if prompted.

The Third Eye (490k) *Freeware*

Hides files in BMP, GIF, and PCX files. Includes encryption and nice user interface.

WeavWav (173k) *Freeware*

Software that can hide secret data in .wav files. Very basic interface.

ImageHide (1.1 mb) *Freeware*

Windows-based program which hide files in a number of different formats without increasing file size.

The tools on these sites were both powerful and sophisticated. S-tools 4 even allowed users to drag and drop interactively with the program, allowing a user to create hidden data within digital images and digital audio files without needing to know how to navigate the user interface. Jeremy selected a picture from a folder on his hard drive and dragged it onto the S-tools interface. He wanted to walked through the process one more time to ensure that he understood how it worked. Jeremy had brought pictures of his various family members from home that would allow him to experiment with more of the tools.

Practice Picture

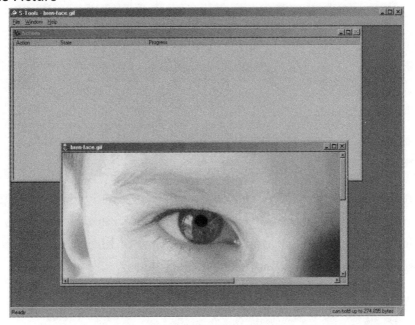

Once the image had been loaded into the S-tools interface, Jeremy noted how the application told the user how much data could be hidden in the carrier file that was loaded. Using the image he had just loaded, there was enough space to hide 274,895 bytes of data. In order to test the various tools, he had created a test text file that he named Jeremy.txt. He would hide his test file in different format carriers and then remove the information again. Selecting the text file, he dragged it onto the top of the carrier image he had already loaded into the software. A small password prompt popped onto the screen. This would be the password used to encrypt the data before it was hidden inside the image.

Hiding 461 Bytes

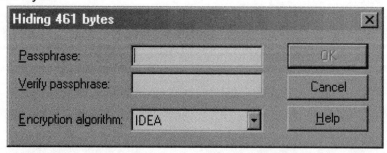

Jeremy typed in a password of *password* and chose to use the default encryption method of IDEA. When he was done, he clicked the OK button and watched as the software processed the information he had given it. After just a few seconds, a new version of his image popped into the S-tools 4 interface with a heading of Hidden.

Picture with Hidden Data

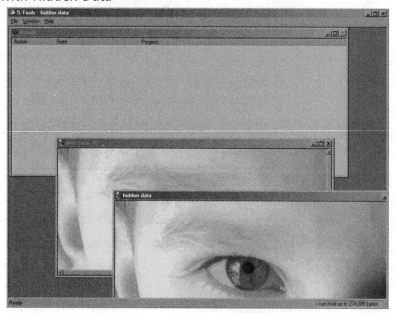

Clicking the right button on his mouse, Jeremy was able to bring up an alternate menu, allowing him to save his new image with a new file-name. Jeremy picked a name and saved the file to his hard drive.

Saving New Image

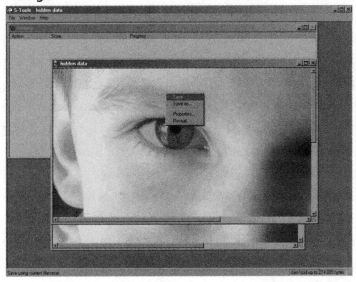

Jeremy closed out the application when he was done and brought up a command prompt under Windows. He had questions about how the information was hidden and the effect it had on the file size. To compare the size of the two images, he ran the *dir* command at the prompt for all the .gif files. The file size had changed dramatically, considering that he had hidden only a simple text file. But without the original file to compare to, how would he ever know there was information hidden in the second image?

Command Prompt

```
Command Prompt                                              _ □ X

H:\>dir *.gif
 Volume in drive H has no label.
 Volume Serial Number is 0000-0000

 Directory of H:\

09/18/2004  05:48 PM          196,087 bren-face.gif
09/18/2004  05:54 PM          239,176 bren-face2.gif
               2 File(s)          435,263 bytes
               0 Dir(s)   153,452,544 bytes free

H:\>_
```

Most of the steganography applications that used image files worked similar to this one. Some of them were capable of hiding information without increasing the file size, and in some cases, the size of the resulting file was actually smaller than the original. There were white papers on the topic all over the Internet that explained the concepts of algorithms. Each tool was written by a different author, and thus used a different algorithm to hide the information inside the carrier. Jeremy expected that some of the applications were more efficient than others because of the algorithm they used and the way they were coded.

But there were other types of covert channels that didn't actually utilize steganography, per se. Their methods were completely different. One of his favorites had been the manipulation of text and words in a message to create something entirely different. Using these tools, Jeremy could create spam e-mails, full text documents, and even scripts to a fictional play.

The first such tool he found was a spam generator built into a web site that would create a spam-type e-mail from a message a user entered into the web site. The site was called Spam Mimic and was based on an engine published by Peter Wayner in his 1996 book, *Disappearing Cryptography*. The authors of the web site had created their own *spam grammar* to be used in the engine and built a web page around the concept. Jeremy opened his web browser and typed the address for www.spammimic.com. Arriving at the page, he clicked the button for *Encode*.

Spam Mimic

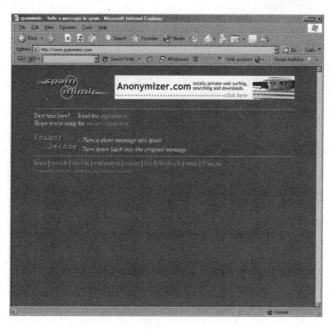

The web page switched to the page created for encoding user messages and Jeremy typed a quick, simple test message. *It doesn't need to be anything complex, just something to test the engine again,* he thought to himself. The entire idea of manipulating words and text in such a way to obscure the real meaning intrigued Jeremy immensely. Words were the most basic form of communication. The ability to continue using words without a huge hit on usability could mean that these types of ciphers were more popular than most people would imagine.

Encoding User Message

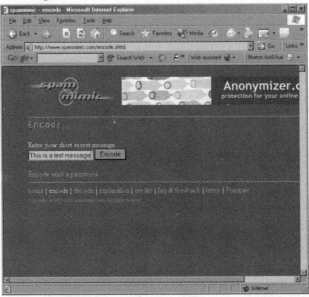

When Jeremy had finished his short message and pressed the Encode button on the browser window, the browser icon began to spin again before displaying his encoded message. The realism of the spam, at first glance anyway, was amazing. With the sheer numbers of spam that crossed the desktops of Internet users around the world, one more message would likely be disregarded and ignored completely. There was potential in this method to communicate with multiple numbers of individuals and never be able to track specifically for whom the message was intended.

Generated Spam Message

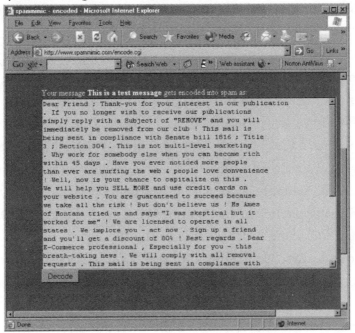

Jeremy glanced again at the output and realized that there were distinct patterns within each spam message that was generated. He could assume only that there was a flaw in the design of this particular engine. Scanning the e-mail, he noticed that there were multiple introductory lines and greetings in his message, even though his initial input had been relatively short. But he had to admit to himself that the tool created a genuine enough looking product that most people instantly delete the message.

There was a market for e-mail lists. Companies looking to capitalize a little more from the mailing lists they had gathered were in a position to now sell those lists to anyone they wanted to. Sure, there were some repercussions and some perturbed customers, but the extra revenue in their pocketbook served as a good an incentive as any. Over the last few years, this had resulted in mailing lists that included millions of e-mail addresses that could be bought for relatively little money.

Jeremy couldn't help hypothesizing about the potential uses for such a system. Obviously, there were financial incentives for some organizations, but what about a group, like the one he was investigating? What were the possible uses for something like this? His first thought was how inexpensive these mailing lists actually were to purchase. A group wanting to hide their communication could simply buy a list from an existing organization and add their own group member's e-mail addresses to the list. By entering their message into the Spam Mimic interface, they could create a suitable e-mail that could then be sent to millions of addresses, including the actual target addresses. Most people would simply ignore the message completely, but those individuals who were already in the know would find some hidden value in the message.

The thought that was frightening to Jeremy was its simplicity. Users on the Internet had already been trained to ignore spam messages. In many cases the e-mails were caught at gateway interfaces that removed potential spam before it ever reached the user. For a few hundred U.S. dollars, anyone could create a mechanism like this for communicating secretly, yet publicly at the same time.

That thought reminded Jeremy of another tool he had downloaded from the Internet, *Sam's Big G Play Maker*. Unlike Spam Mimic, this tool was loaded onto a user's computer under the Windows operating system. And unlike the previous tool, which was intended to mimic the look and feel of a genuine spam e-mail message, the Play Maker software converted your message into a script for a play. He closed his web browser and opened his My Computer icon to browse to the new application.

He had installed the software on his D:\ drive and quickly found the start-up icon in the application folder. Double-clicking the icon brought the software to life on his screen instantly. The software was coded into a very small binary executable that apparently used very little memory on the system.

Sam's Big G Play

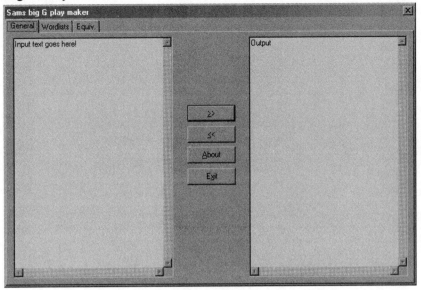

The interface to the software was simple and easy to understand. There were three tabs on the window: one for General, one for Wordlists, and a third for Equiv. The General tab was easy enough to use, allowing users to input their messages in the left pane of the window, click the double right-arrow button, and view the output in the right pane of the window. The process was supposed to work in a similar fashion when used in the reverse. So if Alice sent Bob an e-mail message with a play script in it, then Bob could cut and paste the script into the right pane and click the double left-arrow button to decode the message. Jeremy had to admit that the idea was a good one, but its implementation was weak. He decided to toy with the tool once more, and entered a short message into the right pane of the window.

Real Test from Jeremy

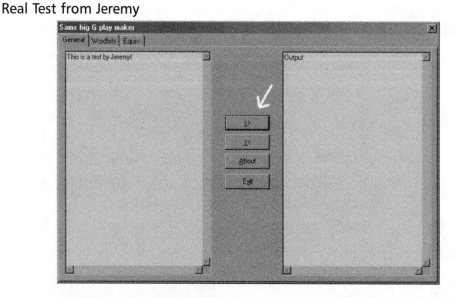

When he had entered his short message, Jeremy clicked the double right-arrow to convert his message into a play. The output was simple, but could pass for a legitimate script assuming no one really spent any time reading the output. A cursory glance at the final product would likely be ignored by the normal user as some extremely boring script written by a coworker with a little too much free time.

Output

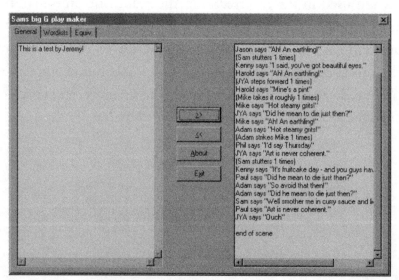

Jeremy had been so amused by this particular tool that he played with it at length, learning that the tool used nothing more than simple substitution to create the final script. Substitution was a relatively weak form of protecting text messages, but especially so with a default equivalency embedded into the tool. But Jeremy had to give kudos to the author of this tool. Instead of embedding a default static list of phrases and words, the user was allowed to customize the settings. Using this function, it would certainly take more time to break the encoded message. Two separate users only would need to share the same settings used in the tool in order to create more realistic scripts and make them more difficult to recognize. Jeremy clicked from the General tab to the Wordlists tab.

Wordlists

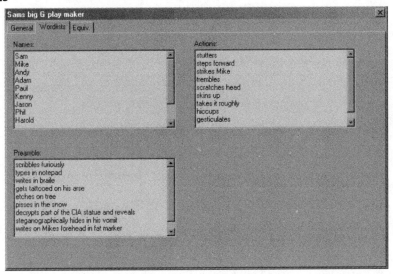

The names would all need to be changed, as any default settings would be immediately recognizable by a true analyst. But changing the names, the preambles, and the actions would help solidify the story line being used in the conversion. *Heck, done correctly,* Jeremy thought to himself. *You could almost come up with a script that made sense if you put the effort into selecting the right terms and phrases.* The tool had limitations, surely, but there was also some inherent value with using the tool. He clicked the next tab, Equiv., which defined the equivalency within the tool. The equivalency defined how each character typed into the input pane would be reflected in the output pane. In most cases, the information in the right pane defined the phrases that would be stated by the names stated in the Wordlists tab. Again, it seemed to Jeremy that, if done correctly, the final output script could look legitimate.

Final Output

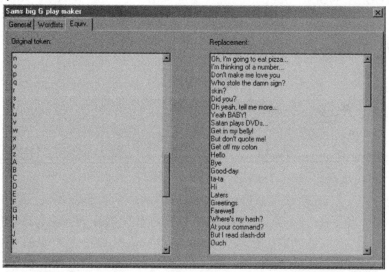

But what methods could be used to send these scripts out that wouldn't draw so much attention? E-mail was an obvious answer, but if a user was sending large numbers of e-mails containing these scripts, it might draw attention to them. The other, less obvious answer was to use an online forum or USENET newsgroup to communicate the scripts. These types of forums were publicly available, but the traffic would be so disjointed as to discourage too many users. Individuals who had prior information about the channel would be able to download the scripts to their local machines and decode the messages.

Jeremy glanced at his watch; just after 10 P.M. *It's probably time to head home,* he told himself. *I can work on this more tomorrow, and I don't want to make mistakes because I'm getting tired.* Jeremy closed the application and logged out of the computer. After packing up his belongings, he turned out his desk lamp and walked out of his small cubicle toward the front door. It had been a long day, and he still wasn't sure if he was really making any progress on the case.

October 3, 2004

Jeremy rolled over in his bed and buried his head under a pillow, trying desperately to escape the bright sunlight now forcing its way through the thin blinds protecting him from the waking world outside. But his mind had been powered on, and he knew there was little chance of further sleep this morning.

His thoughts of the night before were still blurry in his mind. He could recall leaving work and making a quick stop at Taco Bell on his way back to his small apartment. But exhaustion had consumed him as he walked through the door, and there was little left in his mind about what had happened after that. Pulling his head out from under the pillow and sitting up against the small pine headboard, his eyes squinted involuntarily as they came in contact with the bright sunlight.

Something caught his attention as it fell to the floor at the foot of the bed, the remnants of his late night snack. Wrappers from Taco Bell littered the floor and end of the bed, along with various elements of shredded lettuce and cheese. He had been very hungry when he came home last night, but not hungry enough to overcome his exhaustion before the final soft taco had been consumed. It now lay in a haphazard, cold lump at one corner of his bed. *Great, now he had a mess to clean up.*

He reached for the television remote control and flipped the channel to the Headline News. As he stared at the pictures on the screen, trying to wake his mind up fully, it wandered off again, beyond his control. The research on covert channels and steganography had been consuming his every waking moment. It was an exciting new world that until recently he had never known existed. Now he had a new hobby.

There was a reporter on the television giving the latest sports scores and predictions for the professional football games scheduled for tomorrow. The background noise was comforting and blocked out the kids on the sidewalk below apparently making as much noise as their small bodies were capable of. He swung his legs over the side of the bed and sat straight up, stretching. Standing up slowly, he felt the tattered carpet underneath his feet, and grimaced as his toe touched a patch of errant salsa. *It's time to get around so I can fiddle with some more of these tools.* He had to give his recommendations on how to proceed with the current case on Monday. Unless something miraculous happened this weekend, he wasn't going to have much to present to Neil. The pressure of failing on his very first *real* case was eating him alive, but the desire to learn more about covert channels had become an internal driver, motivating him on. He walked across the room and headed into the bathroom. *A quick shower, some breakfast, and we'll be ready to go.*

Jeremy sat down on his now made-up bed. It had taken him over an hour to get showered and dressed, though much of that time had been spent cleaning up the mess from the previous evening's snack. He had discovered, much to his own chagrin, that vacuum cleaners were woefully unprepared for ground-in cheese and taco meat, so the process had proceeded by hand until the entire mess was eliminated. But now he was free, and it was Saturday. The rest of the day was his, and he had plans for those precious hours.

He had spent the majority of the last two weeks researching covert channels, learning everything he could about how they worked and were implemented. If there was any communication taking place right in front of the American people, it had to be on the Internet in the form of hidden information. Initially, he thought he had stumbled upon a gold-mine, the answer was lying right in front of him. But as he had spent more time researching the topic, he had learned that life was never as simple as you might initially hope. There were dozens of different forms of covert channels, taking on a variety of forms and implementations. *How am I ever going to figure out what they're using unless I get more clues*, he thought to himself. He refused to let himself get frustrated by the process, but instead preferred to continue learning. *I'll get this. I know I can.*

Jeremy reached down and grabbed his laptop bag from its resting place near his headboard. He pulled the Sony Vaio from a protective sleeve built into the laptop bag and set it in front of him on the bed. The dull gray exterior of the laptop obscured the nature of the laptop itself. It was loaded with Windows XP Professional, which was the standard on most new laptops sold to government agencies these days, but it was also dual boot. Jeremy had loaded Slackware 10.0 on the laptop as an alternate research platform.

He powered on the laptop and watched as the Vaio logo flashed across the screen in shades of blue and white, followed shortly after by the LILO prompt. LILO, short for Linux Loader, acted as a boot agent, allowing a user to boot into multiple operating systems built onto the same computer. The simple red box held only two options, Linux or Windows. Jeremy highlighted the option for Linux. Today, he would research some Linux tools that created slightly more complex forms of covert channels.

Some of these forms included things well beyond the standard and more well-known steganographic techniques seen in the majority of tools. Two forms of covert channels in particular were of interest to Jeremy today—TCP covert channels and steganography involving actual executable binaries. Both of these techniques were best researched on the Linux platform primarily because of the flexibility and power available to a user under the operating system.

The first tool he would look at was named *Hydan*, and was originally released in 2002 by Rakan El-Khalil. The term hydan was based on an Old English word meaning *to hide or conceal*, which seemed perfectly apropos to Jeremy, considering the circumstances. He logged in and started up the Gnome interface. Once it had loaded, he brought up a terminal window and su'ed to the *root* user. He had untarred the hydan archive file in the /opt/hydan directory, so he changed into that directory and performed a directory listing using the *ls* command. Most of the files listed were either the actual programming code files (.c) or their associated header files (.h), which provided more information that would be used during the compilation process. A file named CHANGELOG had been included, which tracked the development of the product from its early stages in 2002 to the current release. The author of the software had even been kind enough to include an example text message that could be used by the end user to test the software, called *msg*.

File Listings

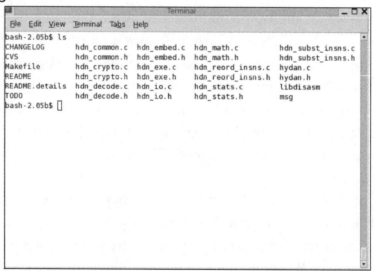

The default files included a README file giving basic rules for compiling and using the application. Hydan was a nongraphic program, requiring it to be run from the shell prompt. The core file to this process was the Makefile. This one file laid out the entire process for the *make* command, making compilation by the end user extremely simple. Jeremy performed a *make* command in the /opt/hydan directory and watched patiently as the application was compiled and an executable product was created. There were no significant compilation errors during the process, and soon a 32-bit executable had been created.

32-Bit Executable

```
                          Terminal                        _ □ ✗
 File  Edit  View  Terminal  Tabs  Help
 ar rc libdisasm.a libdis.o i386_invariant.o vm.o bastard.o i386.o
 ranlib libdisasm.a
 make[1]: Leaving directory `/opt/hydan/libdisasm/src/arch/i386/libdisasm'
 gcc -Wall -Ilibdisasm/src/arch/i386/libdisasm -g  -DVARBITS     -c -o hdn_common.
 o hdn_common.c
 gcc -Wall -Ilibdisasm/src/arch/i386/libdisasm -g  -DVARBITS     -c -o hdn_embed.o
  hdn_embed.c
 gcc -Wall -Ilibdisasm/src/arch/i386/libdisasm -g  -DVARBITS     -c -o hdn_decode.
 o hdn_decode.c
 gcc -Wall -Ilibdisasm/src/arch/i386/libdisasm -g  -DVARBITS     -c -o hdn_stats.o
  hdn_stats.c
 gcc -Wall -Ilibdisasm/src/arch/i386/libdisasm -g  -DVARBITS     -c -o hdn_crypto.
 o hdn_crypto.c
 gcc -Wall -Ilibdisasm/src/arch/i386/libdisasm -g  -DVARBITS     -c -o hdn_subst_i
 nsns.o hdn_subst_insns.c
 hdn_subst_insns.c:552: warning: `_address_add_visited' defined but not used
 hdn_subst_insns.c:575: warning: `_find_addr' defined but not used
 gcc -Wall -Ilibdisasm/src/arch/i386/libdisasm -g  -DVARBITS     -c -o hdn_io.o hd
 n_io.c
 gcc -Wall -Ilibdisasm/src/arch/i386/libdisasm -g  -DVARBITS     -c -o hdn_math.o
 hdn_math.c
 gcc -Wall -Ilibdisasm/src/arch/i386/libdisasm -g  -DVARBITS     -c -o hdn_exe.o h
 dn_exe.c
 ▯
```

Jeremy performed another *ls* command to verify that the new executable did indeed exist. The resulting directory listing showed a new file named *hydan*. Because this was new software for Jeremy, he ran the executable by itself to get the default operating parameters. The program looked simple enough to run. He had been surprised how simple the compilation process was for an end user. The command required no more than an input, a message to hide, and an output. *This should be fun.*

Hydan

```
                                    Terminal                        _ □ ×
 File  Edit  View  Terminal  Tabs  Help
ln -fs hydan hydan-stats
bash-2.05b$ ls
CHANGELOG        hdn_crypto.c  hdn_exe.c   hdn_reord_insns.c  hydan-decode
CVS              hdn_crypto.h  hdn_exe.h   hdn_reord_insns.h  hydan-stats
Makefile         hdn_crypto.o  hdn_exe.o   hdn_stats.c        hydan.c
README           hdn_decode.c  hdn_io.c    hdn_stats.h        hydan.h
README.details   hdn_decode.h  hdn_io.h    hdn_stats.o        hydan.o
TODO             hdn_decode.o  hdn_io.o    hdn_subst_insns.c  libdisasm
hdn_common.c     hdn_embed.c   hdn_math.c  hdn_subst_insns.h  msg
hdn_common.h     hdn_embed.h   hdn_math.h  hdn_subst_insns.o
hdn_common.o     hdn_embed.o   hdn_math.o  hydan
bash-2.05b$ hydan
Usage:
        hydan host_file [message_file]

Takes in a binary executable (host_filename) and stores the
message in message_filename inside of it.
Takes input from stdin when message_file is not specified.
Resulting application is output on stdout.

Ex: ./hydan /bin/ls <msg> ls.stegged

Use hydan-decode to retrieve the hidden message
bash-2.05b$ []
```

The instructions showed using the default *ls* command as an example, but Jeremy decided to copy the actual command to the local directory, to protect his system from a potential error. Once the file had been copied, he used the *ls* command to verify it was there and then decided to try the application out. He typed out his test command *hydan ./ls ./msg > ls.stegged* and pressed his Return key. Hydan immediately prompted Jeremy for a password to use during the encryption phase of the process. Hydan would take the text message given by the user and encrypt that information using the password entered at the prompt. In order to pull the information back out of the executable file at a later date, the user would have to know the correct password. The hiding process took only moments to complete.

Hiding Process Complete

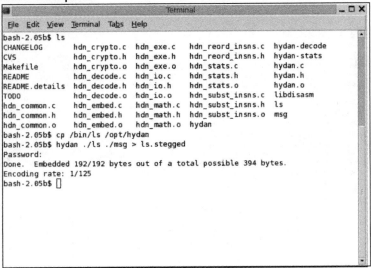

```
bash-2.05b$ ls
CHANGELOG          hdn_crypto.c  hdn_exe.c   hdn_reord_insns.c  hydan-decode
CVS                hdn_crypto.h  hdn_exe.h   hdn_reord_insns.h  hydan-stats
Makefile           hdn_crypto.o  hdn_exe.o   hdn_stats.c        hydan.c
README             hdn_decode.c  hdn_io.c    hdn_stats.h        hydan.h
README.details     hdn_decode.h  hdn_io.h    hdn_stats.o        hydan.o
TODO               hdn_decode.o  hdn_io.o    hdn_subst_insns.c  libdisasm
hdn_common.c       hdn_embed.c   hdn_math.c  hdn_subst_insns.h  ls
hdn_common.h       hdn_embed.h   hdn_math.h  hdn_subst_insns.o  msg
hdn_common.o       hdn_embed.o   hdn_math.o  hydan
bash-2.05b$ cp /bin/ls /opt/hydan
bash-2.05b$ hydan ./ls ./msg > ls.stegged
Password:
Done.  Embedded 192/192 bytes out of a total possible 394 bytes.
Encoding rate: 1/125
bash-2.05b$ []
```

Jeremy read through the final text output of the application, noticing that the software dumped out numbers stating the amount of information that was embedded into the carrier file. But Jeremy found himself curious about how the carrier file had been changed during the steganography process. The size of the carrier versus its original counterpart should not have changed, according to the author of the software. He decided to test this by comparing the two files and their size. According to the *ls* command, both files had the same number of bytes, but their file dates reflected the actual creation dates for each file. Jeremy confirmed that the date on the new file, *ls.stegged*, reflected today's date. The author's documentation stated that there should be no real method for determining if a file was a carrier created by Hydan. But Jeremy knew that the software was still very new. There was still a chance that someone would figure out a method for detecting the steganography, but it would certainly take time if the software worked the way the author stated.

Final Text Output

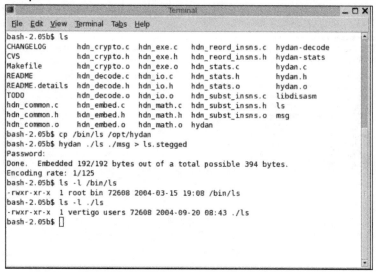

Hydan embeds data into a carrier by altering functions and algorithms within the application without impacting the functionality of those functions. Jeremy had read in the README file that the final executable should provide the same operation as the original, but the process to get there had been altered. The software came with another executable called *hydan-stats* that would present the user with information on the number of operations within the executable that had been altered. Jeremy ran the program against his new carrier file, *ls.stegged*, to find out what the output would tell the end user. The statistics represent every algorithm that had been changed within the executable. Jeremy skimmed through the output, more from pure curiosity than actual understanding of what the output meant.

Skimming through the Output

```
bash-2.05b$ ./hydan-stats ./ls.stegged
File              : ./ls.stegged
Code size         : 49394 bytes
Embeddeable insns : 394 bytes
Number of functions : 22 (7 bytes)
-------> Encoding Rate: 1/125 (1/122 with fns)

Total embeddeable insns: 394 bytes
Total number of fns     : 22 (7 bytes/file, 7 bytes/total)
Total encoding rate     : 1/125 (with fns: 1/122/file - 1/122/total)

mov32:
        mov   r/m32, r32: 595
        mov   r32  , r/m32: 162
addsub32-3:
        add   r/m32, imm8: 534
        sub   r/m32, imm8: 544
xorsub32:
        xor   r/m32, r32: 270
        xor   r32  , r/m32: 48
        sub   r/m32, r32: 34
        sub   r32  , r/m32: 52
addsub32-2:
        add   r/m32, imm32: 12
```

The final piece of the puzzle that Jeremy wanted to test with Hydan was the ease of decoding information from a carrier file. Complex tools seldom became popular enough to see widespread use among Internet users. The software had to be effective and easy to use. Using the *hydan-decode* executable, Jeremy attempted to decode the hidden message. The software prompted the young man for his original password in order to pull the message back out of the executable. Once the password was entered, the message was dumped to the screen in plain text.

Message in Plain Text

```
bash-2.05b$ ./hydan-decode ./ls.stegged
Password:
the quick brown fox jumps over the lazy dog
the quick brown fox jumps over the lazy dog
all work and no play makes xvr a dull boy.
all w0rkx0r and no pl4yz0r makes xvr a dull foo.
bash-2.05b$ []
```

Jeremy changed out of the current directory, back into his own home directory. There was still one more form of covert channel vying for his interest, channels under network protocols. Numerous tools were available on the Internet whose function was to mask unauthorized traffic on TCP/IP-based networks. These tools include creating channels using protocols such as ICMP, TCP, IP, HTTP, SMTP, and others. Some of these applications would hide the message inside each network packet as it was sent out, such as Covert_TCP. Others used protocols that were allowed through perimeter security devices, such as firewalls, to transmit the payload data.

Problems with Covert TCP

Creating covert channels within TCP is a convenient means for hiding information. But at the same time, there are inherent issues which, until recently, have slowed growth in this area. For example, the mechanisms coded into applications such as Covert_TCP are difficult to understand for normal users. In addition to understanding the host operating system being used, users also need to understand how to compile the source code into a suitable executable. This meant that if the software was used on a different platform than the one on which it was originally written, the user would need to understand how to modify the code to compile on their own platform.

The other issue with this form of covert channels, until recently, was the speed at which the channels could operate reliably. Covert_TCP works well, but it transmits data at a very slow rate. Because these channels operate outside the normal realm of the TCP protocol, the benefits of TCP's connection-oriented architecture are lost. For example, if users send a payload across the Internet using Covert_TCP, they are restricted to sending a single byte of information per second. The computer at the other end won't know the order in which to reform the message embedded in the network traffic. Sending the message at a speed of one byte a second ensures that one packet arrives at the destination prior to the next packet being transmitted. This speed restriction makes Covert_TCP impractical for sending large amounts of data.

Jeremy had downloaded several of these tools from various web sites and stored them all in a directory on his Linux partition. Most of the more useful tools for creating network-based covert channels are written for various forms of the UNIX operating system, including BSD and Linux. Although Covert_TCP was one of the original tools and easily the most popular, it was written for the 2.0 Linux kernel, and Jeremy was running a 2.6.7 kernel. He was technical, but didn't have the basic experience and knowledge in network programming that would allow him to port the software successfully. But his options weren't limited, as many new tools had been released in recent years that would allow him to test other techniques for creating these channels.

The dominating concept within the newer tools was to send a payload via protocols that were never designed to carry that type of information. For example, there were applications that could create tunnels across the HTTP protocol that was normally utilized for web traffic. These tunnels would allow any other type of traffic to traverse the network by embedding the information in standard HTTP traffic across popular web ports, like port 80, 8080, and 443. The most useful of these tools he had downloaded was Covert Channel Tunnel Testing, or CCTT.

CCTT was written to allow flexibility in the channels created and used by the end users. One computer attached to a network would be loaded and configured as a server. Another computer on the network would be configured to act as a client communicating with the server. Each installation of the software could act as either the server or the client, based on the configuration. The configuration of the software would define what protocol the server and client would use to communicate, what port they would utilize, and how the tunnels were encrypted. Tools like this could easily be used to bypass the standard perimeter security, such as firewalls and routers, by using ports and protocols known to be allowed in and out of the target network.

Jeremy began his experiment in network channels by copying the CCTT file to a separate directory and unzipping it. The tools were all archived in a similar fashion. First, all the individual files in each application were gathering together into a single file called a tape archive file, or .tar file. Then, the .tar file was compressed, or zipped, to reduce the size of the file for transmission across the network or storage on removal media.

Beginning His Experiment

When the file was unzipped, the individual files in the .tar file needed to be restored to the current directory. Jeremy used the Linux *tar* command to restore the contents to his test directory and watched as each file was pulled out and placed on his drive. The output to the console as the *tar* command ran showed the placement of each individual file, including all subdirectories under the current directory. Jeremy could tell by watching the output that the application had been created in a standard Makefile configuration, which hopefully would make installation quick and easy. File names like *configure, Makefile.am,* and *install-sh* were indicative of the *make* process. The operation took only a few moments to complete and returned Jeremy to a Linux shell prompt, awaiting further input and instructions.

Files

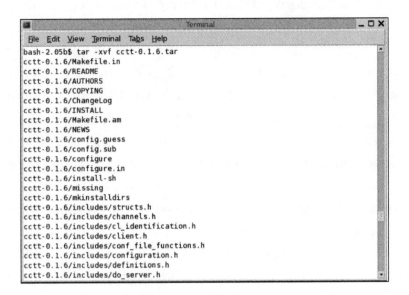

The *tar* operation had created a subdirectory under Jeremy's current directory called cctt-0.1.6. This would be the primary application directory. He changed into the new directory and performed a directory listing to see how the program was laid out. Many of the directories used in the Makefile process were similar across applications. Directories like *includes, docs,* and *src* were common.

cctt-0.1.6

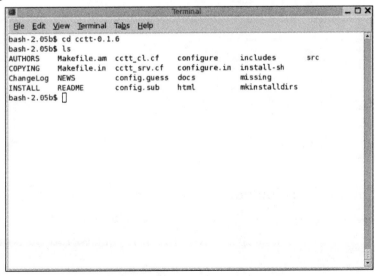

The first thing to do would be to configure the installation script for his platform. This operation would create a Makefile specifically configured for his computer and operating system. Again, the process was fairly normal across most of these types of installations. Jeremy typed the *configure* command and watched as the software went through the process of determining the platform, locating appropriate compilers on the system, and identifying the processor in the computer. Programmers had created this configuration process to make it easier for users to install their applications without making manual changes to the Makefile. Without this process, users would have to search their system for information required to install the software, whereas now the application would perform these activities on their own. Users with less technical experience were now able to install and compile software in this format. Jeremy silently thanked whoever had created this process. He wasn't totally sure whether he would have been able to install the software using the old methods.

Configuring Installation

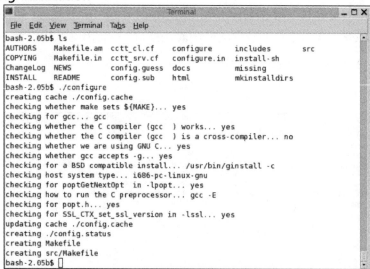

Once the configuration process was finished, it returned his shell prompt. Jeremy typed the *make all* command. The *configuration* process had created the Makefile that defined how the software would be compiled.

The *make all* command used that same Makefile to actually perform the compilation based on the details of the computer it was running on at the time. The compilation process took longer than the configuration process, but was still only a couple of minutes. Jeremy was able to watch as the compiler followed the instructions and created each individual program file based on the information it knew.

Watching the Compiler Work

```
                              Terminal                        _ □ X
 File  Edit  View  Terminal  Tabs  Help
bash-2.05b$ make all
Making all in src
make[1]: Entering directory `/home/vertigo/cctt/cctt-0.1.6/src'
gcc -I. -I.    -I/usr/include/   -g -O2 -DSSL -Wall -Wunused -c main.c
gcc -I. -I.    -I/usr/include/   -g -O2 -DSSL -Wall -Wunused -c functions.c
gcc -I. -I.    -I/usr/include/   -g -O2 -DSSL -Wall -Wunused -c verbose.c
gcc -I. -I.    -I/usr/include/   -g -O2 -DSSL -Wall -Wunused -c error_and_debug.c
gcc -I. -I.    -I/usr/include/   -g -O2 -DSSL -Wall -Wunused -c args.c
gcc -I. -I.    -I/usr/include/   -g -O2 -DSSL -Wall -Wunused -c conf_file.c
gcc -I. -I.    -I/usr/include/   -g -O2 -DSSL -Wall -Wunused -c channels.c
gcc -I. -I.    -I/usr/include/   -g -O2 -DSSL -Wall -Wunused -c channels_function
s.c
gcc -I. -I.    -I/usr/include/   -g -O2 -DSSL -Wall -Wunused -c show_cctt_prompt.
c
gcc -I. -I.    -I/usr/include/   -g -O2 -DSSL -Wall -Wunused -c conf_file_functio
ns.c
gcc -I. -I.    -I/usr/include/   -g -O2 -DSSL -Wall -Wunused -c conf_file_CHANNEL
_PROXY.c
gcc -I. -I.    -I/usr/include/   -g -O2 -DSSL -Wall -Wunused -c conf_file_PROTOCO
L.c
gcc -I. -I.    -I/usr/include/   -g -O2 -DSSL -Wall -Wunused -c conf_file_PROXY_M
ODE.c
gcc -I. -I.    -I/usr/include/   -g -O2 -DSSL -Wall -Wunused -c conf_file_PROXY_M
ODE_LIST.c
```

In the README file, there was information on utilizing the CCTT tool. The instructions explained to Jeremy that the software could act as either a client or a server, based on which configuration file he fed into the software at startup. As he read through the documentation, he found that the sample configuration files had been included in the main CCTT directory but needed to be edited before the application would work. Jeremy brought up the server configuration file, *ccct_srv.cf*, under his *vi* editor and read down through his configuration options to see what was available to him.

The file gave him options to use a variety of proxy servers on the Internet that would relay his traffic, further easing the ability to tunnel his traffic around perimeter security devices. He started at the top of the file and worked his way to the bottom. First, he uncommented the protocol line that defined the use of TCP as the primary protocol. Next, he had to turn on the identification mechanism that would identify the client and server to each other. This was based on a weak keyword function where both the client and the server shared the same keyword. Jeremy uncommented these lines and left the default indent keyword of *simsim* in place to simplify the process.

He continued through the configuration file, uncommenting the necessary functions and adding information where it was needed. It took him a few minutes to arrive at a suitable configuration for the server before moving on to the client configuration file, *ccct_cl.cf*, which was also located in the parent CCTT directory. The format of the two files was very similar, although the client configuration file had much information left in it to edit.

Client Configuration

```
# 24/01/2003
#
# Configuration file for server.
#   Take a look at docs/confs/srv_*.conf
#
#

# Protocol used between client and server or client and proxy
PROTOCOL=tcp

# Allowed proxying list : If the client use proxy_mode,
# Server checks that the client proxying request is set
#PROXY_MODE_LIST=ssh:127.0.0.1:22
#PROXY_MODE_LIST=http:127.0.0.1:80
#PROXY_MODE_LIST=smtp:10.1.1.7:25
#PROXY_MODE_LIST=pop:10.1.1.7:110

# Set the identification type and key
# must be equal in server and client configuration files !
# set to : clear_ident or basic_ident
#IDENT=basic_ident
#IDENT_KEY=simsim
```

Running the *cctt* command from the shell prompt gave Jeremy a list of the command line options that could be used with the tool. He decided to run the server with the simplest options possible just to get it up and running. The network address of the server was given on the command line, along with the desired port number the server would be listening on if a client called. The last option Jeremy gave the software was the location of the configuration file that would be used during the application's start-up. He pointed the software at the server configuration file and watched as it started listening on the port he had designated. The process had been very easy up to this point. Jeremy was impressed. If the creation of network-based covert channels was this easy, it would definitely be something in wide use on the Internet.

cctt Command

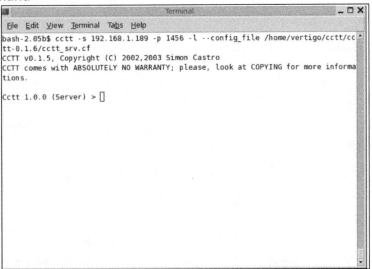

Once the server was running and listening on port 1456 as he had defined, he looked through the various options he had access to from the CCTT server prompt. A failed attempt at using a question mark (?) as a help command told Jeremy that he would need to use the *help* command to find information on the options available. He typed the *help* command and watched as the list of commands scrolled onto the screen.

List of Commands from Typing *Help*

```
                           Terminal                    _ □ X
 File  Edit  View  Terminal  Tabs  Help
bash-2.05b$ cctt -s 192.168.1.189 -p 1456 -l --config_file /home/vertigo/cctt/cc
tt-0.1.6/cctt_srv.cf
CCTT v0.1.5, Copyright (C) 2002,2003 Simon Castro
CCTT comes with ABSOLUTELY NO WARRANTY; please, look at COPYING for more informa
tions.

Cctt 1.0.0 (Server) > ?
ERROR / [Server] : Command '?' doesn't exist !!!
Use help to list commands.
/ ERROR
Cctt 1.0.0 (Server) > help
Cctt - Covert Channel Tunneling Tool - v0.1.6 (23/04, 2003)

Valid commands are :
  help                        display help
  show connections            display current connections
  show params                 display initialisation parameters
  kill connection X           Kill connection on Sd X
  kill manager X              Kill manager of Sd X
  tell client X 'something'   Send 'something' to client on Sd X
  quit                exit
Cctt 1.0.0 (Server) > []
```

Over the next few hours, Jeremy played with his new toy. As he realized, there were plenty of different means for creating covert channels on a network. Any port or service could be mimicked, at least from a cursory network traffic level. Information was protected within the tunnel through use of the shared keyword defined in the server and client configuration files. Once a tunnel was created, any form of traffic could be fed through it.

Jeremy had learned a great deal about the possible forms of covert channels that could exist on the Internet. Some were simpler to use, and thus, more likely to be in use in the terrorism case he was working. Others, although more robust, would require a more technical user on each end of the channel being used. He doubted very much if those tools were in use yet, but the potential existed. With the rate at which technology was evolving, there would be a time when these tools became the standard for covert channels on the Internet. But for now, he decided he should probably concentrate on the easier and more accessible forms, like steganography within digital images and audio files. He may be wrong, but he had to start somewhere, and this was as logical a starting point as any other.

That was enough for today; there were other things he wanted to do. He could resume working on the case on Monday. Jeremy's stomach growled loudly, and he realized he hadn't eaten in quite some time. *It's time to get out of here and get some fresh air*, he thought. He suddenly realized that he missed having friends like Kyle around to go do things with. Once he had started work, Jeremy and Kyle had lost touch; Kyle had accepted a job on the West coast. *We'll have to reprioritize things*, he thought to himself. With that, Jeremy logged out of the computer and shut it down for the day. It was time to take a break. Although he didn't really feel like it yet, he was hoping he was making some sort of progress on the case.

Chapter 12: Facing the Truth

October 9, 2004

Layla lay in her bed, crying again. She was desperate; her mind was split down the center into two completely different and conflicting mind-sets, and she was definitely *losing it*. One side of her had been created years earlier by her father and tormented her day and night. She had a purpose based in hate, excused by religion, and a requirement for her to be cold and uncaring. The other side of her longed to be gentle and tolerant; this side of her wanted to forget the failure of what had been her childhood and develop a new purpose in life. Her youth had been stolen from her, as had her future. Regardless of the pain she now felt pulsing within, she finally was able to attain a clarity of mind that had eluded her before. Jeremy was right; she did have an opportunity for a real future that she would decide, a future she wanted to reach out and take into both hands and protect.

She had been so confused for so long. She could always hear her father's screaming voice in her ears, motivating her with fear of physical punishment. Then there was the supposed anger of Allah that paled in comparison to her father's wrath should she eventually fail. There had never been any playgrounds for this young girl. There were no friends waiting outside to kick around a soccer ball or poke fun at the neighborhood boys. There was only the fear and incessant mantra of twisted purpose hammered into her, and now, the longing inside her to escape.

Layla rolled away from the window and lay on her side, facing the pale colored walls. As with the rest of the apartment, the walls were boring, showing only slight brown stains through age. But the window reminded her that there were living people outside, innocent people, children, families. It reminded her of the children who had died in the recent terror attack in Iraq. Visions of her own brother, lying dead in a pile of rubble filled her mind. *How did I end up here?* The pain of losing her brother to a randomness had been difficult to bear, and had only intensified exponentially by the anger of her father.

Her mind slipped back to that day. A friend of her father's, she had long since forgotten his name, rushed to the door of their small home on the east side of Ramadi. There had been an explosion near the university. Her father's face had turned bright red, and the young child version of herself had watched as tears filled his eyes. No one knew at that point that her brother had been involved in the explosion, not for certain. But there is a bond between parent and child that reaches deep within the parent, and somehow, her father *knew*, and had said "He's gone; I can feel my son's life force is gone from this world."

Their car had rushed across town toward the university. The images in her mind reminded Layla of when her brother played with her outside their home. He would laugh and toss her around in the air above his head, making her gleefully dizzy. Their mother and father would watch from a window in the house, smiling at the two playing in the dusty evening sun. Layla bit her lip as the pain of her loss returned. Ironically, her brother had preferred to stay near home to study even though he had been granted scholarships at universities in London and Germany. He had loved his family deeply and wanted to stay close in case of any emergencies that might befall them.

The small family's car stopped near the university, but was unable to get nearer to the site. Military vehicles blocked the small alleyway, and armed Americans guarded the site. Her father stepped out of the car and walked toward the rubble, ignoring the shouts of the soldiers, who then let him be when they saw that he was intent on finding a lost victim.

Although she was only eight years old, the scene was etched in her mind like an old black and white photograph, turning yellow around the edges. Rocks, stones, and shattered pieces of handmade brick were scattered in a large circle around the area. Shards of glass poked up through the rubble taunting the men who climbed across the piles. A large hole occupied the space approximately where the door might have been in the small shop. From what she could understand with her young mind, a very large explosion had ripped the shop from its core and left pieces of it strewn about the alley.

The neighboring buildings, although damaged badly, still stood. The owners paced around and inside their small shops, crying at the destruction; their entire lives were destroyed by the events of the day. The building across the street, a small market that once sold food to the locals, was now buried underneath pieces of the small coffee shop that used to reside across the way. Layla could remember not seeing any blood on the rocks, and there were no bodies lying nearby, but there was a smell in the air that she did not recognize.

Her father had joined the other three to four men who were already climbing the rocks of the haphazard piles of rubble, trying to find survivors, or the remains of the dead. The piles were deep, and it would take time to reach the bottom. Over the next few hours, more men joined in the search, and soon a line stretched down the alley, with rocks being passed from man to man until a new pile was formed at one end of the small alley. Women wailed as they stood and watched. The men carried on their work, few saying much at all, but nearly all of them praying silently to Allah, their lips moving only slightly.

Layla closed her eyes. The tears were streaming down her face, soaking her hair and making it stick to her face. That single day of her youth would change the rest of her life. She sat up in her small bed and took the small glass of water off the nightstand. A small stream of water ran down her chin as she poured more into her small mouth than she could swallow at once. When the glass was emptied, she set it back on the small nightstand, her mind already wandering back in time once more.

The first body pulled from the wreckage that day was a small baby, the small blanket still wrapped around his tiny body. A sharp rock protruded from his small back, and his clothes were matted with blood, still wet. His head was bald as the black hair was just starting to grow in. He was so young, and the scene had made Layla cry instantly. A person can see a pile of rubble and understand that something has happened, but once they see a victim, a body, their minds are forever changed. Her father had taken the child and handed it gently to one of the women crying at the side. She took the baby and wrapped it in black cloth. The women prayed over the child, crying to Allah to give the baby peace.

The second body was a woman, still holding a bag that had once held groceries from across the street with an additional smaller bag strung around her shoulders and around her neck. The men pulled the woman from the wreckage; her leg was completely gone. They kept their composure and carried her as carefully as they could manage, across the rubble to a clear area off to one side. As they moved, a few small items fell from a hole that had been torn in her bag. A small baby toy rattled to the ground at Layla's feet as the men passed. *This is the baby's mother,* she remembered thinking to herself in shock. *Who would do this? Who would kill an innocent mother and her child?*

But the scene was about to get much worse. From inside the shell of the broken coffee shop, a man hollered to the others. Part of the roof had collapsed as the support wall had been blown away, leaving a pile of rubble near one side of the shop. Layla could barley make out the shape of a hand, sticking up limply from the rocks. The men gathered around the area, pulling rocks quickly and passing them down the line, from man to man, until the rocks had been removed. She could still hear the sound erupting from her father's lungs, a sound made by animals in the desert, but never a man. She watched silently as each rock was removed, freeing the body from its prison.

A number of terrible things will happen to most people during their lives, but nothing compares to the death of a child. The pain and emptiness felt by a parent sears their insides, shredding their hearts and leaving them feeling numb and empty. A child serves as the focal point of every hope the parents have and a bottomless flask into which the parents pour every ounce of their love. Losing a child can cause a man to lose his mind at the same time, and so it would be on this day.

Layla could vividly see her father clutching at the hand, screaming in agony as the other men carried his son from the wrecked building. Her brother's face stared up at the sky, and his arms hung limp at his side. Blood stained his clothes, and his legs hung at odd angles as he was laid down on the street, away from the rocks. That was the day her life changed completely. From that day forward, she was not a child. She was allowed nothing more than to revenge her brother's death.

She wiped her eyes and pulled her wet hair from her face. Looking back on it now, she wondered why she had been allowed to stand and watch the entire scene. She had been no more than a child herself. But the scene was surreal, almost a dream. A young child playing spectator to a horrible event, never truly understanding the significance of what had happened that day or the impact it would have on thousands of lives in the future. But she was grown now. The pain had been real. The impact had been mortal.

The funeral had been held three days later. Time had been needed to repair the young man's damaged body and prepare the arrangements. Her father had spent three days in silent misery. He avoided contact with her and her mother. No one approached him and he approached no one else. The anger was building inside his now empty heart, replacing the love that had been torn from him. But on the day of the funeral, her father had appeared calm, almost casual, just another spectator in this morbid life event. On that day, her father had walked to her and lit a fuse to a bomb inside her destined to explode years down the road. But fuses burn with flame, and it hurt her inside to carry such a horrible hatred inside of her for so long. It was against her nature and denied logic. She could not let this go any further. Human life was sacred. Greed and paranoia result in death and pain. She would play no further part in this.

Layla reached for her cell phone and dialed Jeremy's number. She had tried to let him be these last couple of weeks as she knew he was working nonstop on a project, but she needed to talk to a friend. Quite possible the only friend she ever really had. The voice on the other end was both terrifying and comforting at the same time as she realized what she needed to do. As soon as she heard his voice she blurted out, "Jeremy, I *really* need to speak with you. People will die if we don't. I can't live with that."

"What? Layla? What's wrong? Are you okay?" came Jeremy's reply. "You sound as if you've been crying. You're not hurt, are you?"

"No, physically I'm fine. Mentally and emotionally I'm having a rough time right now." Layla reached over and grabbed a tissue from one side of her bed and wiped her eyes. "I know you're busy with whatever top secret work you can't talk to me about, but I really just need to talk to you about something."

"Look, Layla, it's really not that big a deal. People graduate everyday from colleges around the world and make their way into the working world, to real jobs. No one has died from it yet, at least not immediately. From what I understand, you have to be in your forties before work will kill you on some random stressful Monday morning." Jeremy laughed out loud, obviously enjoying the joke he had just made, but realized suddenly that the voice on the other end was silent. This was serious. Layla always wore her emotions quietly, letting him into her world a little at a time, but he could always elicit a laugh from her. This was serious "Okay, I'm sorry. Talk to me. What's wrong with you?"

Layla took a deep breath and tried to relax. *It's no good,* she thought to herself, *I'm never going to be comfortable again until I get this off of my chest.* "Jeremy, I have a long story to tell you. It's going to shock you. There are parts of it you probably will never believe, but if I don't tell someone who can help me, people will definitely die."

Jeremy's skin was crawling. There was an eerie tone to Layla's voice, one he had never heard before. The hairs on his arms were beginning to stand on end. "Okay. We can work through this. I'm your friend; that's what I'm here for. Tell me what you need, and I'll help you."

"When I was young, my brother was killed when an American mortar round went astray and blew up outside the door to a coffee shop he was sitting in. He was killed instantly." Layla wiped her eyes again. It stung inside to actually talk of these events out loud to someone. "His name was Ahmed, and he was a student at a local university in Ramadi. No one is really sure why the Americans were firing off rounds or whether it was a freak accident. But suffice it to say, many people in our city were angry by the apparent attack." Layla paused, trying to catch her breath.

"When my father heard about the attack, he rushed to where the coffee shop used to be, with me in tow. I was still a young girl back then, but I can remember the scene vividly. The young mother who had died from the blast. Her small child—a rock stuck in his frail body." She started actively crying again, knowing she wasn't making sense.

"Go on, Layla. It's okay."

"Looking back now, I remember feeling very sad for the young woman and her baby. But the worse was yet to come. Shortly after they had pulled the two bodies from the rubble, they found another body." Layla was fighting inside to regain her composure. If she broke down now, she'd never make it to the important part. "My father was screaming in agony before I ever even saw the body. Together with several other men, my father brought the body of my brother past the edge of the debris and laid it on a blanket, laid out by some of the local women. He was completely distraught, my father."

"There were people crying for days afterward. All I can really recall is the near constant wailing of members of my family as they mourned. My father said nothing to me, preferring instead to sink down into his own solitude. Several days later, we had the funeral." She took a deep breath, feeling a sense of relief as the years of pent-up pressure and secrecy easily rose to the surface.

"When the funeral arrived, everyone was visibly grieving; everyone that is, except my father. For some reason, he seemed to have come to terms with what had happened. He came to me later that day and put his hand on my shoulder. It felt so good to have his attention again. But he wanted something from me."

"What did he say, Layla? What did he want?" Jeremy was tied to Layla's words, hanging on each syllable as it flowed from her lips.

"He told me that eventually I was going to attend the university in my brother's place, and I was going to avenge his death. It never occurred to me at that time what he *really* wanted me to do."

Jeremy was silent with the possible implications her words might hold. She continued.

"For a decade my father tormented me with the idea that the West had killed my brother and would try to kill all my friends and family before they were through. He had been spending more and more time at a very small mosque in town, one known for harboring men who despised the Americans. His thoughts grew more and more angry. My days were filled with extended lectures by my father about the evils of the West and how they must be destroyed in the name of Allah. It was my father's grudge, hidden within a religious veil to conceal the truth behind his words.

"A few years ago I arrived in Canada to attend school. One of the first things I did was to adopt a new name on the Internet, one that would not sacrifice my true identity. I used this name in e-mail, on web forums, in newsgroups, and in IRC. My time online was spent consorting with other angry Muslims who wanted to hurt the Western peoples." She took another drink of her water. The words were flowing much easier now.

"Believe it or not, it's actually quite difficult to find many people willing to take a violent stand against the United States, or even the West in general. Islam is generally a very peaceful religion, but men have a means to bend even the more enduring truth and make it something terrible. In time, I had associated myself with multiple online personalities who believed the same rhetoric that I had bought into. To this very day, they all believe me to be a man, Salah Aldin.

"I'm not sure how much you know about most Middle Eastern cultures, Jeremy, but for the most part, and with very few exceptions, women are considered second-class citizens. Men rule the workplace and the home, sometimes with an iron fist. Women have a place raising children, making meals, and cleaning. The Internet allows me to be anyone I want, or need, to be, including a man. Men will listen to other men, especially when they agree. I pretended to be a man online because I wanted these other men to follow me, to do what I asked of them, to potentially make the ultimate sacrifice for me and their God."

Jeremy was growing increasingly concerned. "Layla, you're just a student. I don't understand where this is going."

"I needed them to follow me because I was coordinating an attack against American interests, its people, Jeremy."

Jeremy's heart stopped cold. *This can't be*, he thought. *I have to be dreaming. This is Layla, not some random terrorist.* "Please tell me you're kidding. You're not like that and you know it. You're just really stressed out right now because you're getting ready to graduate. Maybe you've been watching too much cable news. Please tell me this isn't true."

"I'm not kidding, Jeremy. For over a year now I've been building a team over the Internet, communicating with them, stroking their egos and priming them for the day that would eventually come. But for many years more I have been fighting an internal battle for my soul. That war has finally ended. I need your help to ensure that no one innocent dies. I don't know whom else to go to."

"Why now? Why me? Surely you have others you can turn to." Jeremy was worried now. She really was serious.

"It's because I knew you had gotten at job with the government there in the states," she replied. "And because you're the only true friend I have. I can't let this happen, and I have the key to helping stop this before anyone gets hurt."

Jeremy realized with a start that he was holding his breath and let the air out of his lungs. He drew another deep breath, unsure of what to say or how to respond. "Layla, I think I know what to do, but I need you to stay where you are. Can I call you back in a few minutes?"

Layla was in a daze. Now that it was out in the open she felt numb, in a trance. Through the fog she heard Jeremy's voice again. "Layla! Please... say that you'll stay where you are. I'll call you back shortly."

"Okay." That was all she could muster before hanging up the phone.

Stunned, Jeremy stared off into space. *Could there be a connection?* The possibility hadn't escaped him that Layla could be one of the individuals involved in the case he was currently working at the office, but he didn't want to jump to any conclusions. She had admitted her activities to him herself, but what if she was just under a lot of pressure and having a nervous breakdown? *Man, I don't know what would be worse; I'd hate to drag her all the way to Washington, D.C., if this is all just some delusion.* He finally managed to convince himself that, at the very least, he needed to get in touch with Neil and find out what the protocol for this type of thing was. *Maybe he can give me some advice,* he thought.

Jeremy picked up the phone and dialed Neil's cell phone. The phone rang sharply on the other end as he waited for an answer.

"This is Neil."

"Hey, Neil; this is Jeremy. I've got an issue, and I need some advice from you on how I should proceed."

"This sounds serious, guy." Neil adjusted the volume on the phone so that he could hear Jeremy better. "What's up? Is this a personal or a professional issue?"

"It's actually professional, and it's a long story." Jeremy sighed and then continued. "You have a few minutes? You're never going to believe what I'm about to tell you."

The tone of Jeremy's voice hooked Neil into the conversation immediately. "Yeah, I've got time. Let's talk."

Jeremy prepared the story in his head. *It's as important* how *the story is told as what the story is about,* he reminded himself. "Okay, well, here's what's going on ..."

Chapter 13: Taking Command

October 13, 2004

It can be difficult to sit idly by and wait for the inevitable. The truth can be standing directly in front of you, staring you in the face, and still be invisible when your mind refuses to accept it. Every man is born with some degree of hope and faith, but there's always a limit; the line where the gap has grown too wide for even a leap of faith. Discovering where your own internal limits are can be frustrating and painful. Believing that someone you depend on and trust let you down completely is hard to accept. Our own internal emotional defenses refuse to allow the acceptance of those realities. But in time, the truth becomes impossible to ignore, and that's when the anger sets in. Jimmy was sitting aboard the cruise ship, in his room, having already made the transition from hope to anger.

How the hell can the man abandon something that was obviously so important to him? This thought ran through Jimmy's mind, over and over. Salah had disappeared several weeks ago, leaving no trace, no guidance, and no warning. Jimmy's repeated attempts at e-mailing the young man had been met with utter silence. Regardless, the project was currently at a standstill and something had to be done. The group needed leadership if the project was to continue. He had to get things back on track, and he needed to do it quickly. Salah was worthless, a coward, and Jimmy hated him.

The normally bearable stress associated with the project was reaching a fever pitch now that Jimmy was feeling abandoned so close to the target date. He wasn't used to being a leader. Motivating people was not what he did well. As he looked around the small cabin space where he slept, his mind was focused internally on what his next steps should be. He had gotten an e-mail from the group's contacts at Al Qaeda one week ago, asking about their progress. They were concerned that there had been no recent communication from Salah since the last payment. They had their own goals with this project and were not likely to accept failure as a viable option. *Had Salah run off with the money? Was the entire project a cleverly planned hoax? Would Salah hand them all over to the enemy?* Jimmy had assured the Al Qaeda contacts in an e-mail several days ago that the project was very much for real and that he would be replacing Salah as the leader of the group. Jimmy was frustrated by the little information he actually had about the disappearance of Salah, but gave the contacts everything he knew up to this point. They wouldn't like it; he was sure of that much, but there wasn't much left to do.

Despite his hesitance, he knew deep down that he was left with only one choice now. He was going to have to step up and take control of the project. There were dozens of men out there risking their lives for what they believe in, and they needed someone to manage the project. There was no telling what Al Qaeda would do to someone they thought might be a danger to their own agenda. If Salah jumped ship on the project, what was to say that Jimmy wouldn't as well? He didn't want Al Qaeda to doubt him, so his e-mail had been intense, written with his own sense of drive for the project. *The group is still intact, and the first phase of the project will be carried out as planned,* he had told them. He hoped they believed him. If Salah got Jimmy into hot water with Al Qaeda, Jimmy would track him down and kill the man himself.

His first task had been to reassure the others in the group that all was well and that he was taking charge. He explained Salah's absence by saying the man had lost his nerve and abandoned the project. *He did not have total faith in Allah,* he had told them. Many of the men in the group were devout Muslims, much like Salah had professed to be, and Jimmy needed to be one of them if he were going to lead them. *Do not be so weak in your belief. Allah* will *help us through this. It is* His *mission.*

Jimmy's second task had been to get the men on the cruise ships back on track by helping them decide how they would strike. One of the men already had conceived of how he was going to build and place the device on his own ship, but the plan had flaws. The other man had not come to any decision and had apparently been waiting for further instructions and guidance. Jimmy accepted the situation and stepped into his leadership role, providing the two men with further instructions about possible materials to use and where to place the devices. He had even warned them to be on the lookout for anything suspicious, in case Salah had uncovered their plans. *Stay alert and don't give away your identity.*

Jimmy had also decided what chemicals he would use to create the toxic cloud on his own cruise ship. They were all easily accessible for most individuals on the cleaning crew. Combining the ingredients would require a suitable container and placement within the ventilation system. Because of the large quantities of food consumed by the passengers during each voyage, the cruise lines purchase all of their food supplies in bulk. One of the most used consumables is milk. But unlike the milk purchased at local supermarkets, cruise ships buy their milk by the bag. Large plastic bags with spouts are filled with milk at the dairy and placed inside cardboard box containers that are then loaded into milk machines. Passengers went to the milk machines, lifted a metal pressure handle on the outside, and filled their glasses directly from these bags. These bags, when emptied, were placed in large recycle bins outside the kitchen area that was readily accessible to the cleaning crew on the ship.

He had decided to fill the milk bag with a dangerous combination of chemical cleaners that were known to create toxic fumes after being exposed to each other for a period of time. A variety of toilet cleaners, carpet cleaners, and detergents for washing the sheets on passenger beds would be used. With very little effort, a trusted individual could create a lethal toxic cloud, poisoning passengers and crew members alike. He already had access to all the chemicals and had snagged several milk bags earlier during this same cruise. The placement of several of these devices would ensure a thicker field of poison in the area.

But he was still faced with the placement of his devices. His original thoughts on using something in the engine room had proven to be fruitless, as access to the room was difficult to come by, even with acquaintances in the area. There also wasn't nearly enough ventilation exposure from the engine room as he had first thought. He wanted to affect a large common area that would be used by a majority of the passengers soon after they were finished with their trip into port. The best targets for this were the various dining areas. Yes, he would need to find suitable vent shafts that would fill the dining areas with the toxic smoke.

Jimmy's cleaning shift was due to start in another 45 minutes. He would have to wait to send another e-mail to the group's contact, but he still had time to run by the computer room, put his name on the schedule sheet for computer time, and grab himself something to eat prior to going to work. *At some point,* he thought, *I'm just going to have to buy a laptop. I hate having to share public computers with these disgusting Americans.* It wasn't so much that the computers in the lab were difficult to use, but in most cases, users were limited to an hour a day. If he were going to manage this project and the phase afterward, he'd need to have his own computer that he could work on with some privacy. There would be a lot of information to get out to the rest of the team, including some changes to the way information was dispersed. But the first phase of the plan was about to come to fruition and Jimmy had limited tools with which to work. He wouldn't have to deal with working from a cruise ship for much longer.

If he followed the original schedule, he still had two days to finalize his plans and make sure that every one was still on track, despite the lapse in management. But after what had happened, he was starting to reconsider. *It might make sense,* he thought, *to have everyone act as soon as possible in case Salah had compromised the group's plan.* They could not afford to lose their advantage, the element of surprise. He pushed a wave of anger back down into his stomach and tried not to think about Salah so much. The feelings would be distracting, and he could not afford to lose his focus, not now.

His ship was scheduled to dock at port tomorrow, their first stop, and Jimmy was going to plant his devices and leave the ship, never to return. If he timed it correctly, he could be off the ship and away to safety before anything odd was noticed. He wasn't due to strike until their second port of call, which was in two days, but he wasn't taking any chances.

Jimmy decided to schedule his last computer time for his lunch break that evening. It was then that he would send e-mails telling the others what had happened and how they would proceed. Al Qaeda would be pleased to hear that things were moving along as planned.

Jimmy quickly made his bed, changed into his blue and white crew uniform, and stuffed his dirty clothes into his laundry bag. There would be time tonight for any last-minute planning he needed to get done. He wanted to look around the ship one last time, while most of the ship's passengers were still sleeping. There were locations around the cruise ship that would provide adequate transport of the toxic smoke, but there were others that would better carry the payload to a large base of passengers. That was the end goal, after all, wasn't it—the widest dissemination of the payload, the highest level of fear and terror with the least amount of effort and risk? He double-checked to make absolutely certain that his backpack was set aside, ready to be packed with the few items he needed. He'd be taking that into town tomorrow. All his other belongings, clothes, toiletries, and a few minor personal items would be left behind. To everyone else, it would look like a normal excursion into town for one of the crew members. He smiled to himself despite the stress. *This is all going to be okay.* Walking to the door, Jimmy shut off the cabin light and locked the door behind him as he left the room.

The young woman was strikingly beautiful as she sat at the old wooden conference table in the center of the room. He had visualized an ugly woman with mussed hair and the remnants of two weeks' worth of dirt still on her face, but she was anything but that. She wore what he would consider to be the standard wardrobe of any young woman her age—

faded jeans and a T-shirt. White tennis shoes adorned her feet, and there were signs that she had been wearing makeup before she started crying.

Her dark black hair hung loose and fell across her shoulders, light reflecting off of it. The dark eyes set in the center of her face were red and bloodshot, tears still coming down in streams. She was tired and worried. Her olive skin held a pale hue that told the man she might not be particularly healthy right now. As he walked across the small room, the young girl never even looked up to see who had entered the room. He pulled out one of the wooden chairs across the table from her, set a bottle of orange juice in front of Layla, and put his coffee, laptop, a yellow pad of paper, and a voice recorder on the table in front of him. He switched on the recorder and tapped the small microphone at its top to ensure it was working. The red light blinked at him, indicating that it was picking up the tapping.

As he sat down in the hard chair, he began to talk. "Layla, my name is Neil. I work with Jeremy." Neil hesitated a moment and was met with silence. "Layla, I want to help you. I understand you feel like you're in over your head, but there is still time to fix this. You understand that, don't you? Here, I brought this juice for you. I thought you might need something." He pointed to bottle on the table and tried to smile as best he could. The stress emanating from this woman was intense, and he could tell she wasn't well.

Neil watched patiently as Layla wiped her eyes with a tissue and looked up at him. There was pain in those eyes. She had seen terrible things in her life and that pain was seeping out of her in unending streams. "Yes. I understand," she answered him. "I'm just having a difficult time understanding how I came to be in this situation. But yes, I want to help. I want to stop this before anyone else dies."

"Good," Neil replied. "I'm sure with your help we can stop this." Neil was angry about the plan, but he was trying very hard not to disrupt the investigation by scaring the young woman and causing her to stop talking. He had very strong opinions about a great many things, and to him, carrying out deadly plans against innocent people was the coward's way to fight. He had spent a lifetime working to help the American people, people he considered truly good people, for the most part. But he also understood a little something about human psychology. Children are susceptible to brainwashing. Their minds are so weak and impressionable that almost anything sticks with enough reinforcement. This young woman sitting across the table from him was proof of that.

"Look, Layla. I'm not going to sit here and pretend that I believe what you were doing was justified in some manner. We both know that's not the truth. My gut instinct is to be truly offended that you ever even planned to kill innocent people. But what I will say is that I believe, according to the information you gave Jeremy, there were circumstances in your youth that have led you down this path. And we did verify your story, just so you know." Neil watched her carefully as he spoke, measuring her body language. "But the fact remains that on your own, you came to the realization that what you learned as a child was an error in judgment. That, my girl, is your saving grace. That's why we're willing to work with you to make this right."

"How did you find out about my past?" Layla didn't look terribly upset. In fact, she looked as though she already knew the answer. But Neil decided to answer anyway.

"Jeremy shared your story with me." Honesty was the best policy after all, and they needed Layla's help. "We verified the story about your brother through news archives. You know that he has only your best interest in mind, right?"

"I believe that, yes," came the reply. "I guess I just wanted to hear it outright. Jeremy is a good man."

"Yes, he is. And he cares deeply about you. He's worked out a deal that will minimize your liability if you can give us enough information to stop the attack you mentioned and help catch the ones behind the plan."

"I was the one behind the plan," she began. "I arranged everything."

"Yes," Neil answered, "but you have had contact with Al Qaeda, correct?" Neil was busily booting up his laptop to take notes while Layla continued to speak.

"I believe it's Al Qaeda, yes. They have provided funding for the others who need it to maintain their positions. But I suppose, honestly, that I can't prove it's really Al Qaeda. All I have is an Internet address that I use to log in to a server on the Internet and communicate with them."

"Are you willing to share that information with us, Layla?" Neil didn't want to share this next piece of information with her, but he had to. It was his responsibility. "I need you to understand something very important, Layla. Are you listening?"

"Yes."

"Good," Neil sighed before he began speaking again. "I cannot guarantee that you will not be brought up on charges for your actions in this case. Nor can I say without a doubt that you won't go to prison. What you've started is an extremely serious crime. American citizens have been put to death for lesser crimes than killing hundreds of people. But what I can tell you is that, based on the information and help you provide the U.S. government, you will likely receive more leniency. If we can prevent the tragic death of innocent people, we can improve your standing in this matter. Do you understand what I'm saying, Layla?"

"You're saying that regardless of how much I help, I'll likely never be a free woman again." Layla took a deep breath and sat up straight. She wasn't doing this to get off the hook. She could just as easily have continued the project and never been caught. "But that's not why I'm doing this, Neil. If I wanted to be free, I would have just disappeared into the shadows and never said a word. No one would have ever suspected a thing." She took the bottle of juice in front of her and popped open the lid, taking a deep swig. Neil sat patiently while Layla replaced the lid on the bottle and then continued speaking. "At this point, I really just want to stop all the madness. The voices in my head grew quieter after I first spoke to Jeremy, so I truly believe this is the right thing to do. I'm interested in saving lives. There are a lot of things in my life that I now know are wrong. There are also plenty of things that I regret. I can't change the past, Neil, but I can help change the future."

"Okay, I can understand those sentiments. And believe me, Layla, we will do everything we can to help you for helping us." Neil sighed and closed his eyes momentarily, focusing his thoughts. "Try to understand that some people will hate you just because of what you've started. It doesn't matter that you're attempting to stop a moving train and putting your own neck on the line. And even though we'll try as best we can to keep your name from hitting the newswire, there are always leaks."

He shifted in his chair, feeling quite out of control at this moment. There were simply too many variables to this entire situation that made it nearly impossible to wrap his brain around it. He rubbed the spot right above his eye, a habit he hadn't revisited since his earlier days in investigation. Neil looked across at the table at the young woman in the chair across the table from him. She smiled at him pensively. But Neil couldn't decide whether he liked Layla or not. And he had to admit to himself that it really didn't matter whether he liked the girl. He had a job to do or people could lose their lives.

"Thank you," came her reply. "Will Jeremy be involved in this?"

"Jeremy will no longer be involved in this case because of your personal relationship. It's not that he doesn't want to help you as much as he can. He'll be doing research and supporting you in the background, but until this case is closed, he's got to keep his distance." Neil and Jeremy had already had this discussion. Jeremy was still young to the department and wanted very much to help his friend. But the simple fact was that he would not be allowed. The slim chance was always lurking there in the shadows that emotion might destroy logic, giving way to irrational behavior based solely on his feelings for a friend or lover. It would have been this way even if the personal relationship were between Neil and Layla.

But Jeremy had never argued the point, which made Neil proud of his still-young partner. Jeremy possessed a concrete understanding of what was prudent, even in a situation that was extremely personal to him. His only request to Neil had been that he be kept informed of the progress, which was the primary reason that Jeremy was being allowed to do background research on the case.

Neil's mind snapped back to the present. Realizing the young woman was watching him and waiting for him to continue, he began speaking. "Why don't you help me understand the technology you were using to coordinate the attack," Neil started again. "Jeremy tried to help me out by explaining what he knew at this point, but he's still very new to the covert channels arena. I have no doubt he'll be an expert in short order, but time is not a luxury we have right now."

"I understand," Layla replied. She sat up in her chair, determined to make this as clear as possible. And although the idea of spending the rest of her life behind prison bars didn't necessarily appeal to her, the idea of one more innocent child dying in a war she no longer had faith in was more than she could bear. "The broad area of technology is called covert channels. Basically, these channels of communication exist because people have found ways to use technology in ways that are outside the original design of the medium. For example, digital images are standardized under different image formats, like .GIF and .JPG."

"So they're all created the same way, just with different information to reflect the different image. Is that what you're talking about?" Neil asked.

"Yes, that's pretty much it. The original architects of these image formats didn't count on anyone coming along later and being able to hide information in those images without affecting the visual content in the images. Their goal was simply to create a method for storing and displaying photographic image information in a digital format that could easily be shared. They never built their image formats to be resistant to modification because that was never a design requirement. Who would have thought that someone would come along later and use an image file to hide information?" Layla struggled to come up with a suitable example, one that Neil would easily understand. "If I have a text file that I want to keep anyone else from looking at, I can now hide that information in a digital image. And if I ensure that the information is small enough, it won't affect the quality of the image and can't be detected with current technology. So few changes are made to the image that you'd never know the information was there. Does that make sense?"

"Are you saying that hiding a very small bit of information in another file will be impossible to detect?" Neil was perplexed. "If the information was created on a computer, it should leave some sort of signature, right?"

"There are definitely some forms of steganography that leave signatures, yes. But the more modern forms do not leave any detectable mention of their existence. And if the images are not distorted by having too much information crammed into them, you might never know that any information is hidden in there. Current technology on the detection side of the house is still very immature. I'd imagine with time we'll be more adept at detecting these discrete payloads within their carrier files. From what I understand, there are a couple of software tools today that help automate the detection of these types of steganography. They might be able to help by detecting images that fall reasonably outside the expected bounds of the image format."

Neil groaned out loud. This was growing more complex by the minute. "Are digital images the only target for steganography?"

"Well, actually, no." Layla reflected a moment before continuing. There were so many different paths to take with this conversation, but she wanted him to understand. He had to understand. "Okay, without getting into too many of the details, let's just say that most binary files can be used for steganography. That includes image files, audio files, and executable files on nearly every operating system available on computers."

"All right, I understand that. So that's steganography. What are some of the other forms of covert channels?"

"Remember how I said that covert channels use technology in ways they were never intended to be used?"

"Yes."

"Well, think about network protocols. Do you understand how computers on a network communicate?"

"Yes," came Neil's answer again. He had taken several networking courses over the past decade and was fairly comfortable with the general concepts of how it worked. "As long as it's not overly technical, I can follow a conversation on protocols. I have a fairly decent general understanding."

"So you know that each network transmission consists of a number of packets, each with various header information. At the end of those headers comes the actual data that's being transmitted across the wire."

"Yes, I do," Neil replied confidently.

Layla continued. "But where else could you hide information? There are other places within the transmission that give us ample opportunity to insert data."

"I guess you've lost me. I thought that the data segment was the only place you could insert data."

"That's exactly why covert channels work, Neil. People have grown so used to seeing things a certain way that they end up with virtual blinders on and can't see the other possibilities that exist." She watched as Neil's forehead furrowed again. "The designers of the network protocols never saw this as a problem either. The headers themselves can provide great mechanisms for hiding information, and no security products on the market today can reliably detect those forms of channels on the fly. And remember, each operating system has to be able to create or alter information in those headers if it wants to communicate on the network. They're basically inserting information into the headers. All we have to do is make them insert the information we want them to insert."

"Okay, so we're just changing the information that the operating system was going to insert into the header before placing the packet on the wire," Neil asked.

That's right. But again, this is only one other possible form of covert channel. There are literally hundreds that are being experimented with each day on the Internet. Another very popular form is the text channel."

"Okay, so we're changing gears here. What's a text channel?"

"Text channels come in a variety of forms and are very easy to create. Text manipulation is one of the most popular because it's so easy to use. There are even web-based tools for creating these types of channels. How often do you read the spam e-mails that gather in your inbox each day?"

Neil didn't really need time to answer. As with most things, he had strong feelings about spam e-mails. The constant flow of useless trash that emptied into his home e-mail account was a daily source of irritation. "I don't read them at all. I delete nearly every e-mail that comes from a name or agency I don't recognize. Of course, the spam filter catches much of it before I ever see it, but my home account gets inundated. Why do you ask?"

"If I wanted to hide a covert message in a channel that would basically be ignored, a spam e-mail would be the perfect fit," she answered. "Hardly anyone reads them. And on those rare occasions when someone actually does read one, they hardly ever make much sense. What better form of covert communication than one that everyone on the Internet has already been trained to ignore? Pavlov's law applies to human behavior quite well. We are, by nature of our own intellect, conditioned to destroy or ignore those minor annoyances in our lives."

"I suppose you're right about that," he replied. "I don't even waste time thinking about them anymore. They just automatically get deleted without a second thought." Neil hated to admit it to himself, but this young lady had a sharp mind and made some very valid points. *Good God*, he thought suddenly. *I wonder how many of those e-mail messages that look like spam are actual messages?* The thought of the sheer potential was overwhelming. Curious about how prevalent this form of channel was, he asked, "So these types of channels are already out there?"

"There are logic engines already built and operational that will create a custom spam e-mail, play script, or basic spreadsheet file based on a message you type. In fact," she continued, "there are books already on the shelves that provide the code to these types of logic engines. And if you're not that technical, you can simply visit a web site that has already posted an application for public use."

Neil's face was starting to turn red again. Layla knew he was contemplating the potential impact. She continued before he had the opportunity to begin speaking. "Think about it, Neil. You can send that message to as many people as you like, millions even. The key is that there are certain target people in the world who would be looking for that message. They would know it was coming. Everyone else is likely going to delete it before even looking at it. Weak forms of encryption, called null ciphers, also use text manipulation."

Neil's mind was trying to wrap itself around the incredible diversity of potential channels that could be created and used to communicate. There were already more in existence than he would have wagered and this conversation could easily continue for hours, but he needed to get to the point quickly. Innocent lives could very well depend on how long it took to get this information, and he found himself side-tracked by the conversation. "Okay, so instead of getting caught up in all the details, why don't we talk about what you have been up to until this point? We can go into more detail later, if we have time."

She nodded in response and started at the beginning. "Well, as I told Jeremy before, after my brother died, my father decided to use his only other child as a weapon against the people he felt were responsible, the Americans. He started spending a great deal of time with a local group of extreme Muslims. My father had always been a religious man, but he had never been extreme up to that point, not that I can remember, anyway."

"Okay, I'm with you. Go on."

"When my father started attending this particular mosque, all my time at home was spent doing chores, learning the intricacies of the Islamic religion, or studying computers. He was training me to be his tool, his ultimate revenge. I accepted the lessons my father was teaching me as if they were the complete truth. Now I understand that the elders in the group had misinterpreted the words of the prophet Mohammed. Allah does not condone violence unless it's provoked and justified." Layla paused and took another drink from her bottle. She looked at Neil to ensure she was giving him the information he needed. She found that he was typing information into his laptop. Assuming she was on the right track, she continued.

"Several years ago I applied to a college in Toronto, where I could continue my studies and work on the plan I had devised, based on my father's guidance. When I started, I had only my father's interests in mind. But over time I realized that my father's ideals were not necessarily my own, and I started questioning them, you know? I didn't own those thoughts; they were my father's, and he died shortly after I arrived at college."

"I understand," Neil replied. "It's a maturing process. Children often pull away from their parents and their upbringing in an effort to better understand what it is that they need from life. Please, continue. I'm listening, just taking notes at the same time."

"Anyway, I was the ever-faithful daughter, following my father's voice blindly even though my mind started fighting back. But once I got to college I was caught in a conundrum. I couldn't do the work myself, but how would I find others whom I could trust? It's not like I could just start walking up to kids at school who looked as if they were of Middle Eastern descent and start a conversation about how to strike out at America. To make matters worse, I was functionally handicapped in Arab society. I literally had very little room to move around, intellectually."

Neil looked up from his laptop after hearing this. "What do you mean, handicapped?"

"The Middle East, for the most part, is still very sexist. Women don't have a place in the governing of their country and tend to have significantly fewer rights than men. Women raise children, keep the house, and cook meals. But that was my father's plan from the start. If I could somehow use my knowledge of computers and the Internet to gather a following of men who were willing to follow my plan, I'd somehow be beyond detection. After all, who would ever expect a woman to be capable of not only masterminding a plan like this but also making it successful?"

He sat and watched as Layla finished. She was smirking, but it was obviously not a smirk of humor. She was offended, and the tone of her voice was slightly vicious. Neil smiled politely and nodded for her to continue her story.

"To make a long story short," she continued, "my best bet was to work fully online, where no one could see me or hear my voice. The original plan was to attack Western interests directly from the Internet. Power plants, hospitals, financial institutions, and more; they're all vulnerable. Dozens of proprietary systems litter national governments all around the globe. Up until a few years ago, most people never really considered the security implications of having a power plant near a major airport or connected to the Internet. And for the most part, the evolution to a more secure operating environment is moving slowly and can be painful to adjust to."

Neil finished typing in his last note, stood to stretch his legs, and stared at Layla, a question hanging there in his eyes. "So, Layla, you're telling me that your original idea was to attack American infrastructure?"

"That was never really my plan," she responded. "It's just a possibility that I had initially considered, mostly owing to the simple fact that many of the Arabic men on the Internet who hate America think along those lines. Every battle is a face-to-face confrontation with them, even if it's online. But I wanted the attacks to be subtle and unseen. Only the planning would occur online. The attacks would still be personal."

Neil grimaced, noticeably annoyed by the casual manner in which Layla was discussing her plans to attack his homeland. But somewhere inside he had to admit that he understood why she had done all this, even if he didn't agree with it. He took a deep breath and motioned for her to go on with her story.

"So my problem was that of maintaining my anonymity during all of the planning and coordination activities that would need to occur. I was to be only the leader, protected by the shadows on the Internet. A commander doesn't normally fight the battles on his own. If he died, no one would be left to lead the army that supports him, and the war would be lost to the enemy. And quite honestly, I didn't know enough Muslim men with the technical ability to carry out attacks like that. And if I were going to train them, it would need to be online, where they could never see my face. But it certainly would have helped if I had been able to work with them in person."

"But you being a woman would really have caused issues with that?" Neil asked.

"Correct. But the West should look for scattered attacks directly on American networks in the next couple of years, with extended information assaults not long after. After all, the common opinion is that most folks in the Middle East aren't capable of this type of activity. We've lagged behind in technical ability because our economies don't support the level of integration that you see in the West. Now would have been the perfect time for that type of assault, from strictly a war planning perspective. If you want to be successful at an attack, you should appear incapable of such an attack."

Neil took a sip of his coffee and set the cup back down. "Why is now such a good time? You lost me."

Layla smiled, genuinely this time. "No offense, Neil, but Americans tend to be extremely arrogant. They feel invincible, like nothing can really reach out and touch them. If you combine that with a general feeling that your enemy has no real capabilities, it creates the perfect situation for an attack. Sun Tzu once said in his book, *The Art of War*, 'Hence, when able to attack, we must seem unable; when using our force, we must seem inactive; when we are near, we must make the enemy believe we are far away; when far away, we must make him believe we are near.'"

She watched Neil's eyes as they flitted across the computer screen in front of him, his fingers flying across the keys. He was taking detailed notes of their conversation. She waited until he was finished typing and had looked at up her before she continued.

"Because Americans don't feel threatened, terrorists are more capable of causing damage." Layla looked into Neil's eyes, but wasn't sure if he totally understood what she had just said. "Look, you feel like you don't have much to fear. Sure, you know there is someone out there who would just as soon shoot you in the face as serve you tea, but it's a very vague and distant connection, right?"

"I suppose that's true," Neil answered partially to himself. "I guess it's because we don't have a particular person to point at and say, 'that's my enemy.'"

"Okay, good point. What you've done is create the perfect circumstance for an attack. You've done all the mental work for the attacker before the thought to attack ever entered his mind. In the American mind, the attacker is way off in some foreign land with no measurable means for crossing the oceans, making himself a home here, and carrying out an attack. That would take intelligence and financial resources that most of the West doesn't believe exists in the Middle East," Layla smiled subtly. "For the most part, that's true. Much of the Middle East has neither the resources nor the desire to come to America. But there are a few with enough money to share and the charisma to light a fire under the belly of even the laziest man. The enemy is not so far away as you might think, Neil. They're not going to bang on your gates and tell you they're out there. They've been allowed in, with you permission. They've taken up residence. They are one of you. They're your friends, your neighbors.

That's the very reason that the events on September 11, 2001 were so successful, the perceived American invincibility."

"That's a pretty scary picture you paint, Layla." Neil reached nervously for his cup of coffee, his hands shaking. He had been in this line of work for many years and thought he knew a lot about the job. But when it came down to it, he was just as naïve as the rest of the country. But he was becoming more and more agitated by her rhetoric. It bothered him much more that she might actually be correct. "Can you please tell me how you planned and laid out this attack? I need as much information as you can give me so we can stop these attacks before anyone gets hurt."

Layla nodded her head. "Since I wasn't really in a position to perform direct attacks against actual network systems, I decided to engage in the traditional terrorist activity where people are normally blown up, lots of other people freak out, and the world finally pays attention to our plight. I was clinging desperately to the beliefs that had been instilled in me as a child, even as I found myself questioning them. We, the Arab people, were victims of the West's aggression and it was time to stand up for ourselves. The world had long since proven that no one else would. I wanted to use the Internet even though I wasn't using it as a source for our attacks because it would demonstrate to the world that America did not have superiority in cyberspace as many might believe. So I decided to do all of my coordination and planning via the Internet."

"Why were you so interested in using the Internet? Would it have been easier and safer to avoid anything that could be traced back to you?"

"The Americans believe they created the Internet. It makes them feel like God. It's their baby. Using their beautiful, darling creation against them and right under their noses would be a spectacular show of stealth on our part and a significant sign of weakness on yours. And what safer method for communicating could there possibly be? There are hundreds of millions of people on the Internet, all pretending to be someone they're not. It would be very difficult to find a single person among all those others."

Layla took a few moments and adjusted in her chair. She was growing less and less comfortable as the clock on the wall ticked on. "Anyway, the best way for us to communicate in the open and without anyone knowing that we were even communicating was via covert channels. So after some in-depth research into the topic, I gathered a team together, with the help of a friend, and we developed a system of sending messages back and forth."

This was the first that Neil had heard of a friend being involved, and he was understandably concerned. "Who is this friend? What was her involvement?"

"I believe him to be a man, not a her. He goes by the name Jimmy, at least online. I don't honestly believe that any of the team members use their real names when they communicate. And each of them has been asked to use public Internet terminals. But Jimmy was the first person whom I met online who agrees with me. He has suffered similar losses in his family to the West and wanted to taste vengeance. We trusted each other, and he helped me gather the rest of the team. Jimmy is very motivated to make this happen. He carries a lot of hatred for the Western world within his heart."

Neil took another deep breath. Here he was, confronted by someone who had once hated him without knowing him. She was someone who had consorted with others who hated America. The threat suddenly seemed so much more real now. A quick glance up at the clock brought him back to his senses, and he fought to refocus his questions. "You mentioned a team, Layla," Neil replied. "How many people are we dealing with here?"

"There were 27, last I heard," she answered back. "But I stopped communicating with everyone a couple weeks ago. I would assume that I've lost my access to the system and that Jimmy has taken over at this point."

"Twenty-seven," Neil exclaimed, shocked by the high number. "You managed to gather 27 men around you, on the Internet, who were willing to participate in a plan like this?"

"Yes," Layla responded. "I might have been able to find more, but I was paranoid and preferred to keep the number small."

"So how were you communicating with the team?"

"We started out on an Internet Relay Chat channel on EFNET. Then I moved on to e-mail. Gradually, we moved into more technical arenas. Soon, I started to maintain a web site that I used to pass messages to the team. It's one of those free web sites given out by companies that want your business or the sponsorship money from placing banner ads. The page is designed to look like a normal American family's home page, used to post vacation pictures from around the world. It's innocuous and innocent looking. Anyway, that's where I post the messages."

"Do you just post them in the open, in a message forum?" he asked.

"No, the messages are hidden within images using steganography, similar to what we just discussed. The only exception is the scheme used. Jimmy and I created a much more complex scenario so that it would be more difficult to accidentally stumble across the information. There are 10 images on each new web site I put up. The images have to be opened in the correct order and with the right key. You can't get the message out otherwise."

Neil looked up from his laptop, obviously confused by what he was hearing. "I thought you said there was just one payload per image file. Why would you have 10 images on the web site? Are there 10 different messages posted at any one time?"

"No, actually, the data in the images is protected by a password," Layla answered. "Nine of the images use the same password. When the information from the other nine images is put together in the correct fashion, it will give you the password to open the tenth image containing the actual message for the team."

Layla sat up in her chair again. Her back was starting to bother her in the wooden chair. She opened the bottle one last time and emptied its contents and placed it back on the table. "Anyway, there are actually two phases of the attack. You should know about both. If the first one fails, they'll still pursue the second phase."

The hair on the back of Neil's neck stood on end. Two attacks! "Layla, can you please tell me about those?"

"The first phase was never intended to cause mass casualties. The primary goal was simply to scare the hell out of the Americans. I thought that if I could make you all feel insecure, the second phase would hurt more."

"What is the first phase, Layla?"

"They're going to attack three cruise ships, simultaneously. Not with explosives, just toxic gases. Blowing a hole in a ship would be too difficult for a single person, whereas compromising the ventilation system would be much easier, assuming that person worked on the ship." Layla watched as Neil squirmed with discomfort. She, too, was feeling the sting of hundreds of innocent lives hanging out there in the balance. There was something else he needed to know. This was not going to end after the first phase, and she didn't have the information for the second phase because she had walked away from the planning. "Neil, I don't have any idea what the second phase of the attacks will be. We were going to work on that after the first phase was complete."

Neil stood up from his chair. He, too, was having difficulty staying seated. It was also becoming increasingly difficult for him to be nice to a person who obviously had planned a great deal to harm American citizens, even if she did come to them before the attacks. He took a deep breath and tried to clear his mind and release some of the stress that was quickly building inside his spine. They needed her if they were going to stop these attacks. She also could provide information that might help take a bite out of Al Qaeda. Whether she was brainwashed or not, the activities she had participated in were cause for permanent imprisonment, if not worse. But she did come to them. She didn't want these people to die anymore than he did. She was correct in stating that she easily could just have disappeared into the shadows and never looked back. Neil took another deep breath as Layla watched quietly, under-standing the sudden flush of his face.

"Layla, please continue. You'll have to understand this is very difficult for me, but we need the information you have if we're going to save lives." Layla nodded, tears starting to well up in her eyes. Neil arranged his chair once more and sat down at his laptop in a weak attempt to appear less confrontational.

"The first phase will be carried out by three men. Each one of them has been employed by his respective cruise ship for almost a year at this point. They will likely be trusted members of the crew by this time. They'll have friends that believe in them, and they'll have excellent work histories with the organization. Their job was to create a liquid solution, a soft chemical bomb if you will, that creates a toxic cloud of gas and spreads throughout the ventilation system of the ship. We knew that there would be casualties, but mostly just passengers getting very ill and very scared. The goal is mass American panic."

Neil looked directly at Layla. He needed to know if she was lying. "Layla, when are the attacks in the first phase supposed to take place? It's very important that we know what we're dealing with."

"In two days."

Neil's eyes closed. This is bad, he thought to himself. I have two days to stop attacks on three different cruise liners. How the hell are we going to do that? "What cruise lines are we talking about here, Layla?"

"Tropical Cruise Lines, Caribbean Dreams, and Glacier Bay Cruises. We chose three completely separate organizations to limit our exposure." She wiped at her eyes once more.

"Do you know what names they're employed under, Layla?"

"No. They all use pseudonyms online. I'll certainly give you the names they use online, but I don't know any of their real names or even what they're using while working on the ships. As I said before, they could be male or female as well. There's just no telling." Layla was begin-ning to get frustrated with herself. She had intentionally built a tremendous amount of anonymity into the plan in order to protect the individuals on the team, but now she was facing the possibility of people dying, people like her brother who were not involved in the war. Their blood would be on her hands, and she wondered to herself if she could live with that. "I do know that all three ships are out on cruises at the same time, just in different parts of the world. But I don't even know what they're going to end up using to create the toxic gas. I did some research and sent various options to them, but what they end up using is completely up to them."

Neil reached into his shirt pocket and pulled out a silver pen and laid it on top of the yellow notepad, still sitting on the desk next to his laptop. Pushing the notepad across the table to Layla, he asked, "Would you please write down the names these individuals use online, as well as any other pertinent details you can remember about the information you gave them regarding the creation of these gas weapons?"

Layla reached for the notepad and took the pen from on top and began writing. Neil watched intently as she scrawled the information he had asked for on the top piece of paper. When she was done she replaced the pen and pushed the notepad across the table toward Neil again.

"What are the names of the ships these individuals work on?" he asked as he pulled the pad of paper back toward himself. Neil knew that if they could warn the cruise line companies and get information to all the ships, they might still have a chance to stop this. But there were so many ships.

"I don't know, Neil. I really don't. I never cared as long as they did what they said they would." Layla began to weep softly again and dabbed at her eyes with the tissue that was in her lap.

Neil sat back in his chair and thought for moment. *I wonder how many ships each cruise line has out on the water at any one point?* Suddenly, his mind grasped the only hope they had left. He stood up and shut the cover of his laptop. Walking over to the door, he opened it and motioned for the guard outside. "Please take her back to her cell. I need her local. I need to go make some calls. Please give her what she needs to be comfortable, within reason." The guard accepted his orders and stepped into the room as Neil started to leave. He was a burly man with a military haircut wearing a standard American military battle dress uniform. The patch sewn into the left breast stated plainly, U.S. Marines. The black side arm was clearly visible at his side.

Just when he stepped outside the boundary of the door, Neil turned back to Layla. "Layla, Thank you for your help. I just hope it's not too late to save these people's lives. I'll be sending someone along shortly to gather the exact technical details about how you've been communicating and how to retrieve the information from the web site you were using."

Without waiting for her response, he turned and walked down the hall out of her sight. The guard took her by the arms and helped her up. Reaching behind his back, he pulled the silver metal handcuffs from their pouch and brought them to her wrists. Layla never resisted, giving in fully to the experience. Once she was handcuffed, she was led by the guard, back to her cell to wait.

How did I end up in this situation? she thought. This wasn't the first time in the last six months that she had questioned her reason for living. The two sides of her brain, split since her childhood, were still at war inside her head, although the light of clear logic and understanding was rapidly overwhelming the dark shadows of her childhood. The voice of reason was fighting constantly, pushing back against the voice of her father's ghost. Her brother was an innocent young man when he died. The small baby she had seen was an innocent. The baby's mother, another hapless victim, lay nearby, murdered in a meaningless war. There were many other innocents in this war. *What are we fighting for?* she wondered. She would not allow more people to die in a war over which beliefs were right or wrong. Killing is wrong, unless it's justified. That's what the Holy Book was trying to say all along. She would give these men all the information they needed. No one else would die by her hand.

The lights went off in her cell, and she lay back on the small bed, the rough sheets rustling against her. She absently wondered to herself whether Jeremy would ever be able to forgive her. Was there a chance that he truly understood her conflict? Would she ever be a free woman to walk to the streets of the world again? She closed her eyes and fell into a deep sleep. Her father's voice would not be heard tonight. Layla had successfully exorcised his ghost and moved past her painful childhood to become a woman.

Chapter 14: Racing the Clock

October 13, 2004

Jeremy watched silently from a chair across the desk as his partner continued his conversation with the last cruise line company. They had been calling each and every company over the last 90 minutes. He had been surprised to find so many cruise line companies operating in the United States, many of which he had never heard of before. Some went up North to the colder climates to show passengers the whales and icebergs. Others were content with endlessly cruising the tropical climates down South. There were even some companies that took extended cruises to Europe or the Mediterranean. Most of the calls Jeremy had finished a few minutes ago were to companies that Layla had not mentioned. It was a matter of making sure all their bases were covered. If Layla had made a mistake or had been given wrong information about which cruise line it was, he wanted to be prepared. Now he was just waiting to hear what Neil had found out. As he waited, he stared down at the photocopy of the piece of paper that Layla had written on just a couple of hours ago, his shock still resounding through his body. *Layla?*

"Yes, that's correct, sir. I'm sure you can understand the gravity of the situation. The sooner you can get me a schedule of ships that are currently out and when you expect them to be in port, the better chance we have to stop this nightmare." Neil paused, listened to the voice on the other end of the phone. "No, I'm sorry. I've given you all the information I have at the moment. Can you get me a crew roster as well? No, I need that ASAP. We have a list of possible names that we'd like to compare the roster against. Someone is going to die in the next few days if we don't do something, and I'd hate to think it was because I couldn't get you to cooperate with us on this. Great, I'll wait for your call back in a few minutes. Thanks again."

Neil hung up the phone a little harder than he had intended, not totally satisfied with what he had heard. The cruise lines were taking their time getting him the information he needed. He wasn't sure they really understood the enormity of what they were facing. *Even after 9-11 people don't totally get it,* he commented internally. There wasn't really much choice in the matter for the cruise line companies, though. They *had* to cooperate; people's lives were in danger, and the federal government was involved.

Neil's supervisors had passed the information up the channels, and the National Threat Alert level had been raised, but very few details were being given to the public. It was standard procedure to keep those details from leaking out. The government had it all under control, but wanted people to be on the look out for suspicious activity. Giving out too much information would only cause unnecessary panic.

The department in general was responsible for following the investigation, but a couple of other federal agencies had been made aware of the situation and were providing backup support. The Coast Guard had the quickest access to the cruise ships in the water and had been informed of the full situation. The National Security Agency had been alerted so that it could watch for potentially relevant intelligence data. The cogs and wheels of the federal government had been set in motion and were grinding away efficiently while the public at large sat at home and work, intently watching news on the war in Iraq and the U.S. presidential elections between President George W. Bush and Senator John Kerry. Most would pay little attention to the increase in Alert Level.

Layla had been cooperating completely, and Neil was satisfied that she wasn't attempting to hide anything. At least her body language wasn't giving her away like it might for normal people. She currently was talking to a computer forensic specialist in the department. They had spent the last couple of hours discussing the details of the web site she had created, including the password used to hide the information in the images. The amount of information hidden in the images was very small and had left little to no distortion in the files. Without Layla's help, the technical team would have had little luck in determining which image had the target message and in pulling it out effectively.

With all the possible cruise lines companies busily trying to gather the requisite information, Neil could now focus on another matter—clarifying Jeremy's actual relationship with the young woman. Even if Jeremy was completely unaware of the situation, he had a personal connection with her. Their superiors wanted every detail of that relationship reported back to them, and Neil was in the uncomfortable position of being the young man's supervisor.

"I don't get it, Jeremy. Explain to me again how you and Layla met. With everything that's gone on over the past 24 hours, I'm getting my details confused." Neil tried to smile wryly but came off looking slightly embarrassed instead.

Jeremy knew this was likely to come back around, but was still slightly irritated by the question. "I've already told you. We were in school together. She is a lot of the reason I managed to keep my grades up during the last couple of terms. She used to help me with my schoolwork. If she hadn't helped me out by studying with me, I might have lost this job when my grades dropped." He was embarrassed enough to have needed help in his studies, but having to repeat it was an awful exercise for Jeremy.

Neil smiled again, more naturally this time. He understood how difficult this was on his young friend. The truth was that he trusted his friend completely, but the questions still had to be asked. "And you never saw any of this coming? I mean a person doesn't just spontaneously become a terrorist. She never mentioned anything to you that would have given you a clue? Did she do anything that seems odd, now that you look back on it?"

Jeremy sat back in the chair across the desk from Neil and sighed again. "No, Neil. It was a total surprise. In fact, when she first told me I was certain she was just jerking my chain. There's no way I would have ever pegged her for a dangerous person. I've spent hundreds of hours talking to her. She's a friend. But when you look back at all the stuff she's been through, you can almost understand how she ended up like she did."

Neil knew it was the truth. *When the hell are those cruise ship companies going to call me back?* This line of questioning was beginning to irritate Neil as much as it was bothering Jeremy. "There is never an excuse for murdering innocent people, Jeremy. But I understand that you never saw this coming either." Neil was growing tired and losing his tenuous grasp on his stressed emotions. It bothered him even more to know that he was letting his emotions get in the way. *Whatever happened to just doing my job as best I can?* he thought to himself. "I'm sorry, guy. That was uncalled for. I'm still not totally sure how to address this entire thing. But I am glad that you decided to distance yourself from all this. In reality, I have a difficult time seeing her as a threat either. She's giving us every bit of information we ask for, and more. And she's broken down into tearful fits more than once. That's not really the attitude of someone who enjoys the fact that someone they hate, their enemy, is going to be killed. But regardless, thanks for not putting me on the spot by asking to get more involved. Your work in the background with the research is a tremendous help."

"There's no way I could get involved any more than I already was. I'm fairly certain there's some kind of conflict of interest there." Jeremy tried to smile and break the gloom, but it wasn't working. Neil was too strung up over this ordeal. He was as well, but he refused to believe that Layla was deceiving them. The idea wounded him deeply for some reason, and he chose to believe she was genuine in her intent to put a stop to all of this. "Look Neil, we'll get it. The cruise lines know this is for real. It's serious, and I'm sure they'll react appropriately. We really don't have any reason to believe they're going to ignore us. And Layla had been helping as much as she can. We've kept her pretty busy talking to analyst after analyst and she hasn't complained one time. I'm not even sure she's slept since we brought her here." Neil was rubbing his forehead, right above his right eye, with his hands. Jeremy could tell he had a headache and was having difficulty relaxing from the tremendous stress. "I know it probably doesn't make you feel any better, Neil, but she did come to us. We have the opportunity to stop this. Whatever her reasons for starting down this path, logic prevailed and won out in the end." He adjusted in his chair and ran his fingers through his hair. It had become a nervous habit during his last few semesters at college, and it manifested itself every time the young man was disturbed or stressed.

"Oh, I know," Neil replied. "I just wish we had found out sooner. If she's telling us the truth, we're cutting it very close. I want those jerks caught, and I want them caught in the next 24 hours. Layla said the attacks were supposed to occur in two days. If that's true, I wouldn't expect the terrorists to strike until all the passengers were back on the cruise ship. Terrorizing people would require that there were people near by. We'll likely want to search the ship completely while it's at port."

At that moment, the black office phone on Neil's desk gave a shrill ring, and the red lights on its face began to blink, causing the already nervous Neil to jump slightly in his seat. *Geeezus*, he said to himself as he calmed his nerves. He shot Jeremy a self-conscious smile as the phone rang again, the young man laughing silently at him as he put the receiver to his ear. "This is Neil. Yes. Uh-huh. Okay, that's great. What were their names again? And you're docking when? Great! I'll go check the fax machine and give you a call if I don't receive them."

The idea that cruise ships could make phone calls was amazing to Jeremy. I suppose the technology has been around for years, I just never really thought about it much, he thought. He sat back and watched silently as Neil continued his conversation with the invisible persona on the other end of the line. "No, I don't want you to do anything differently than you normally would, at least from a noticeable security perspective. We're not sure who the involved parties are at this point, and we don't want to alarm the passengers if this all turns out to be a false alarm. No, they're not supposed to act for two more days. Yes I understand. It might help if you let some of your more trusted, senior crew members know what's going on and make some preparations in case this whole thing happens sooner than we expect.

Neil pulled out a desk atlas from his desk door as he listened intently to the voice on the other end. "My recommendation is to monitor the primary points of recirculation into the ship's ventilation system. I know that's not a lot of help, but we need you to dock as soon as you can. Okay. All right, I'll have the Coast Guard trail you in from this point, but they're going to try to stay out of sight. You're getting close enough to U.S. coastal waters that it won't be anything too obvious. Yes, I'll have our agents waiting at the port to meet your crew. Thank you again. I'll keep in touch and let you know if I hear anything else."

Neil put the receiver back in its cradle, more gently than the last time. He was still rubbing his forehead as he scribbled some brief notes on a pad of paper in front of him. "Well, I feel a little better now. At least they have some advance notice and may be able to prevent these attacks."

"So, what's up?" Jeremy asked his partner and friend inquisitively. "I could hear only one side of the conversation."

"Well," Neil started, "They do have some on-board security folks who can help out, and apparently they've been augmented somewhat since the September 11 attacks on the World Trade Center and Pentagon, but they're saying that there's no way that so few people can actually watch an entire ship. There is a security system of cameras installed on the ship, but they admit that some of those cameras are down and there are holes in their coverage around the ship. Some important areas that could be used as attack points aren't covered yet by surveillance equipment. They're planning on using their available trusted crew members to watch those areas to offset their security weakness."

"Wow," Jeremy answered back. "I didn't even know they had security cameras. So how many ships are actually out right now?"

"Two of the companies that Layla mentioned have three ships out right now in various places around the world," Neil began intently. "This last company has only one ship out currently, and it's now scheduled to dock at port in the next 36 hours. We've managed to work it out so that the ship can dock at an unscheduled port in the next 24 to36 hours and make it look like a bonus stop to the passengers."

Jeremy ran his fingers through his hair again, self-consciously pulling his hand away from his head when he realized what he was doing. The truth of the matter was that Neil was right; they were cutting this extremely close. He realized, just then, that he was sitting straight up in his chair so he sat back and relaxed against the back of the chair. "All right, so what are we going to do from here?"

"Most of the security measures put in place on the cruise lines keep the perimeter of the ship safe from attack. For instance, they've implemented a no-float safe zone around the ship that averages about 100 yards out from the ship. There are a few instances where the cruise lines have automated tracking of both passengers and crew members. So when the ship comes into port, they know who is still on the ship and who is not. But one of the companies admitted that this system doesn't always work correctly owing to breakdowns in the system. So it's not always going to be possible for the ship's crew to have accurate information."

Jeremy was watching Neil's face for signs of stress, but it looked as if the man was starting to come to terms with their situation. "What about folks on the Federal watch list? Are we going to be able to find out if these folks are on board based on that list?"

"Well, there's the trick with this whole plan that Layla put together. She's managed to create a scenario where the watch lists, for the most part, won't apply. The various cruise lines apparently have implemented a check system where each passenger and crew member is checked against the Federal watch list and the INS records to ensure that no unsavory types get aboard the vessel or have the ability to easily flee the country. But the individuals who signed on for this terrorist project have no prior record. They're most likely not on any Federal watch lists simply because there's no reason. There is the chance that a mix-up in identities, such as individuals having similar names, could cause them to be stopped, but for the most part, the watch list is an imperfect Band-Aid."

"Who's getting all the technical details from Layla? We know how she was communicating with everyone else, right? We just don't know all those little bits of information we'll need for evidence. If her group really was using covert channels to communicate, those channels likely were protected with passwords of some sort."

"Neil sat back in his chair and considered Jeremy's words. If the targets on the cruise ships somehow caught wind of the fact they were being watched, they easily could abandon the plan. Without sufficient evidence, every single one of them could walk off totally free. "Why don't you work on figuring out how the channels were set up. You're right about needing evidence. If we can't prove beyond a shadow of a doubt that the suspects were involved in those plans, we'll get eaten alive by the lawyers." Neil was becoming anxious for a different reason now. He could see this becoming a public relations nightmare if it wasn't handled correctly and according to the books. "Look, I need to make some calls. I'll come over to your desk in a bit and let you know which direction we're going to head on this one."

"Sounds good." With that, Jeremy gathered up his laptop and walked toward the door. "It's going to be okay, Neil. This is all going to work out."

"I hope you're right."

Jimmy was nervous. His roommate had come back from his shift early talking about how there was rumor of a terrorist attack on some cruise ships. "Sounds crazy to me," he had told Jimmy. "But they've completely cut off access to the bridge and engine room to everyone but those folks who work there." That would certainly complicate matters. But the truth of the matter was that no one had done anything yet. It also told Jimmy that somehow Salah had been caught and given up at least some of the information about the attacks.

Cursing silently to himself, Jimmy sat on the floor of his cabin, putting a change of clothes into his backpack. The small black backpack wouldn't carry a lot, but he only wanted a single change of clothes when he left the ship. He shoved most of his cash into the pocket of his uniform and left the rest in his footlocker. It would look too suspicious if anyone decided to nose around and found that his clothes and money were completely gone.

His roommate had left shortly after passing the news on to Jimmy. He was just 22 and still heavily into the party scene on the ship, but he had adopted Jimmy as his friend. Young men his age were notorious for talking too much, and in this case, it may have saved Jimmy's life. He pulled a small compass from his pack and watched as the dial on its face turned toward the north. Facing toward Mecca, Jimmy bowed and prayed silently on the floor of the cabin. He wasn't usually a religious man, but the recent news from his roommate had him sweating bullets. It couldn't hurt to have a little divine intervention if he was still going to pull this off.

After a few minutes of praying, Jimmy stood and brushed the wrinkles out of his uniform with his hand. His shift would be starting in just a few more minutes, and he knew he had to attend the shift briefing with his supervisor before he could begin work. He grabbed his backpack and walked toward the door, turning out the light as he left the room. Good bye, he reflected as he walked down the crew hallway for the last time.

"Hello, Jimmy; come on in." The manager's voice was warm and friendly as he spoke to the young man from staff tables. "Not everyone is here yet, so we're still waiting. How are you doing today?"

"Not bad. I went to bed early, so I'm all rested up and ready to go." Jimmy smiled and walked over to the chair next to his roommate and sat down.

"That's good to hear," his manager replied. "Well, I'm going to grab some coffee before we get started. Be right back." With that, the man got up from his chair and walked over to the coffee pot that was strategically placed on a table near the far wall.

The manager was a plump man in his 40s named Brian. His uniform was clean and pressed, and his blonde hair was combed straight back from the forehead. Jimmy remembered the first time he had ever met the manager, many months back when he was hired. The man had been friendly and had encouraged Jimmy to get involved in the crew activities in order to make friends. He was a funny man who was constantly cracking little jokes here and there, trying to keep employee morale high. Jimmy resisted the urge to smile, chastising himself for letting any emotions play into this project. For all he knew, the manager could be one of the victims of his plan. But it had to be done, regardless. Allah would have it no other way, and neither would Jimmy.

He steadied himself mentally and looked around the room. His friends around the table all smiled apprehensively, obviously aware of the rumor. Voices chattered, and Jimmy could pick up bits and pieces of the various conversations. Only a few were talking about the rumors; the rest either had not heard yet or chose to simply ignore the rumors as meaningless gossip. After all, when you work so closely with so many young people, there is a constant stream of rumors and gossip that fills the hallways.

The clock on the wall in the staff break room showed 10 minutes remaining before the meeting was supposed to begin. His roommate leaned over toward Jimmy and whispered in his ear. "Hey man, Kenny says those rumors are worthless." He laughed quietly and continued on. "I don't really believe it either, but it should be interesting over the next few days to see how this all plays out. Heck, I bet they don't even mention the rumors."

Jimmy smiled back at his friend, feeling relieved. "I hope you're right, buddy." Jimmy laughed nervously. He knew this entire situation had just grown much more complex, but he hoped that everyone else at this table would ignore the conversations as well. "I think it's just a hoax. Someone probably got really bored and started this rumor to watch the waves." He laughed again and was joined by his friend and another young man who had been listening in on their conversation.

"I heard that same thing," the third boy laughed. "Oh well, as long as I still get a port pass, I'm good to go. I don't see how anyone could get past all of us, anyway. I've been hoping to visit the local market at the next port. Christmas is coming up quick and if I can pick up some presents for quite a bit less money, that would be great."

Jimmy's roommate laughed and agreed. Jimmy sat and watched everyone else at the table intently, smiling occasionally and saying hello to his friends. There was really no big feeling of nervousness or fear in the room, instead the initial excitement was beginning to die down, and the conversations were switching to topics that centered on weekend plans and visits to the next port. He sat back in his chair and watched as the shift manager opened his notebook.

"Good evening, everyone," began the manager. "Let's go ahead and get started so we can get to work." He waited as the others around the table slowly finished their conversations and sat up in their chairs, ready to begin the meeting. "Okay, so there aren't a lot of new items for tonight's shift. The Captain mentioned to the managers that there was some concern about the ventilation system. He didn't give us any specifics at all. We were just told to ensure the vents were clean and properly positioned. It was probably just a passenger who complained about dust collecting on the vent over their table in the dining area. So let's just play it safe and check the vent screens in all the common areas and keep an eye out for any of the vents that look like they might need some extra attention."

Jimmy's blood ran cold. Coincidence? What were the chances that they would want the vents doubled-checked if they didn't already know? It could be just a bizarre coincidence, but it sounded suspicious to Jimmy. But he had the opportunity to work this in his favor. He was on the night crew after all. The manager didn't suspect Jimmy, or he would have never asked Jimmy to check the vents. He took a deep breath and tried to relax. Everything was going to be fine. It had to be.

The manager took a sip of water and looked at his notes. "Since we work on the night shift, everyone here is welcome to a port pass tomorrow, assuming there are no emergencies. Right now I've got Robby, Jimmy, Kelly, and Stacy on the call list. Let's just try to get everything straight tonight so we can all enjoy the time in port tomorrow."

Jimmy felt a surge of adrenaline when his name was called. The apprehension was roaring in his ears. Do they know, he wondered silently. He smiled back at the manager, and nodded his head to acknowledge he had heard what was said. "We'll have this ship in great shape." Inside, Jimmy reconciled the fact that he might be denied his pass tomorrow. It would certainly cause issues if that happened. Without a pass, he would have a difficult time getting off the ship. "We've never lost a port visit yet," he quipped at his manager.

"Oh, I know, Jimmy," replied his manager. He smiled back at the group. "But it's standard procedure. You all know that. The Captain has been sort of skittish lately, so there's no telling what will set him off. So let's just make sure everything is top shape, and we'll all be in the markets tomorrow. I've posted the schedule on the bulletin board in the cleaning room. Please take a look and make sure you know what you're supposed to be working on tonight. Are there any questions before we go?"

The group was growing restless and no one was going to ask any questions. These people wanted to quit wasting time and get to work. Jimmy could tell that he wasn't the only person worried about potentially losing his day out in port. Stacy was sitting quietly across the table, looking agitated. There were other people in the room who were concerned about not getting off the ship tomorrow. It hadn't happened in the time that Jimmy had worked on the ship, but he had heard stories from his associates about instances in the past when the Captain had denied them leave.

"Well," the manager began again. "If there are no questions, why don't we go ahead and get to work. I'll be making my rounds while you work. If you have issues or questions during the shift, give me a ring on the cordless." The manager folded his papers back into his folder and stood up. "Okay, let's get to work."

Jimmy waited until a few of his coworkers got up before he stood up himself. When he stood up, he adjusted his uniform and headed next door to the cleaning room where all the cleaning carts were kept. The other members of his cleaning crew were streaming through the door into the room next door, and Jimmy jumped in line and followed suit. He walked over to the bulletin board and waited until he could see the papers on the board. Scanning for his name on the list, he sighed with relief to see that he was scheduled to clean the common areas. Nothing had changed. He was still a trusted member of this crew. More importantly, he still had the access to the common areas he needed. With only a few people scheduled to clean the common areas, Jimmy wouldn't look suspicious if he were inspecting the vents. In fact, he was likely to get a few extra thanks from the rest of the staff. He smiled to himself and took a deep breath.

Jimmy walked over to where the carts were kept and loaded it up with the appropriate supplies. He stuffed his backpack into the bottom portion of the cart where he normally kept it. There was a set routine that he followed each night he worked, and he was sticking to that routine in case anyone was watching. As he started to wheel his cart from the cleaning room, Stacy stopped next to him and handed him a Phillips screwdriver. "This is in case you need to readjust any of the vents. I can't miss the pass into town tomorrow, dude. I have a date." She smiled at Jimmy and continued speaking. "All four of us in the common areas now have screw drivers, in case we need them. This totally pisses me off. It's not our job to fix those vents; it's the job of those dorks in maintenance."

Jimmy smiled back at Stacy. "Yeah, but none of us want to miss the port pass." He reached out and took the screwdriver and placed it into his cart, next to the cleaning supplies. "It's all cool, Stacy. Don't sweat it."

"Thanks, Jimmy," she replied.

Jimmy watched as she walked away with her cleaning cart in front of her. He smiled again, this time to himself. Perfect, he thought, before pushing his own cart from the room toward the commons.

Chapter 15: Losing Control

October 14, 2004

"Jesus Christ, Jeremy!" Neil was obviously perturbed. "I need you in the office, and I need you here *now.*"

"Okay, calm down. I'm on my way." Jeremy held the phone closer to his ear. It was difficult to hear Neil's voice above the cars driving by on the street next to him. He stood up from his table on the patio of the small eatery he was at and motioned to the waiter that he would be right back. Opening the door to the inside of the restaurant, he headed to the men's room. "Tell me what's going on. I need to pay my lunch tab, and I'll be right in."

"They struck early, that's what." Jeremy could tell that Neil was stressed to the extreme. "You know I can't give you any more details than that on an unsecured line. Get in here. Please."

"All right, I'm coming in now." Jeremy walked back out of the men's room and went back to his table. He motioned to a waiter who was standing at the register near the door. "Excuse me, waiter. I need to get my check so I can pay; I've got to run. Can I also get the rest of this boxed up?"

"Absolutely, sir," came the reply. "I'll be right back with your check." The waiter took the half-eaten plate from in front of the young man and made his way to the door. The man returned a couple minutes later with a paper bag, apparently holding Jeremy's remaining lunch, and the bill. "Thank you, sir. Come again soon."

"Thanks," Jeremy responded as he put some cash on the table with the check. "Thanks for your help."

Neil looked up to see who was entering his office. He was still on the phone when Jeremy walked in, not 15 minutes after he had called him. Jeremy walked over to the chair across the desk from Neil and sat down, waiting for his phone conversation to end. Neil's face was red, sweat beading up on his forehead. A bottle of aspirin sat on the desk next to the phone. He shot Jeremy a half-hearted smile, a look of *thank you* more than anything else.

Neil hung up the phone and wiped the sweat from his brow with a handkerchief that had been sitting in his lap. When he was finished, he looked up at Jeremy. "I'm sorry I was short with you, dude. I'm feeling a little overwhelmed at the moment. All three ships have been identified, but we've got all American cruise ships headed to coastal waters now with Coast Guard escorts, just in case."

"Deaths?"

"None so far, but there are some sick folks out there. I don't know yet what they managed to string together for the attack, but it hasn't killed anyone yet. One of the ships was in port when the devices went off. Luckily, most of the passengers were off in town having a good time. It's mostly just crew members who are ill on that one."

Jeremy was stunned. "You said *devices*. Does that mean there was more than one on all the ships?"

"No, there was only one device on the other two ships," came the reply. "Security on one of the ships was able to catch the guy before he released the chemicals. But two of the guys were off the ship before anyone knew any better. They've both been identified, though. All the ships had a complete crew recall after the incidents, and only one guy on each ship has been missing."

"Is anyone following up with Layla to see if she knows these guys by their name or if she can help us locate them?" Jeremy was sure Neil had already done everything that was appropriate, but he wanted to be sure. *Besides,* he thought, *it probably helps Neil to just talk.*

"Yes, someone is with her now trying to get more information about this phase and the next. We've already seized her computer; it came in this morning, and the analysts are going through it now." Neil rubbed his forehead above his right eye and continued speaking. "The problem here is that she doesn't have a lot more information. The second phase wasn't even planned out yet, just discussed in general. Hell, she doesn't even know when it's supposed to occur."

"That's not good," Jeremy responded.

"Well, in her defense, she's been at work with the analysts for days trying to get them up to speed on all the different forms of channels she and her partner discussed. All she can tell us about the second attack is that it's supposed to be carried out on a popular public event in the United States. They hadn't even talked specifics yet. But she's not taking this easy. The analysts tell me that she's answering every question they ask her, but that she's not giving them much time to ask questions. She just keeps showing them everything she knows."

"Are you starting to trust her, Neil?"

"I'm starting to believe she isn't lying to us. Now whether that could be construed as trust or not, the jury's still out on that. She's just a *very* lucky young woman that no one died because of this. She's still considered a terrorist, Jeremy. Her future doesn't look bright. You need to know that."

Jeremy winced internally. He had been afraid to ask Neil. Layla was his friend, but they were now officially on different sides of the fence. To the United States government, she was a terrorist and would be held accountable as such. "That's okay, Neil. I understand. I'm still loyal to my country. At least she's still trying. How is her emotional state holding up?"

"She seems to be fine. We've got her on a 24-hour suicide watch, just in case."

A sudden thought occurred to Jeremy. "Neil, someone has taken over this group of terrorists. They're inside our borders. That's a scary proposition. Are there any clues to who may be pulling their strings now?"

"Actually," Neil began, "we don't have a clue. The web site that Layla was using before has been inactive since she quit working with it. We're monitoring the hit logs, but there's not much out there right now, just a lot of random hits from search engines that managed to crawl the site. That's why we've got her showing us everything she ever researched, planned, or even discussed with anyone in her group."

"Right now," he continued, "there are about 50 analysts researching every single one of her ideas. They're following through on every detail trying to catch a shimmer of light in the darkness. So far we don't have anything."

"What has the group talked about in the past that we're trying to follow up on?"

"Oh, let's see," Neil replied as he pulled his laptop computer closer to him. "Well, we're scanning on the online auction sites because they had discussed that at one point. Do you know how many online auction sites there really are? My gawd!"

"There are the newsgroups, which are supposedly like message boards. From what I understand, they're fairly old technology but are still widely used and accessible. The problem here is that there are literally thousands of them; each group could have thousands of messages in it."

Jeremy winced at the numbers. "It's not looking good, is it?"

"Well, Layla was right about one thing she mentioned to me. It really is like finding a needle in a haystack. If more terrorists start using technology like this to communicate, we're going to have a hell of a time finding them."

"No kidding. What are the other areas we're looking into? There can't be that many more, can there?" Jeremy was already a little unnerved by the number of possibilities that already had been listed. But deep down he knew that the Internet was a huge beast and that the terrorists could be hiding in any little crack or shadow, away from the prying eye.

Neil glanced back at his computer again. "Oh yeah, there are tons more. She was apparently a very busy girl. Web sites were near the top of her list." He looked up at Jeremy who was nervously running his fingers through his hair again. "I like the fact that you've managed to pick up nervous habits along the way, like I have. I can read your reactions better." Neil grinned to himself. "I take it from your expression that I don't need to remind you just how many web sites actually are posted to the Internet."

"No, you don't. This is really ugly."

"Sure it is. But once you rule out all the legitimate businesses, American religious and political sites, and a few others, we're left with only a few hundred million. Let's see, what's next? Oh yes, peer-to-peer networks. That's a nice one. How the hell are we supposed to manage that?"

Jeremy thought for a second before replying. "Can we get in there and monitor the traffic somehow? There has to be a way into the network so that we can see what's being sent out."

"The analysts have looked into it, and apparently a few of them are familiar with the technology. In some cases, we're able to browse the hosts that are sharing files, which is how all the kids these days are getting busted for sharing music files. From what I understand, there is a team of several analysts already scanning the network looking for files." Neil rubbed at his eye again and closed his laptop. "The list goes on and on, everything from proprietary instant messaging servers to real-time broadcast servers."

"Neil, what are the analysts using to scan through all this information?" Jeremy was confused. "There is likely to be a vast amount of possible targets and many more pieces within each one of those."

"They've got a few tools that they can use. Most are commercial, though. The team leader for the research analysts, Tyler, showed me a couple of the tools they're using when I went down there earlier. Let me give him a call. We can go check their progress, and you can check out their software." Neil picked up the receiver and dialed the extension to Tyler's desk.

"Hi, Tyler; this is Neil, upstairs. Can we run down and see how things are going? I'd like to show Jeremy the tools you are using. Sure, okay, we'll be down shortly." He put the receiver back down on the phone and looked back at Jeremy. "We're good to go. I just need to stop by the food court downstairs and grab some Mountain Dew for the analysts." Neil stood up from his chair, unplugged his laptop, and grabbed it and his notepad. "Apparently they've run out."

"Should we be leaving? Aren't we waiting for more information on this first attack?" Jeremy wanted to see what the analysts were doing, but he couldn't see just leaving the investigation hanging out there. "I mean, this is our case, and I'd hate to let it drop. Especially since it's my first *real* case."

Neil smiled back at Jeremy. "Relax, the first phase was handed off to another team downstairs. They're running the follow-up investigation. They've got my cell number and are supposed to call when they find out something. For now, we've got orders to find out what the second attacks are, including where, when, and how. Now, come on; I'll need your hands to help carry all those cans." With that, he turned and walked toward the door, with Jeremy following closely behind.

As Neil walked through the door, trailed by Jeremy, a dark-haired man popped his head up over the side of his cubicle to see who had come in. "Hey, Neil; come on in. I was just getting ready to scan an image of the computer we got from Layla's flat in Toronto. We're trying to find out exactly what tools she's been using. So far, everything she's told us seems to be checking out."

Neil smiled and walked toward the open side of the cubicle. "Hi, Tyler. Okay." Jeremy followed behind Neil, distracted slightly by the tables of computers and parts lining the wall to their left. The cube they entered was actually double the size of a normal cubicle and appeared to have had one of the divider walls removed at some point in the past to make room. An extra worktable had been moved into the area for investigative work. Tyler was currently bent over a computer case sitting on the work-table, trying to insert a USB key drive into one of the free ports on the front of the case.

The walls of the cube were lined with certificates and degrees. Jeremy looked with interest at a patent certificate hanging on the wall next to a master's degree from Carnegie Mellon. When he had finished, Tyler stood up from the computer and shook Neil's hand. "I'm glad you could come down. It will be interesting to see what pops up."

"Tyler," Neil began, "this is Jeremy, my partner. Jeremy, meet Tyler Richardson."

Tyler pulled the rolled up sleeves of his dress shirt up past his elbow and reached out his arm to shake Jeremy's hand. "Nice to finally meet you, Jeremy. You've managed to get yourself into quite an investigation here." Tyler laughed warmly.

"A pleasure to meet you, as well, Tyler," he replied. "I hear you have your hands full at the moment. I hope things are going well."

"It's not bad, at least not yet. I expect things to get a lot more difficult once we get past this initial investigation. We're just in the general information verification phase." Tyler looked at both Neil and Jeremy, apparently trying to include them both in the conversation. "Everything we've found so far agrees totally with what we've been told from the interviews with Layla. Once we get into the detailed analysis, things could potentially get pretty messy." He smiled. "I was just about to run a content scan on the hard drive of her computer to see what tools she really has installed."

"What are you scanning for?" asked Neil curiously.

"Well," he began, "I've already gone through manually, looking over the hard drive from a cursory level. But we need to know everything about the software installed on this computer that relates to our investigation. So basically, we're looking for any suspicious tools. These could include both applications that are capable of helping create various forms of covert channels or a variety of hacker tools that could be used to case a target on the Internet. Manual checks are great, but to do them as detailed as we would need would take a tremendous amount of time. And from what I understand," he said looking to Neil, "we're sort of behind the eight ball on this one because we don't know much about what is supposed to happen next. Is that correct?"

Neil frowned slightly, frustrated by the reality of the situation. "You're correct. We don't know much at all, aside from the few general details that Layla has been able to provide."

"I didn't realize that there were actually tools to scan for applications like that," asked Jeremy. "Is this an open source tool?"

Tyler smiled. "The tool is actually a commercial product. We tend to use it in forensics investigations involving hacking suspects and the like. But the tool also comes with a database that allows us to scan for steganography software as well. Would you like to see it work?"

"Sure," replied Jeremy with a grin on his face.

"Okay." Tyler turned back around and set the keyboard out in front of the computer monitor, along with a mouse. "The software is called Gargoyle and is from a company name Wetstone Technologies out of New York. They've created databases full of hash values for all the files associated with most of the popular hacking software out on the market. So we just use their dataset for the steganography applications and set the software to scan the entire drive. We're working from a drive image here, and I'm running the software from a USB key drive to avoid possible further contamination of the drive contents."

Tyler moved the mouse pointer to the appropriate icon on the desktop and double-clicked. A splash screen with a picture of a gargoyle popped up above the desktop and was replaced only moments later by the Gargoyle interface. "This, gentlemen, is Gargoyle," Tyler said.

Wetstone Gargoyle Main Interface

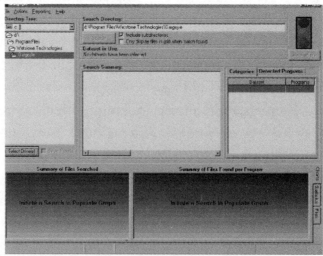

"Show us how it works, Tyler," said Neil, apparently also absorbed in watching the demonstration.

"Well, this is the main interface. We can use this window to choose the type of scan we want to run against the computer. Since we're running from a directory on my USB key drive, any reports we save will be saved on the key instead of the hard drive. Gargoyle comes with about 15 datasets that you can use. Each one checks for different applications or software on the target computer. If you look at the list here, you can see the datasets used to scan for things like spyware, key logging software, Trojans, or even denial of service tools. For this scan, we're going to use the stego.mdb dataset."

"What's actually contained in those datasets?" asked Jeremy. "Are they actual database files that can be opened and viewed under applications like Microsoft Access?"

"Absolutely," replied Tyler. "They're normal database formatting. Here, let me show you what it actually looks like on my computer." He turned from Layla's computer and moved toward his own desktop. Finding the Microsoft Access icon on the desktop, he double-clicked and selected the open file option from the menu. It took him only a moment to find the Gargoyle database files. He selected one at random and clicked open, watching contently as the file opened under Access.

"The actual layout of the database was created by the National Institute of Science and Technology. It's part of the National Software Reference Library. Basically, Wetstone went out and created SHA-1 and MD5 hashes of the various files associated with each piece of software in its datasets. If you look at this window, you can see that each file is listed along with its file size, CRC32 error check, and the operating system it works under."

View of stego,mdb File

SHA-1	MD5	ProductCode	CRC32	FileName	FileSize	OpSystemC
FF462B337B3AE9CAF6C7D587C52C5FAD78DFEFB4	5107417963380E8D1CF80F1925C91F3F	36	00046E24	Zayime.dat	7502	WIN2000
FF462B337B3AE9CAF6C7D587C52C5FAD78DFEFB4	5107417963380E8D1CF80F1925C91F3F	276	00046E24	Zayime.dat	7502	WIN2000
F02779B5F6423A64C42E8CFFB5DAA792F49F4500	42DE3DE2DC177AB691B6D59F4B82A195	156	004F52BA	support.h	2113	WIN2000
FFEB84FB5F67C6742A5A5D17AC03A1587ED55D38	3C1BE7A0789B330B2DF86C7658229661	281	007A7F55	index.dat	32768	WIN2000
D3DAA79C00A97F870DAADEF7EA1165452EB6F52E	FE0FB703411CB69C18F1D9D4DFD8F5DE	26	007FF2F0	CWSPARAM.EXE	13776	WIN2000
16A28AC3227AF30EC414F96C06D20D6CA7C1B7E3	E2C812CBF5593F588441296DA1710CA7	249	008721E0	rm20help-3_1.htm	4890	WIN2000
28766B8791737D6148F8396BD516E57CA0B44063	4C19F3028081824DCED569C8384B7C97	93	008F0195	blowfish.dll	69120	WIN2000
A80D67A057919B9F14CC818BD23DF7CC4256ABD8	3842B218744592A179E82E6660199818	161	009E4041	java_net_SocketImpl.h	612	WIN2000
414E1B75CA52A1474669BF0E63EE26EA0E265982	DB3C070A2078B747F63737E8D2E5C8DC	133	00A2B59A	SNOW.EXE	62464	WIN2000
81E076F84E030251C7B68B77192CC8EA113D6859	3E772F710DEAF3BD331915AC0341676B	130	00A8DABC	SMBTest_Rescale.cpp	6376	WIN2000
90BF9F1E2940BEAA2A238EC2DFADC1BDE621DC02	28B6BF379FA249969329CCE1D62B96E7	227	00B0EBD8	SCYTALE.SIG	152	WIN2000
EB77C0AE97FEC45B1B1515AD87548AB11246C032	0C2C1D8D65BEA4BF3BB612B7F030A6B8	249	00BB76E6	IEOverlay.gif	271	WIN2000
FC13EF6606686A66079B5BED81C0920D787F55F3	E2D18003CFAF0305EA3C7B5172B8C57F	214	00BE89AD	inwsecr2.exe	1268846	WIN2000
4B09CB152A79D22253A770621A662E56EA4A37EC	F1F1ADD65FCEE96E97C753F44E83427F	279	00C2F7DE	index.dat	32768	WIN2000
C16DC804872074868D0AA4428762B0614A40328	664B1002B932C6630ACBF3A0671C8934	82	00C924AE	UnHide.BAT	376	WIN2000
C16DC804872074868D0AA4428762B0614A40328	664B1002B932C6630ACBF3A0671C8934	83	00C924AE	UnHide.BAT	376	WIN2000
C6064185F2CE87142466EF530E4DD65C20AFAC49	CBD6CE07ACE3813CD1091D5618743ED5	130	00CCBD6B	SMBSP_MedianCut.cpp	7341	WIN2000
0ACF72F9B78194A806D36CFB3B649D8C867B7B21	C0A444358FDFAE8FB9A0B39847C98D35	168	00CE70F3	Image45.gif	21729	WIN2000
0ACF72F9B78194A806D36CFB3B649D8C867B7B21	C0A444358FDFAE8FB9A0B39847C98D35	238	00CE70F3	Image45.gif	21729	WIN2000
DC0114D848EBDE23F1F352808797E119A6F7E24B	9669D7BF8C4A6EFFAF571106DFA21D1D	130	00D34AB2	SMBTestST.cpp	5653	WIN2000
190B6559362F74C16FEF4321DA5EA16217BDDFFC	A886D36593238A0FB47C21EE40E592FB	228	0112BFE4	PGPSTART.TX_	5680	WIN2000
F00517C131B52FE4327C738A956A21D901D2E28B	812079E4A532F60FD6B20E4818766B37	150	01226688	cygmhash-2.dll	233311	WIN2000
F00517C131B52FE4327C738A956A21D901D2E28B	812079E4A532F60FD6B20E4818766B37	151	01226688	cygmhash-2.dll	233311	WIN2000
F00517C131B52FE4327C738A956A21D901D2E28B	812079E4A532F60FD6B20E4818766B37	152	01226688	cygmhash-2.dll	233311	WIN2000
05BE8213E03F46341E645E7130333A5B6978EE90	3EEFAEA6A3EFC845AD086AD94ABB70D4	113	0122F52E	FAQ	3693	WIN2000
3937928AF6881B127617D6E297A304D799951B17	CB1606CE86519BEC2CCF775550E59247	112	014D3F2C	Encode.plq	18550	WIN2000

"So how does it detect software that has been removed?" Jeremy asked. "It looked like it will work fine against applications that are still installed, but it's going to be impossible to find applications that were uninstalled, right?"

"That's a good question, Jeremy," Neil joined in. "How does that work, Tyler?"

"The uninstall function for many applications is really not a complete uninstall at all. In fact, there are often many smaller files that are left on the hard drive. Surely you've run into a situation where you thought you had removed a piece of software only to find the directory still there at a later time, with some token files still inside."

"Okay, that makes sense," answered Jeremy. "But clean uninstalls will not be detected, correct?"

"Most likely not," replied Tyler. "Now that you've seen the format, let's run the scan and see what we find." He moved back to Layla's computer and clicked the File option on the menu at the top of the interface and selected the Open Dataset option from the drop-down menu.

Selecting the Open Dataset Option in Gargoyle

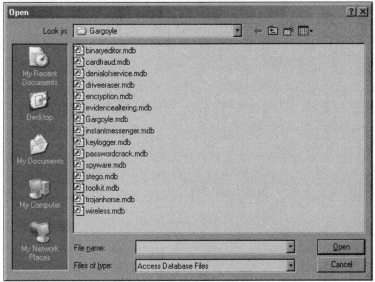

Tyler selected the stego.mdb database file from the dialog box and clicked the Open button. When the main window was the only one left on the screen, he ensured that the correct directory name was in the entry box at the top and then turned to Neil and Jeremy. "Now we'll run the scan on the hard drive to see what's installed. We'll scan the D: drive first. I can scan the other after you leave."

Ready to Start the Scan

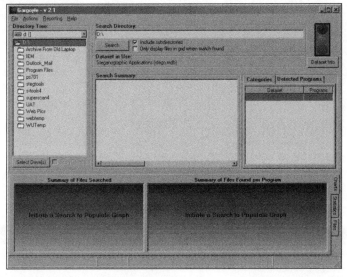

Tyler moved the mouse pointer up to the Search button located near the top of the Gargoyle interface. The Gargoyle Status window popped up on the screen and the three men watched intently as the number of files being checked increased at an amazing rate. "As you can see," Tyler began telling the other two men, "the software tells us which directory is being scanned at the moment and the status bar at the bottom tells us how far through the process we are. This really should take only a few minutes because the target drive is relatively small."

"How long does it normally take to scan a hard drive?" asked Jeremy.

"In actuality, it really depends on the number of files on that drive. It potentially could take quite a while if the drive is large and there are a lot of files on the drive." Tyler laughed softly to himself. "I know that doesn't really answer your question. I've seen a scan take upwards of an hour on larger drives."

Gargoyle Status Window

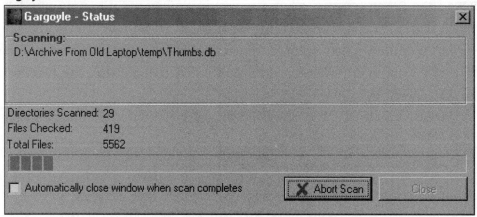

"So how often do you use this tool?" Neil asked Tyler.

"We're actually starting to depend more heavily on it," Tyler replied. "The various datasets that come with the tool are really useful, but the best part is that we can create our own datasets and use them within the tool as well."

"I can understand creating an NSRL-compliant database to use, but what would you put into it?" came the reply from Neil. "Aren't all the tools already in the datasets you get with the tool?"

"Not always. Bear in mind that with the creation of the Department of Homeland Security, the various investigative and law enforcement agencies around the country are now sharing information. We run across new tools on a regular basis that aren't necessarily in the public domain yet. We create the SHA-1 and MD5 hashes for all the files for those applications and put them into our own proprietary datasets. So we do use the ones that come with the application, but it's relatively easy for us to use the tool for other things as well."

"Any chance I can get copies of those extra datasets?" Jeremy asked. "I've been playing with more of the tools lately, trying to get a better grip on what we're dealing with. It would be nice to have those in our collection, as well."

Tyler smiled at Neil. "You're starting to sound like one of my analysts, Jeremy. You interested in a transfer to a new division?"

Jeremy laughed, but Neil just frowned at Tyler. "I don't think so. Not yet, anyway," Jeremy said.

Tyler looked back at the screen to check the status of the software. "Oh look; it's done. That didn't take long at all. Now, let's see what we ended up with."

Scan Completed

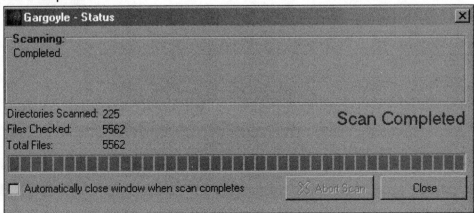

The Gargoyle main interface was now filled with information from its scans on the target hard drive. Tyler looked at the screen and noted there were matches found for steganographic software. "Hey, check it out; there were pieces of nine separate applications found on the hard drive that are used for creating steganography."

"Where did you see that?" asked Jeremy.

"Over here," he replied. Tyler pointed to the right side of the window. "See this box here, with the two tabs?"

"Yes," was the answer from Jeremy.

"Well, what we're looking at right now is the first tab, Categories. This window is most useful when we use multiple datasets for our scans. But from what we're looking at right here, you can see that it found remnants of nine different steganographic applications."

Searching for Stegnographic Applications in Gargoyle

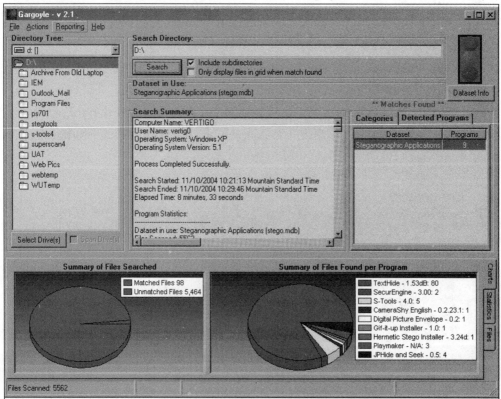

"If we click over to the second tab," Tyler continued as he clicked the tab named Detected Programs, "we can look at the specific application remnants that were found on the drive. Several of these applications I know Layla told us about, but I can't recall whether she mentioned the others. I'll have to check the notes from the interview. But overall, there are no real surprises here."

Neil looked at the output more closely, a question coming to his mind. "But isn't that information the same as what's currently displayed at the bottom?"

"It's close; you're right," came the reply from Tyler. "But the information at the bottom of the window shows us more details about what was found. Notice there are three tabs at the bottom."

"Ahhh, okay, I see now. We've got a better idea of the actual percentage of discovered files are from which application," Jeremy interjected. "I also like how you can see which version of the software was discovered. But is the tool capable of distinguishing between two or three different versions of the same software?"

"In many cases, yes, but not always." Tyler turned to look at Jeremy again. "In some cases, there are files that don't change much from version to version. Sometimes they're README files and other times they're just basic library files that haven't been altered by the author since the last version. But Gargoyle will tell you which versions match that file."

Tyler turned back toward the computer and continued. "Also, we can even see how many files actually matched information in the dataset. So out of 5562 files scanned on the drive, only 98 files had matches in the database for steganography."

The Detected Programs Tab

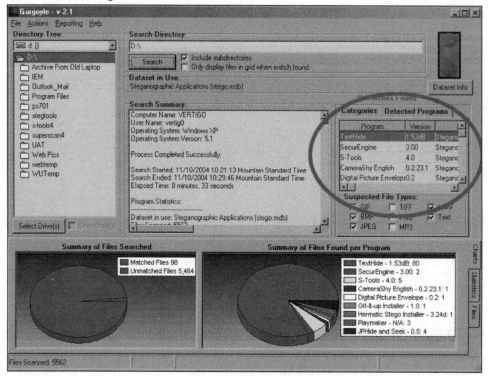

"That was the Charts tab. Let's take a quick look at the Statistics tab and see what else we can find out." Tyler turned back around to the computer and clicked the Statistics tab at the bottom of the screen. "Here we go," he said. "Remember you asked me a few minutes ago about how long it normally takes to scan a hard drive, Jeremy?"

"Yeah."

"Well, here are the actual numbers for you," Tyler replied. "Using the stego.mdb as our dataset, on this computer, with this hard drive, we see that our scan rate was about 11 files per second. It even tells us how many megabytes (MB) of data are scanned per second. In this case we were getting about 7MB scanned per second."

"But all that is probably platform-specific, isn't it?" asked Jeremy.

"Absolutely. A faster processor and more memory in a computer will allow us to scan much faster than if we actually ran the scans on Layla's computer. She wasn't into speed and power. So by imaging the drive and putting that into a faster computer, I can actually get the information I need at a faster rate."

"That makes sense," came Jeremy's reply.

"There is one more useful piece of information I don't want you to miss from this particular tab. The right side at the bottom shows us a bar chart. Those bars represent the actual percentage of files found for each application it detected on the system. This is useful for understanding what was on the computer that could have already been deleted or removed."

"Are there ever false positives with a tool like this?" Neil piped in. Neil had taken Tyler's chair, which had been sitting abandoned near his desk. He was leaning forward in the chair, looking in between Tyler and Jeremy as the other two men went through the results of the scan.

"The only times we've had any false positives in our findings were times when the hashes created for a file in the dataset were created wrong. This happened to us once while we were creating out own dataset, never with the ones that ship with the product." Tyler smiled wryly at the other two men. "I'm sad to say that I'm the one who made the mistake." He laughed dryly. "But we found it during a test of our dataset, so there was no harm. But for the most part, if the hashes are created correctly, it would be nearly impossible to get a false positive. These hashes are a lot like human fingerprints. No two pieces of software have the same hash values because the contents of each file are completely different."

"What if the contents vary by only one letter or character?" asked Neil, leaning back in the gray office chair.

"That one character would cause the file to have a completely different hash. Think of it this way, Neil. You can take a pig and make sausage from it, right?"

"Right."

"And if we run a DNA test on that sausage and compare it with information we had stored previously about the pig, we could verify that the sausage came from the pig, right?"

"Sure, I understand that."

"Well," Tyler continued, "we're using the same concept. The datasets are built using hashes generated from the actual applications we want to scan for. The only hash values that we should run into that match are ones created from identical files. That tells us that the application was, or is, installed on the hard drive we're looking at."

"Okay, I get it now. Thanks Tyler."

"Anytime. Now let's look at that last tab and see what else we have to work with."

Scan Speeds and Percentages

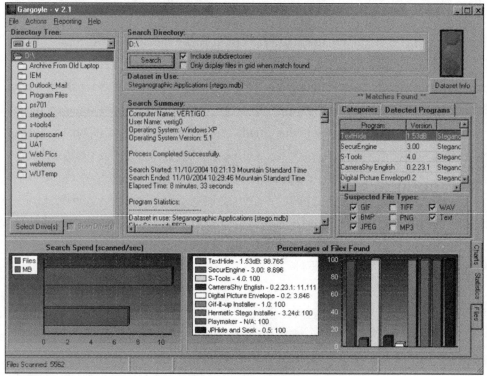

"Okay," replied Jeremy. "What's this last tab?"

"The last tab is the Files tab," answered Tyler. "This is where we find out the specific files that were found on the drive and their relation to the application."

"So," Jeremy continued for Tyler, "we should see 98 entries in the file listing, correct?"

"That's correct. We can get all the information we need about the files that were found, including the application they belong to, the version of the software they belong to, where they're located, their file size, and whether or not the file is included in multiple versions of the same software. Here, look at the file listing."

The Files Tab

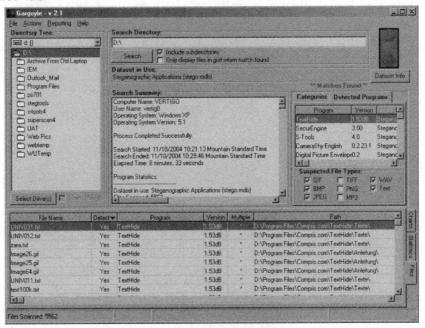

"Hey, check this out, Neil," Jeremy answered. "It even finds example images that are installed with the suspect software. That's pretty cool."

Neil laughed and turned to Tyler. "You might end up with him sooner than you think if you keep this up."

Jeremy blushed slightly and ran his fingers through his thick hair. "Sorry, Neil. This is just really interesting to me."

"It's okay, kid," Neil replied, smiling. "I figured you'd move in this direction at some point."

"And you're welcome anytime, Jeremy," Tyler responded. "We could always use someone else who actually enjoys doing this type of work."

"Thanks," Jeremy answered. "So can we save the information if we want to use it later?

"I was just about to get to that," came the reply. "We have to save and date a report for every scan we run like this. The tool has a built-in reporting function that lays everything out for us in a report that we can store electronically and print out in hard copy, should we need to." Tyler bent back over the computer and moved the mouse pointer to the Reporting option on the main menu at the top of the window. "From here we select Create Evidence Report." As Tyler clicked on his selection, a new window popped up above the main window.

"From here, we enter all the case information we want included in the report." He began typing relevant information, including the case number, his name, and his division. "They make it pretty easy to create these reports, which is great for me because I despise creating documentation from scratch." When he had entered all the information he needed in the report, he clicked the Create Report button at the bottom of the new windows and waited as the report was created and brought up onto the desktop in a web browser.

Evidence Report Creation

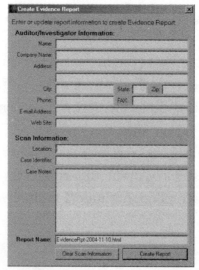

The report was laid out in Hypertext Markup Language (HTML) formatted tables. "See," began Tyler again. "All the information we saw in the interface is now in the report we've created and it's automatically saved with the filename I gave it in the last window. We're not really into that bright green color that dumps out in the reports, but since it's an HTML file, it was relatively easy to write a script that changes the table header colors and adds our division logo to the report."

"Yeah," Jeremy responded, "I'm not so sure I like that color either." He laughed and looked at Neil. "I think I've seen Neil wear a shirt that color to work before." Tyler laughed along with Jeremy while Neil just looked up at the two young men, smiling.

"Okay, I see how it's going to be," he replied. "You're just going to team up on the old guy in the group. That's fine. I have ways of making both your lives miserable."

Evidence Report Laid out in HTML

Both men laughed, apparently already comfortable with each other. "Hey, Tyler," asked Neil. "I have one more question for you."

"Sure, shoot," replied Tyler.

"Well, we know how the datasets are formatted and how the software uses the hashes to find remnants of various pieces of software, but so far the only way we know of to find out what applications Gargoyle looks for is by bringing the .mdb file up in Microsoft Access. There has got to be an easier way to do that."

"Oh yeah, there is. I'm glad you mentioned it, actually. Wetstone puts out new datasets on a fairly constant basis, and we always look through to see what new applications have been added to the databases." Tyler clicked the small x at the top of the browser window to close the report and highlighted the main Gargoyle window with the mouse pointer.

"There is a button over here at the top right of the screen, right under the stoplight. You see that," he asked his coworkers.

"The one that says Dataset info?" asked Jeremy.

"That's the one," replied Tyler. "If we click that button, it brings up information about the current datasets we have loaded." He clicked the Dataset Info button and waited as a new window appeared on the desktop. "The drop-down bar at the top of the window allows us to pick and choose between any datasets we might have loaded at the time. In our case, we have only the stego.mdb file loaded, so there aren't any other choices."

"So," began Neil again, "if we scroll through that list, we should see everything that is scanned for by Gargoyle in that particular dataset?"

"That's correct," answered Tyler. "The applications are listed alphabetically on the left-hand side of the frame. It even goes so far as to list each individual version of each application separately." Tyler scrolled down the window some and came to stop on the entry for the StealthDisk Pro application. "Here is a good example," he continued. "Here we have two different entries for the StealthDisk Pro application. One of them is the actual installed application, and the other entry appears to be the installer file that you would download from the Internet. So if a suspect had downloaded the software but not gotten around to installing it yet, Gargoyle would still be able to detect it." He turned to Neil. "Did that answer your question, Neil?"

"Yes, it did. Thanks, man." Neil looked at Jeremy. "We should probably be going so he can finish up his work. Tyler, do you mind if we stop by every once in a while to see how things are going? I imagine that Jeremy will want to visit every now and then now that you've managed to get him all wound up about your tools."

"That's not a problem at all. Either of you are welcome whenever you like. Just give me a call first to see if I am in a meeting or have time."

"Sounds good," replied Neil. "Let's go, Jeremy. We still have work to do upstairs. We'll talk to you later, Tyler."

"Bye, Tyler," chimed in Jeremy. "Thanks again. That was cool."

"Anytime guys," Tyler replied as he walked them to the door. "And let me know when you get tired of working upstairs. We can always use someone with your drive down here in the dungeon."

"I will," Jeremy replied as he walked out the door to the office.

Tyler made his way back to his cubicle. There was still time to get another scan of the computer done before his day was finished.

Gargoyle Dataset Information

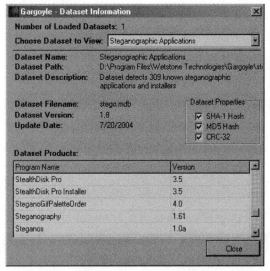

Chapter 16: Heightened Motivation

November 1, 2004

Jimmy was fuming inside as he sat in the old wooden chair in the run-down restaurant. The food here was awful, but then again, he hadn't found any food in the local establishments that appealed to his Middle Eastern palette. A small but steady stream of locals came and went as he sat at the table looking out the window into the dirty street. They were content enough to eat the food. *Perhaps it's just an acquired taste*, he thought to himself.

But it wasn't the food, or even the people, that had him raging inside. It had been over two weeks now since the first phase of the project had fallen apart in front of his eyes. And although media outlets around the world were covering the strange incidents, the United States government was playing it off as another round of gastrointestinal illness similar to what had afflicted the cruise lines in 2002. They were trying to prevent an outbreak of mass panic. The American public was used to seeing news like this. Those few people who claimed this was a possible terrorist attack were discredited with declarations of paranoia and hysteria. It was a huge attempted cover-up, and he couldn't decide which way public opinion was swaying.

He could tell from newspapers and television broadcasts that press agencies around the world weren't sure which way to lean regarding the attacks either. Some were calling it an outright terrorist attack on an American industry that had lagged behind in the push for better security. Others adopted the story the government had sponsored. The news anchor on the small, rickety television hanging on the wall near the bar of the restaurant was speculating about the truth to those rumors. "Authorities are still refusing to comment on the young man of Middle Eastern descent currently being held for questioning in Tampa, Florida.

Rumors are flying today about a possible government cover-up. Could this really have been a terrorist attack?"

Jimmy sat back in his chair and thought again about the last 24 hours of his time on the ship. He had spent hours reflecting on those events, wondering if there was some way, any way, he could have improved the plan. Salah had obviously given away their plans. He had been lured into a trap, but had not been caught. But more importantly, no one had died. There were no real *victims*. There were still a few people in critical condition, but not a single life had been taken. That bothered Jimmy. The first phase had been a failure, a useless folly, in his mind. One of his team members had been captured; the other had apparently escaped. A picture of the captured man appeared in the newspaper as he was escorted from the ship to awaiting vehicles at port. This was the first time Jimmy had ever been able to put a face to any of the names he had been communicating with for so long.

He remembered setting the devices in two different vents in the dining hall. At the time, it looked as if he might not get it done. A fleeting thought had crossed his mind once to scrap the entire phase and just move on, but he simply could not let himself walk away from something that he had worked so hard on. In the end, he had used his time in the men's lavatory in the dining hall to put the cleaning chemicals into the milk bags. He used duct tape to seal the opening in the bag and set the completed devices in their respective vents. The bags would slowly build up pressure and eventually pop a seam, leaking both the gas and the cleaners into the ventilation system.

As he walked through security, down the gangplank, and into town, his first thought had been to get as far away as possible. After a quick visit to a local bank to exchange American dollars for Mexican pesos, he bought a bus ticket to a small town 150 miles inland. The bus left the small tourist port town within an hour of his departure from the ship. Stuffed against the window of the bus by a larger than normal local woman, he stared out at the passing landscape, thinking about his next move and wondering about the others.

But now he was trapped in a small Mexican town, forced to continue the project in less than optimal conditions. There was still plenty of money in his backpack to support him for 12 months in this depressed economy. He also felt safe now, away from prying eyes and inquiring minds. Jimmy had rented a small room above this very restaurant. The rent payment was small, and the owner was glad to have the extra income to help support his ailing business.

Once Jimmy had rested, he ventured into the town to determine what his available resources would be for continuing with phase two. He needed to let the others know he was alive and well. They *would* move on, despite Salah's betrayal. He would use that fact to motivate the team further, push them harder. Success was no longer an option; it was a requirement. Besides, as much as his newfound hatred of his former friend burned hot inside of him, he understood that there were other Al Qaeda operatives in a much better position to exact revenge on Salah. His primary goal right now had to be the continuation into phase two of the plot.

Obtaining a reliable Internet connection here was more difficult than he originally had thought. It bothered him immensely that somehow the Western mentality had absorbed itself into his mind. *Not everyone around the world has a broadband connection to the Internet*, he had reminded himself. His working environment had changed, and he would have to make do. America had a web of thick Internet pipes laid across its soil in all directions, but countries like this lagged behind in technology. A connection was expensive and slow. Still, he *had* managed to get connected several times while he had been here, through a small library two blocks away.

Al Qaeda had been watching the news, too. He had an e-mail waiting for him. They knew of the betrayal. They knew of his broken success. They expected better things for phase two. Jimmy found himself rushing through a planning process in his head, trying like hell to come up with something better, more powerful. They would expect nothing less from him. *Allah does not deserve your failure*, they had said. *He deserves your success.*

Jimmy sat up straight in his chair as a young waitress brought his lunch and set it in front of him. He had seen her working here nearly every day he had been in town. She was a cute, young woman with ravishing eyes and dark hair. He found the dark color of her skin attractive and tempting. Her simple dress was dirty from working in the kitchen, but she was polite and avoided looking into his eyes. Her deference to him made Jimmy smile, despite himself. *Perhaps*, he thought, *I will stay here once my work is complete.* He found her appealing, but distracting. The young woman filled his water glass and walked back toward the kitchen with the metal pitcher. A sigh of relief escaped his lungs as he found his mind able to focus once more on the task at hand.

As he picked at the plate in front of him, he considered possible locations for his next attack. Salah had some good ideas, but he would have shared those. Jimmy needed something new, something better, something not so immediate, but still very close at hand. The two men had discussed large sporting events, which were extremely popular and well attended in the United States. The Super Bowl football game was too well secured because it was a suspected attack venue. The World Series was too close at hand and also too well secured. They needed something chaotic, something random, yet planned out. They needed an event that would be too difficult to secure.

There were so many places, so many events. Americans love to celebrate. There was the Macy's Thanksgiving Day Parade. There were live music, television, and movie award events. Red carpet movie premieres were a dime a dozen in Hollywood. NASCAR races all along the southern half of the country, where the weather was still warm, drew thousands of spectators. Christmas events in major cities around the country, like the Christmas tree lighting in Washington, D.C., or in New York City. There were so many choices, but so many of them were wrong right from the start.

He wasn't certain how long he had been sitting there. The beans on his plate had grown cold. A voice broke through his thoughts, and he looked up to find his young waitress asking if she should reheat his food for him. *Yes, please*, he said in broken Spanish. The young woman nodded with a smile and carried his plate back to the kitchen. *Where can I do this?* he asked himself, again. At times, he wondered if his inability to be intimate with Allah was creating these issues for him. Praying several times a day had become a standard occurrence in his daily schedule, although he admitted to himself that he really wasn't sure if he was even doing it correctly.

Staring out the window, he watched as one of the few cars in town made its way past the pedestrian and animal traffic toward the other end of the street. The people here reflected the life they were leading. Their clothes were made from fabrics of the color of the earth around them. Hues of browns and tans and pale greens hid days' worth of ground-in grit within each garment. It was difficult for Jimmy to maintain his perspective of attacking such a large country as America while being immersed in such a simple lifestyle.

A steamy plate was set back in front of him. He thanked the waitress and gave her a few coins for her trouble. She thanked him for his generosity. Jimmy watched as her face came up to meet his, and his eyes were drawn to her neck. A bright strand of ornamental beads adorned her thin, sweet neck. The beads were bright red and obviously fake, but on her they looked beautiful. A scene was gathering in his mind, a vision of hundreds of thousands of people all crowded together. They were drinking alcohol and singing. Women were baring their breasts to men on the streets. Like a voice screaming inside the back of his head, Jimmy heard the words he had been looking for, Mardi Gras.

If the young woman thought that Jimmy's smile was broad because he was attracted to her, it was fine with him. He *was* attracted to her. It was that attraction that had made him notice the beads around her neck, providing the answer he was looking for. There was simply no way to ensure the complete safety of hundreds of thousands of people crammed into a three- or four-block radius. Their alcohol-induced fervor would provide the perfect cover for an attack. It was not something he had ever spoken with Salah about. Allah had saved the answer for Jimmy until he needed it. *Thank you, Allah.*

When the young waitress walked away again, Jimmy took a drink of water from his glass and set it back down on the scratched wooden table. Finding comfort within himself for finally having a direction, he smiled to himself and began eating his lunch. *I need to start my planning and communicate with the team,* he thought as he ate. *This will be an attack the Americans will never forget.*

He finished the plate of now hot food quickly and downed the remaining water in his glass. He wiped his face on the napkin he had been using and placed it on top of his empty plate. Jimmy stood up from his chair and pulled some money from his pocket, laying it on the table next to the dishes. There was enough extra cash to provide the waitress with a nice tip. When this is all over, he thought, I'll be back for you. He grabbed his backpack from the floor next to his chair and headed toward the door.

Jimmy walked out of the small restaurant and crossed the dingy street to the opposite corner. The library was close and he wanted to do a little research before it closed for the day. Deciding on a target was different from actually planning for the attack. There was a lot of information he would need, a map of the French Quarter, a list of businesses, and the dates and times of events.

He walked up the four stone steps to the library and pushed gently against the old wooden doors. The smell of old paper filled his lungs as he stepped into the room. The library was small, consisting of only a single room, a few tables to sit at and read books, about 30 aisles of books, and two old computers. The books were nearly all in Spanish and beyond Jimmy's very basic Spanish language skills. The computers were based on definitely old technology, but the library was sponsored by the local government and had used its limited resources to acquire a slow satellite connection to a remote Internet service provider.

He walked over to the old desk in the far left corner and took a seat in front of one of the computers enclosed in a tan, scratched case. He pushed the power button on the monitor and double-clicked the icon for the web browser, an older version of the Netscape browser running under Windows 95. But from the dust that had settled on the keyboard before he came in a few days ago, he could only assume that no one else was using these computers. There was a good chance that no one in town really even knew how to use them.

Jimmy entered the address to the Google search engine and waited as the web site was loaded into the browser. *Geeez, this is slow*, he thought. He entered search terms to help him start locating information on the 2005 Mardi Gras; Mardi Gras 2005 New Orleans Schedule. After waiting several seconds, the search returned a list of suitable web sites. He smiled and clicked on the first link, The Official Site of Mardi Gras 2005.

Google Search Results

Jimmy grinned widely as the first link finally came up in the browser. At the top of the page was the first piece of information he would need. February 8, 2005 is Mardi Gras. He pulled a notepad of paper and a pen from his backpack and started keeping notes. He would need to save this information. He normally would have used his USB key drive, but the computer was old, and didn't have a USB port. Scribbling the information he had just found on the first sheet of paper, he began reading through the web site, trying to find the other information he needed. With the speed of the connection, Jimmy knew he would be here for a while. He settled into the chair as best he could, trying to get comfortable. This time, he would succeed.

Chapter 17: Chasing Ghosts

November 16, 2004

Jeremy pressed the small white button just outside the door and waited patiently. He had the clearance required to enter the area, but his badge hadn't been added to the system yet. It just meant that he had to wait until someone came and let him in—not too much of an issue. He heard the sound of the lock click from the inside and the door swung open and the face of a woman appeared. She looked as if she was in her mid-40s and had likely been working in the government for some time. Her clothes were professional, yet casual by most standards. "Yes, can I help you?"

"Hi," he answered back with a smile. "My name is Jeremy, and I came down to meet with Tyler. He's expecting me."

She looked at his badge, checking the clearance level indicated on the badge. Smiling she replied back to Jeremy, "Come on in; I'll take you to his desk."

"Thanks!" He followed closely behind her as they crossed the short distance to Tyler's cubical. As he walked behind her, his eyes were drawn to the hardware lying haphazardly around the office.

"Tyler?" she asked as she stuck her head just inside his space.

"Oh, hi, Janis," Jeremy heard Tyler reply. "What's up?"

"There is someone here to see you," she said. "Jeremy."

"Excellent, come on in, Jeremy. Thanks Janis. I didn't hear the door bell." Jeremy saw Tyler smile at Janis as he entered the small cube.

"Not a problem," she replied with a grin. "I was headed up here anyway. Well, I'll let you two boys talk. Nice to meet you, Jeremy." With that, she turned and walked from the area toward the front door.

"Come on in. Have a seat," Tyler began. "You mentioned an interest in our investigation, and it's been a couple of weeks so I thought I'd invite you down and show you a little of what we've discovered. You have some time," he asked.

"Absolutely," replied Jeremy. He was trying not to sound overly eager, but he was definitely interested in what Tyler's team did. "I've got time."

"Great. I was hoping to show you how we're trying to detect potential methods of covert communication. I'd love to get your input and feedback." Tyler twisted uncomfortably, trying to pop the bones in his back. "I feel like we're trying to push a boulder up an icy slope, Jeremy. The job is just so huge. There is so much information on the Internet and so many possible channels that could be used."

"I know what you mean, Tyler. When I was doing my initial research I was really shocked by the number of hiding places. They could literally post their messages anywhere, and we might never find them." Jeremy ran his fingers through his hair and sighed. "So how *are* you going about finding the messages?"

Tyler smiled slightly. "Straight to the point, huh?" He turned to his computer and pulled up a spreadsheet. "This is the current distribution of our team members, not that you really need this much detail. But I can't keep track of what each person is doing right now, so I had to move it all into this document. I'm tracking 30-plus people now." He pointed with a pen to the first row on the spreadsheet. "These two people do nothing all day but try to find places on the Internet that would work as distribution mechanisms for covert communication. Right now they've identified a list of places and services that this team," he said as he moved the pen down a row, "is investigating. There are significantly more people on this team because we have to do manual and automated scans to find possible channels."

"Sounds like quite a task," Jeremy responded. "It's almost a little overwhelming, Tyler."

"It's very overwhelming, Jeremy." Tyler closed out the spreadsheet and reached back to the rear of his desk, pushing the small black button on the keyboard/video/mouse (kvm) switch. Jeremy recognized the Gnome desktop as it popped up on the screen. "A good deal of our manual checks are focused specifically around finding anomalies in picture files. We've found a few that we suspect of containing steganography, and we've forwarded them to the NSA for processing. But we have yet to find enough suspect images in one area to warrant spending a lot of time."

Tyler moved the mouse pointer up to the top of the screen and clicked down until he found the icon he was looking for. A splash screen for a graphics editor named GIMP popped onto the screen, followed immediately by the application interface. "This is GIMP," Tyler continued. "It's a graphics creation and manipulation software. We've been using it as a tool to help us narrow down some of our manual searches on the Internet."

"You're using a graphics tool? How?"

"Digital image files, when created correctly, follow certain standards." Tyler clicked the File option on the menu and scrolled down to Open File. He browsed through the directory structure, finally finding the files he was looking for. "Let's look at these two files."

"They look the same to me," answered Jeremy as the images came up.

"They are—sort of, anyway. One image is the original file I started with. The second image has information hidden in it via a form of steganography. I used the S-Tools program to embed the information." Tyler brought the second image to the front and continued speaking. "You can see some distortion in the image that has stego, but mostly in the form of noise. See how grainy the image looks?" he commented to Jeremy.

"Sure, I've seen that before when I was playing with the tools myself."

"Ah, good, so you're familiar with how the tools work, at least from a general perspective," Tyler said as he smiled and looked at Jeremy. "But have you ever seen poor digital images that had noise like this in them?"

"All the time. In fact, I've seen some that were worse," Jeremy laughed lightly.

"So without the original file, how would you know to suspect something might be wrong with the image or that it might contained hidden information?"

"I'm not sure," replied Jeremy. "It's easy when the original is in front of you."

"You're right," answered Tyler as he moved the mouse to the menu at the top of the interface. "But there are methods for at least narrowing down the images that might have steganography." After several clicks of his mouse, a palette window popped up on the desktop, showing the colors available in the original image. "Have you ever seen a color palette before, Jeremy?"

"Yes, I have a good idea of what it is," he replied.

"Can you tell me how many possible colors are in the palette of a normal GIF image, then?"

"Don't they have a maximum number of 256 colors?"

"That's correct," Tyler said with a smile. "You sure you don't want a job down here?" He smirked at Jeremy as the young man ran his fingers through his hair. "This image only uses 128 colors, half the palette. You can see from the colored blocks shown that most of the colors are different. A few are close in color, but they're far enough apart in shade and hue to require their own entry in the palette."

"All right, that makes sense. So what does that tell us?"
"Actually, that doesn't tell us anything other than we are likely looking at an original file," answered Tyler. "In order to get the point, we need to look at the second image, the one with the hidden information. So let's look at its palette."

Palette of Image One in GIMP

Tyler brought the second image back to the foreground, and the palette window changed to reflect the colors in that image. "See any difference in the number of colors?"

"Apparently, there are more colors," Jeremy answered, "even though the images still look very much alike."

"Correct. There are actually 256 colors in this particular image's palette. And if you look closely, many of the colors look very close in shade and hue. One of the researchers in the field actually coined the term color buddies to refer to this phenomenon. When information is hidden in an image by S-Tools, new palette entries are created. These extra colors are an indication that we're likely dealing with an image that has information hidden in it because the image no longer follows what is considered to be standard operating procedure when creating and saving a digital image. The color buddies are added when an application uses Least Significant Bit modification to embed information in the image."

"Oh yeah, I read about LSB modification when I was doing my own research at the beginning of this case." Jeremy smiled proudly and continued. "So your team is using this to check images manually for hidden information?" he asked.

Palette of Image Two in GIMP

"It's one of the ways. It's not definitive by any means, but it provides a clue." Tyler closed the palette window but left the two images open on the desktop. "We also look at the histogram of each image. It can be useful, but not always. Let's look at that now so that you can see how it changes between the two images." Tyler moved his mouse pointer up to the Dialogs option on the menu at the top of one image and waited as the small window showing the histogram appeared.

Jeremy looked at the new window that appeared, uncertain about what it meant. He watched as Tyler zoomed in on the image, showing more pixilation within the image. "So you zoomed in on the image, Tyler. What's that for?"

"We're zoomed in so that you can see the actual detail in each of the images," he replied. "Once you get down that deep you can see the actual pixels in the image, which means you have a better chance of seeing deformations in the image caused by the steganographic process." He highlighted the histogram window then clicked on the first image. The graph shown in the smaller window was now the histogram for image one.

"This is the histogram for the first image," he began. "Do you know what a histogram is?"

"Not really."

"Okay. Histograms measure the distribution of the tones, from dark to light, in an image. So, for example, this histogram shows the distribution of the dark and light tones in this particular image. The darker tones are reflected on the left side of the histogram window, and the lighter tones are reflected farther to the right side."

"So since the image is a darker image," answered Jeremy, "the histogram reflects that by showing the colors all on the darker side of the graph. Does that simply mean that most of the colors are darker tones?"

"Exactly. This is a normal histogram for an image that is based in darker colors like this one is. And if you look at the pixilation in the image window, now that we've zoomed in, you can see that the pixels are arranged in similar colors."

"Okay, I can see that," responded Jeremy.

Image 1 Histogram in GIMP

"Now let's look at the second image, the one with the hidden information in it," Tyler continued. "Now, again, please remember that this is not a conclusive means for detecting steganography. It's simply a manual means for analysis. It can help us reduce the number of potential targets that we need to revisit later."

Tyler clicked on the second image and brought the histogram window back to the foreground of the desktop. He zoomed in on the second image, just as he had done with the first image. "Now what do you see?"

"The image looks much more grainy, and the histogram covers more area on the right side of the graph," Jeremy responded back.

"Right," Tyler answered. "The pixels in the image are no longer so evenly matched. The colors look distorted because many of the pixels in the image have changed color. That's why the image looks so incredibly grainy. Instead of smooth areas of similar colored pixels, we now have an image that has several different colors of pixel within each area of the image. What do you get from the image and histogram combined?"

"The pixels that have been altered in the second image tend to be lighter colors, which might explain why the histogram had predominately moved over toward the right side of the graph, where the lighter tones are located."

"Excellent analysis. You're right," said Tyler. "You'd make a great analyst," he laughed. "The lines on the histogram reflect that fact that there are more colors in the light tone category than on the darker tone side. Great work, Jeremy. You're a quick study; that's for sure."

Jeremy smiled broadly. "I'd be lying if I said I wasn't interested in pursuing the analysis work at some point. But I should probably at least finish up this case before I take off and leave Neil hanging. Besides, it's good to have the experience on both sides of the fence, don't you think?"

"Definitely," Tyler answered. "But there is one more thing you should be aware of when you look at images this way. Remember how I said that this is not a conclusive means for determining whether an image has been modified as a carrier?"

"Yeah, I remember that."

"Well, the reason is that there are some digital images that just have been so compressed and mutilated by amateur graphics talents that the images may look like this even if they don't have steganography in them. This manual check was just one of the ways we look. Consider it more of another means of validation. It's not the *only* symptom of the problem, but it's one of them."

"All right," Jeremy replied. "I'll keep that in mind."

Image 2 Histogram in GIMP

"Great. There are some other means for looking for possible targets," he continued. "Each one of them depends on what tool created the steganography. For example, the steganography created by S-Tools on a GIF image will produce a different form of distortion on an image than using something like JPEG Hide and Seek to hide information in a JPG image. Does that make sense?"

"I think I understand what you're saying," Jeremy answered honestly, "but it might help if you had another example for me."

"Okay, that's cool. Let me boot back into Windows so that I can show you another tool we use to hunt for steganography." Tyler closed the two images on the desktop and then shut down GIMP. After logging out of the graphical desktop, he restarted the computer and waited as Windows loaded. This next tool is actually a commercial tool published by the same company that put out the Gargoyle™ product I showed you a couple of weeks ago, WetStone Technologies. It's called Stego Analyst™."

Tyler browsed through the panel on the left side of the Stego Analyst™ interface until he was in the directory on his hard drive that contained his target images. He carefully dragged the thumbnail of the first image and dropped it into the left pane of the right window and then dragged the second icon into the right pane of the same window. "All right, Jeremy, here are two new images that I use for demonstrations like this. These pictures are from the Japanese Sword Museum in Tokyo. The image on the left is the original image, and the one on the right has information hidden in it."

"I can't say that I see any difference between the two images, Tyler," Jeremy laughed embarrassedly.

"That's not unusual. Don't be embarrassed." Tyler looked at Jeremy as he spoke. "I wouldn't expect you to know any of this unless you had been trained or been doing much more detailed research on your own. The simple fact is that there really is no noticeable difference between these two images, at least to the human eye."

"Really," Jeremy asked. "What do you mean? My vision is perfect, but I still can't see a difference."

Tyler smiled. "It's not that your eyes are any less capable of focusing on objects, but that the design of your eye is such that you have difficulty making out particular colors. You might live your entire life without knowing that. To start with, you probably learned something about your eyes when you were a kid in school. The eye detects light and color via cells called rods and cones because of their shape. Do you remember any of that?"

"Vaguely. I do know that those are the cells that transmit light and color from the eye to the brain."

"Good. What you need to understand is that the rods are simply rod-shaped cells that surround the perimeter of the retina and mostly send information to the brain about the black and white colors we see. There are normally over 120 million of these rod-shaped cells situated around the edge of the retina. These are the cells that help your eyes adjust to a darkened room. They tend to be more sensitive to light."

"The cones, however," Tyler continued, "are concentrated in the middle of retina. These cone-shaped cells basically are classified into three categories based on the wavelength of light they are sensitive to. About two-thirds of the cones in a person's eye are sensitive to the longer wave-lengths. This sensitivity causes our eyes to be more adept at seeing warm colors, versus the cooler colors."

"So when you're talking about warm colors you're talking about red, oranges, and yellows, correct?" Jeremy said. He was enjoying the conversation because no one had ever gone this in-depth with him.

"Yes," replied Tyler. "And the cooler colors are the blues and greens."

"All right, I'm with you now," Jeremy answered. "I just wanted to be sure we were on the same sheet of music."

"No problem at all. So to make a long story short, we can't see the discrete changes in the images because most of the changes made during the steganographic process affect those cooler colors, they ones we nor-mally have difficulty seeing anyway. The example I'm using here has lots of cool colors in it, so I don't really expect you to see any changes yet. There are a lot of varying shades of green and blue in those bushes, trees, fence, and rock. So let's look at the tool now. I'll show you how we can see changes in the image that aren't necessarily obvious to our eyes."

"Stego Analyst™ makes it relatively easy for us to go through the images, either manually or automated. We can look at single images, as we are doing here, or we can run the tool against an entire drive or directory of images. That's how we originally found the images on Layla's drive. I'll show you the automated scans later, but let's look at how steganography affects JPEG images."

"Do we look at the palettes on JPG images," Jeremy asked, "as we did with the GIF images?"

"Nope. Actually, we're going to look at some other characteristics of the images. The colors in the palette won't help us because JPG images aren't necessarily locked into a maximum number of colors. JPG images can have as many as 16.7 million colors in their palette, which is considered *true color*. We're going to look at distortions in the other layers of the image, areas the human eye doesn't discern on their own. Stego Analyst™ lets us break the images out into Hue, Saturation, Intensity, and more. It's in those layers that we'll actually be looking for the changes to the image."

Stego Analyst™ Normal Image View

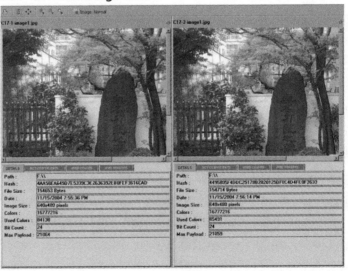

"Do you know how JPG images work?" Tyler asked Jeremy. "It's fine if you don't. I just need to know how much detail to give you."

"No, actually," Jeremy started, "I never got that deep into my research before things went nuts."

"Hmmm, let me think about the easiest way to explain this to you, then," replied Tyler. "Okay, first off, JPG is *not* an image format. It's actually a compression standard."

"Are you saying that images aren't actually created in JPG format?"

"That's right, Jeremy. The raw image data is taken and compressed with the JPEG standard to create a standard .JPG image file. Basically, it divides each image into 8- by 8-pixel blocks. Then the JPEG standard calculates the Discrete Cosine Transform, or DCT, of that block. The result of that mathematical algorithm is called the DCT coefficient, and in its simplest sense is a single color that will represent the colors of all pixels in each 8- by 8-pixel block. It's a color average. The result is that the image loses some of its detail, but can be compressed to significantly smaller sizes."

"Okay, without getting too deep into the weeds," responded Jeremy, "what does that mean for an image that has been modified? I'm interested in how this works, I'm just not honestly sure if I'm ready for all the details yet." He laughed as he considered what he had just said. "You know, it sounds kind of dumb when it comes out like that. I really do want to know everything, but it's probably safer if we take it slow. I don't want to miss anything that might come in handy later."

Tyler laughed with Jeremy. "I totally understand. I'm the same way. I just don't normally have the forethought to slow down and make sure I understand everything fully before I move ahead. Sometimes I just get too excited to learn everything. What it comes down to is that we're not totally certain why this happens the way it does, at least not yet. We have some guesses, but nothing concrete."

Tyler changed the image view inside the Stego Analyst™ tool by clicking the Image button directly above the two images. "Let's look at the Intensity of the images. You'll notice that we can't see much difference between the two images in this view either. The colors in the image haven't changed enough to affect the intensity, which is the basic brightness of the pixel, black being the darkest and white being the brightest. So, as you'll see soon, the colors have changed in hue and saturation during the steganographic process, but their intensity remains relatively unchanged."

"Yeah, you're right," Jeremy answered. "I can't really see any difference in the two images at all. But it sort of makes sense with the way you explained it. If the intensity of the color had changed in many pixels, it might start to be more noticeable to the casual observer looking at the image."

"Tools like this one make it a lot easier to find images that have potential hidden payloads. Without them, I'm not sure we'd ever find anything," Tyler laughed.

Stego Analyst™ Intensity View

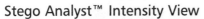

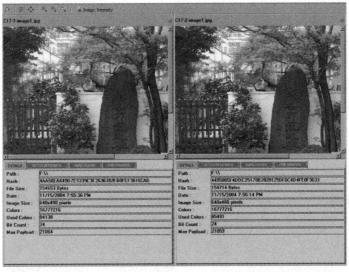

"Let's look at the view of the saturation of the colors in the image," said Tyler as he put his hand on the mouse again. He clicked on the Image button directly above the two images again and scrolled down to the Saturation option. Jeremy watched as the images appeared to change into the inverse of what they were just seconds before.

"As I mentioned before, all we have to go on at this point is speculation about why this occurs. But if you look at the colors in the stone, you'll see that the DCT coefficient has somehow affected the saturation of the colors in those blocks. Saturation is defined as how much gray each color contains. The more gray a pixel contains, the less saturated it is with color. Whatever the applications are doing to hide the payload in the image, it's increasing or decreasing the amount of gray in these blocks."

This last point intrigued Jeremy. "So maybe it's working along the same lines as the LSB modification in the GIF images," he said. "It would make sense."

"That's sort of what we're wrestling with now," Tyler responded with a grin. "But no one really wants to be the one to say beyond a doubt that this is the way it works, you know?"

"Oh sure, I can understand that."

"But regardless of the actual reason," Tyler continued, "we know that images that have been modified with JP Hide and Seek will show these clues. If the payload is large enough when compared with the size of the carrier, you'll have these blocks showing up all over in the Saturation view of the image."

Stego Analyst™ Saturation View

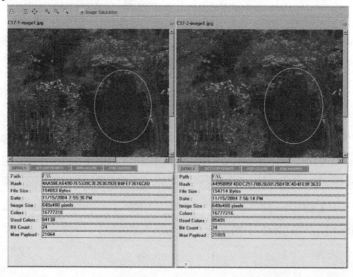

"Let's look at the hue of these two images. You can see the changes in the color of each block more clearly." Tyler gripped the mouse in his hand and clicked through the same sequence of options again, but chose the Hue option from the scroll-down menu instead. The images flashed again quickly as Jeremy and Tyler watched.

"Whoa," said Jeremy, "that's a big change from the last view. You can really see the blocks now."

"Yeah," Tyler replied, "it's pretty obvious now; isn't it? I just wish we knew for certain why the images show these signs when they've been modified. But we're all so far behind on the detection side of things that we're really working with sticks and rocks trying to find people who are working with hammers and axes."

"I was noticing the fact that there are very few detection tools out there right now." Jeremy remembered doing his initial research just weeks before. There really weren't many options for the good guys. "In fact, I'm not sure I had even really heard of this product either."

"Well, we actually got word of the product from a conference we had attended a while back," Tyler responded. "The concept was really cool, and we didn't have anything like it in our toolbox. But I think you're right. There aren't really many options, are there?" Tyler looked back at the current view of the images. The boxy look of the stone in the image was easy to identify and at least it provided some sort of clue. But Tyler couldn't shake the feeling that they were farther behind in the game than even he or Jeremy thought. "I just wish we were further ahead in our understanding. The fact that we know the information is hidden there doesn't replace the fact that it's going to be damn hard to find potential payloads on the Internet."

"We can do it; it just won't be easy." Jeremy smiled at Tyler. "It's really interesting stuff, but it would be much cooler if there weren't real people's lives at stake. To be honest, though, if we don't step up to the challenge and evolve our detection technology to the same level as the creation technology, we're going to be in a world of hurt in the years to come."

"Ain't it the truth," said Tyler thoughtfully. "For now, though, we'll do the best we can with what we have. There are a few people out there working on the problem. But remember, this was all just the manual verification stuff. There's really no way to perform this type of activity on all the potential images on Web pages, newsgroups, and peer-to-peer networks."

"So what do you use instead?" asked Jeremy.

"We've got a couple of automated scripts that we've written and tied into some of the detection mechanisms we've written, but we also use another piece of software that comes with Stego Analyst™. Want to see how it works?"

"Absolutely!"

Stego Analyst™ Hue View

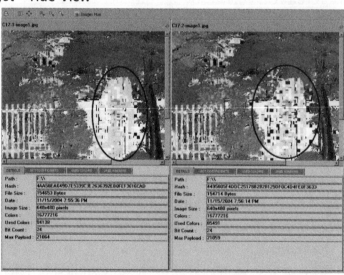

Tyler closed out the Stego Analyst™ interface and maneuvered the mouse pointer back through the Start menu until he came to the program icon he was looking for. "This is Stego Watch™," he said with a smile. "It's helping us scan a good deal of the web, looking for files that might have information hidden within them. It can also be used to scan a computer looking for steganography. We used it on Layla's computer. Once the program identifies suspect files, we do the manual verification with the other tools I've already shown you."

"The software comes with nine sets of separate algorithms that all look for different anomalies within binary files. Some of the algorithms work against images, and some work against audio files. The image algorithms again are split up into palette-based images, or lossy images. Lossy is just a fancy term used to refer to compressed images where information is lost as the size of the image is made smaller."

Tyler highlighted the window that had just popped up on the screen and started speaking again. "This is the main window. There is a trick to the software. It requires you to register the algorithms you'll want to use with the software before it will even let you start a session. When you use the tool in the future, make sure you remember that."

Jeremy smiled at Tyler and replied, "Sounds easy enough. I suppose that even if I forget, the simple fact that the software won't start will clue me in to what I've managed to forget."

Tyler laughed. "You're probably right. There's an indicator at the bottom left of the main window that lets you know if there is an active session or not. It will be red if you don't have a session and green if you have one running. So let's get our algorithms registered with the software so we can get started on the actual scan process."

"Sounds good," Jeremy responded.

Stego Watch

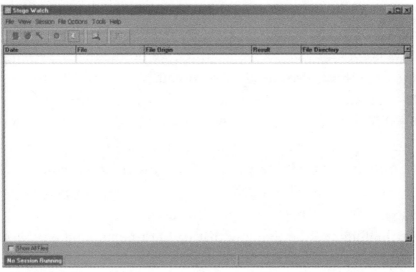

Tyler clicked the File option at the top of the Stego Watch™ inter-face and scrolled down to the first option on the pop-up, Stego Detection Algorithms. "This is how we go about registering the algo-rithms for the software," he stated offhandedly as a new window popped up in front of the main interface. "There are two tabs at the top of the window. One lets you actually register the algorithms, and the other will show you the currently registered algorithms."

The default window showed no algorithms being used with the soft-ware. Jeremy watched intently as Tyler clicked on the Register tab on the new window. A text entry box appeared with the title Dll Name. "This box allows a user to type the path to the dll algorithm file they want to register. If you're not sure what the exact file path is, you can click the Browse button, here."

Stego Watch Algorithm Registration 1

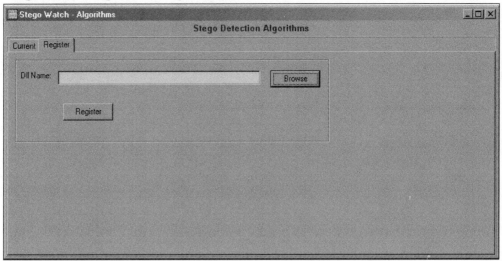

Tyler clicked the Browse button and the Open dialogue appeared. The files in the selection window appeared to be the algorithms that shipped with the product. "Are those the actual algorithms?" Jeremy asked Tyler.

"Yes, those are the default algorithms that ship with the product. It's nice that we don't have to search for them. Let's go ahead and register them all, just in case we decide to use them." Tyler clicked the top file in the list, LossyCheck-A.dll, and while holding the Shift key on his keyboard, clicked the last file in the list. "Okay, so now that all the files are highlighted, let's click Open and look at the currently registered algorithms to make sure everything is kosher."

Stego Watch Algorithm Registration 2

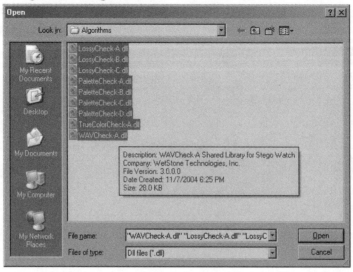

Tyler clicked the Open button at the bottom right-hand corner of the window and watched as the window changed back to the previous window. The only difference that Jeremy could see was the full path to the files he had highlighted was now in the text entry box. Tyler clicked the Register button.

Stego Watch Algorithm Registration 3

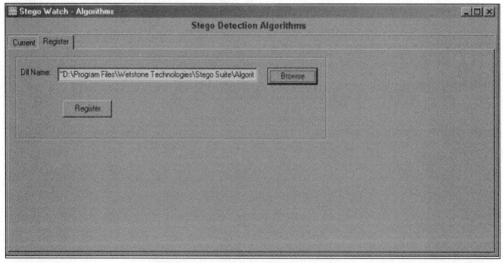

When he was certain the software had accepted the registration of the algorithms he had chosen, Tyler moved the mouse pointer to the Current tab. "Let's see what information it gives us here," he said, looking back at Jeremy. Jeremy smiled back, but said nothing.

Tyler turned back to face the screen again, but continued talking. "The information given in this window is so that the investigator will know what information the algorithm looks for. Since steganography corrupts the normal default structure of the binary file in question, these algorithms look for those deviations from what is considered normal. Sometimes there are false positives, but the software closes the gap between the unknown and the suspect in relatively short order."

"Does your team use it often?" Jeremy asked. He wondered how much use these tools would see in the course of an average day.

"We don't use it every day, no," came the reply from Tyler. "But it's useful enough when we need it that we don't let the license expire. I would guess it gets used one to three times a month now, depending on our caseload. But that's all there is to registering the algorithms. It normally needs to be done only when the software is loaded up the first time. Now let's get down to business."

Stego Watch Current Algorithms

Algorithm	Dll	Level	Paletted	Raw	Grayscale	8-bit BMP	8-l
WAVCheck-A	D:\Program Files\Wetstone Technologies...	Quick					
LossyCheck-A	D:\Program Files\Wetstone Technologies...	Extensive	X				
LossyCheck-B	D:\Program Files\Wetstone Technologies...	Extensive	X				
LossyCheck-C	D:\Program Files\Wetstone Technologies...	Extensive	X				
PaletteCheck-A	D:\Program Files\Wetstone Technologies...	Quick	X			X	
PaletteCheck-B	D:\Program Files\Wetstone Technologies...	Quick	X			X	
PaletteCheck-C	D:\Program Files\Wetstone Technologies...	Extensive	X			X	
PaletteCheck-D	D:\Program Files\Wetstone Technologies...	Quick	X		X	X	
TrueColorCheck-A	D:\Program Files\Wetstone Technologies...	Quick		X			

Stego Watch - Algorithms

Stego Detection Algorithms

Current | Register

"So what's next?" asked Jeremy.

"We need to set up the session options for our scans," came the reply. Tyler selected the session option from the menu at the top of the main interface and scrolled down to Session Options. The two men watched as the session options window popped up.

Session Options 1

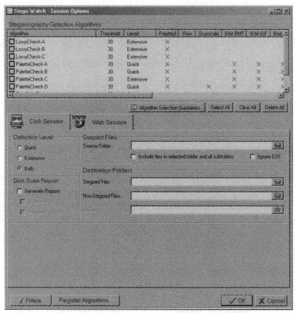

"Wow. There are a lot of options," Jeremy piped in as he saw the window.

"Yeah, they built in a lot of flexibility. You see all those algorithms we just registered, on the top of the window?"

"Yeppers," Jeremy replied.

"Well, you can finally see what each algorithm looks for if you click the Algorithm Selection Guidelines button here." Tyler clicked the button and a new window popped up. Jeremy looked at the new window and saw that it gave detailed explanations about each of the algorithms and what they looked for. "Just in case you need to know which one to use later down the road," Tyler assured Jeremy.

Stego Watch™ Algorithm Selection Guidelines

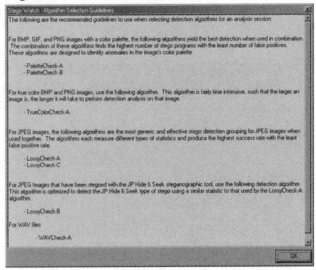

"Why don't we stick with just a few of the algorithms for now. I'm going to simulate a web scan session, then we'll drop back and scan the local hard disk and see what we find," Tyler said as his mouse moved across the interface, selecting all the palette-based algorithms on the selection screen at the top of the window. "I'm also going to skip the scan for audio files just to keep things quick and simple," he finished.

"What's the difference between the quick scans and the extensive scans?" Jeremy asked.

"They're just more aggressive in the anomalies they look for during the scans. They tend to take longer, and it takes more manual analysis to narrow down the potential false positives. We're going to run it, but it's likely to pop up more results than are really there. But since this is just a test run, it won't hurt to show you what the findings look like when the scan is complete."

"Excellent. Well, what's next?" Jeremy chimed in.

"We need to set up the directories to save all the various files in, and we need to specify the web address of the web site we're going to run our test scan against," Tyler answered. "I've got a friend over at this particular organization who knows I'm going to run this scan today. I told him

I'd do it as a favor as long as he promised not to press charges." Tyler and Jeremy both laughed. "We should be okay," Tyler finished.

Session Options 2

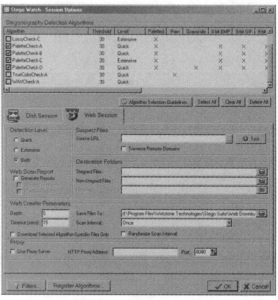

Jeremy watched intently as Tyler entered in the various directories the software would use to save the different files generated during the scans. "Why don't you put all the files into the same directory?" he asked. "It would save you some typing and keep everything where you can find it."

Tyler turned around again to face Jeremy before answering. "It's standard procedure. We want to keep the suspect files away from the benign ones. That way there's no confusion when we're doing the actual manual investigation. The reports directory just keeps all the reports from our scans in a standard location on our hard drive. We date code all the reports when we're done running, and we add in the case number. It's all very easy to follow."

"That makes sense. I had never really thought about it like that," Jeremy answered.

"You'll be thinking like an analyst in no time at all," Tyler laughed. "We just have to get you down here with us." He turned back around to face the computer screen. "Notice that I've got the Generate Report button selected. This tells the software to create a full report for me once the scan has completed. The report it generates isn't exactly the format we'd prefer, but since they get dumped out in PDF files, we can manipulate them without much problem."

"Hey," Jeremy began, "what's the test button for; the one next to the web address you entered?"

"Oh, this?" Tyler said as he clicked on the button.

The two men watched as Internet Explorer popped up on the screen. In a matter of seconds, the web address Tyler had entered in the text box was pulled up in the browser. "It allows us to verify that the web address is the actual one we want to scan. We wouldn't want to be running these tests on the wrong web sites," Tyler continued. He closed out the web browser and said, "Why don't we go ahead and start our scan?"

"Okay," Jeremy responded.

Session Options 3

Tyler clicked the OK button at the bottom right on the current window and watched as it disappeared. The mouse pointer moved up the screen to the Session option on the menu bar. Tyler navigated down to the Start Web Session item on the drop-down menu.

Jeremy watched as the blue status bar at the bottom of the screen moved from left to right, indicating how close it was to completion. He almost noticed that the red indicator bar that had originally stated that no session was currently running was now green, indicating that a scan was underway.

Stego Watch Web Session Running

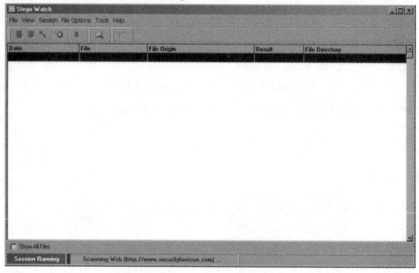

Tyler waited until the web scan was finished before he closed it out and started from scratch. There had been no results in the window after the scan. "I didn't figure we'd find anything, but it gave you a good idea of what happens during a web session. Let's run a quick scan on my hard drive. I know there are images with hidden information on my drive. Most of it's from research, but the results will let me show you how to interact with the findings."

Jeremy watched Tyler step through many of the same options as before, only this time, he chose the disk session option from the menu options. Most of the variables were the same as he had seen with the web session they had just run.

Again the status bar at the bottom of the screen ticked across from left to right. It took a little longer to run this scan. Jeremy assumed it was because there were actually more results. Soon, the results started to appear in the scan window.

Stego Watch Disk Session Beginning

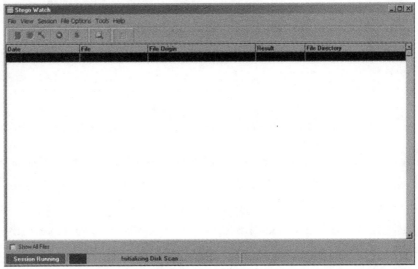

The two men watched as the scan continued running, filling the screen with the results it had found from the hard disk. "Geez, man. How many files do you have on this disk?" Jeremy said laughing.

"I have enough to test with," Tyler said as he smiled back at the younger man. "But honestly, this is a smaller disk. Still, it's got enough test data on it that we'll be able to see some results. See, it's not taking too long. We're already 23% done with the session."

Jeremy laughed and continued watching the screen. Strange symbols aligned themselves next to some of the findings. Others seemingly had no results at all. A few more of the images actually had a percentage designation next to them.

Disk Scan Progress

After a few more minutes, the two men were rewarded with a *Session Ended* dialogue in the bottom left corner. "Ah," Tyler began, "there we go. It's done now." He looked down at the status bar in irritation. "I really thought I had more stuff on this disk, but the scan says I have only 253 files that could be processed based on the algorithms I selected. I must have picked the wrong drive."

"No big deal, dude," Jeremy responded. "At least we have something to look at. Why don't you explain what this all means? Right now I'm making wild-haired assumptions." He grinned wryly at Tyler who grinned back.

"Okay, I get the hint," he replied.

Disk Scan Session Ended

"Let's organize these results a little better," he said as he maneuvered the mouse pointer to the *Result* column at the top of the window. The results shifted. When the reorganization was complete, the top of the window was filled from the top with the images that were rated highest for possible steganography. "There, that's better," Tyler said once the results had been rearranged.

"The results at the top of the list were scored by the algorithms we selected," Tyler began again. "If you recall, we selected all the algorithms that work on paletted images. All the results at the top of the list are GIF files, which are palette images."

"So what do we do now?" Jeremy inquired.

"Well, we could do any number of things. If we highlight a file, we can right-click on it and see our options." He right-clicked on the top file, and Jeremy watched a new pop-up menu appear. The options were simple, but Jeremy noticed one in particular.

"You mean we can pull the image up directly in Stego Analyst™?" he asked.

"Yep, pretty slick, huh?"

"That's really convenient," Jeremy replied. "But aside from the manual verification stuff, which we've already covered, what do all those symbols mean next to each file?"

Tyler laughed. "Heh, I think they've heard that question before. They even built in a legend for all the icons they use for descriptions." He clicked on the Help option at the top of the window and selected the Result Icon Legend from the menu. "These are the icons the software uses to describe the findings."

"Ah, that's cool," Jeremy began, "But can I ask you another question, Tyler? I'm confused about one step in this entire process. It's a process I see as very important if we're ever going to have appropriate evidence in these cases."

Result Icon Legend

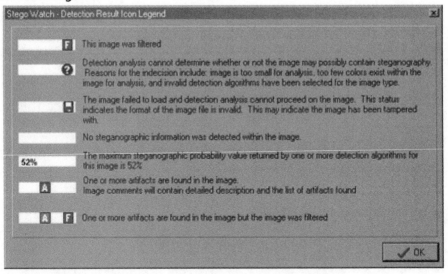

"Sure," Tyler responded. "What's your question?"

Jeremy stopped for a minute to think about how best to phrase his question. "During my own research, most steganography programs encrypt the payload before hiding the data. It seems to me that we don't have much of a case based on the hypothesis that something is hidden in the file. How does your division handle that?"

"You're very right," came the answer from Tyler. "We can't press charges without proof that something was occurring. We actually have two mechanisms for decrypting suspect files. In fact, this software comes with a tool for that, but it's still in the very early phases of its capability. That tool is called Stego Break™. Our other option is the National Security Agency. They do quite a bit of breaking for us when the tool isn't enough to break it."

"Can you show me the built-in tool?" Jeremy asked. "I'm pretty sure the NSA isn't going to share their capabilities with us." He laughed.

Tyler laughed aloud as well. "You're probably right," he said with a smile. "Let's take a look at Stego Break™ instead. We can invoke the program from either Stego Watch by right-clicking on an image or by itself from the Windows Start menu. Let's break it up by itself and show you how it works. It's a fairly useful program, and I know the programmers are working on adding additional capabilities that will only increase its value."

Tyler closed out the Stego Watch™ software and opened the Stego Break™ program from the Start menu. The window that popped up looked quite a bit different than the other WetStone applications. Jeremy thought it looked more like a wizard application. "Is this a wizard application?"

"Yes, it is, in fact," Tyler said. "They tried to make the interface pretty easy to use. So why don't you sit down and work through it yourself."

"Cool," Jeremy said, trying to not sound so excited. Tyler stood up from his chair, and Jeremy moved into his place. Once he got comfortable, Jeremy read through the contents of the window and clicked the Next button. "This really does look simple," he said.

"Oh, it is. We're only going to have one hitch with this piece of software, and that's because I don't have a dictionary loaded on this computer. I totally forgot. Sorry, dude," Tyler said, trying his best to look worried.

"Ha! It's okay. So let's get going on this. Neil is still expecting me back upstairs at some point today. I don't want him to think I've already moved down here without telling him." Jeremy shot Tyler a wry grin.

Stego Break Dialogue 1

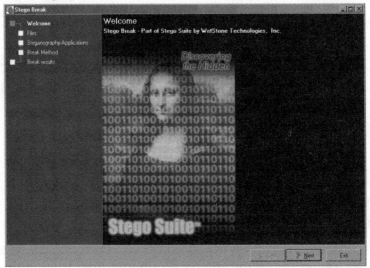

When the next window popped up, it was obvious to Jeremy that the application was looking for files to crack. Reading through the instructions on the screen, he saw that he needed to right-click on the interface and use the drop-down menu to select files to add to the password crack routine. Doing as he had been told, he right-clicked and chose the first option from the menu that appeared. "Where are the files you want me to add, Tyler?"

"The best bet is just to pick an image on the H drive," he replied.

Stego Break Dialogue 2

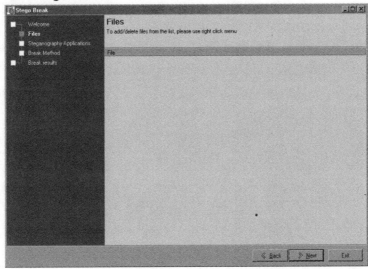

Jeremy browsed through the test computer's hard drive, finally settling on a random image. "We're just doing this to see how it works, right? Since we don't have a dictionary loaded, we're not going to be able to really put the software to the test."

"Well, there are some other options that we'll test, but yes, it doesn't really matter which image you choose this time. I'll give you a DVD that contains some of the dictionaries we use when we do this for real. For now, let's just press ahead and we'll make due with what we have available."

"Great. So here's an image we can use. That should work fine." Jeremy clicked the Next button and moved on to the next screen.

Stego Break Dialogue 3

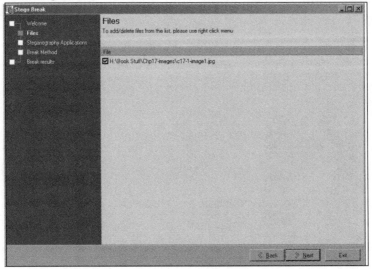

"Okay," Tyler began. "We're looking at the various applications that Stego Break™ has the ability to crack the encryption on. Right now, the software can break passwords for JP Hide and Seek, F5, Jsteg, and Camouflage. I know the developers are still working on other programs as well, but it takes time to develop. But it's like you said before, at least someone is out there trying to solve the problem. Pick any of the applications in the list, but leave out Camouflage. The software can crack all the others together, but it requires that Camouflage be attempted on its own."

"Okay, that's good to know," Jeremy replied. He selected the boxes next to all the applications, with the exception of the Camouflage, then he clicked the Next button.

Stego Break Dialogue 4

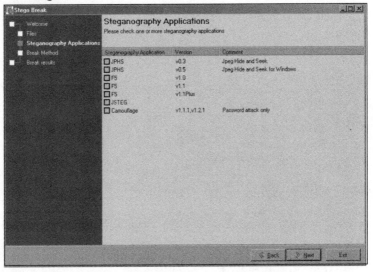

Stego Break Dialogue 5

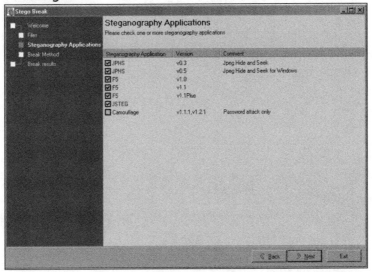

"There are three options on this screen," Tyler began. We can use existing dictionaries to crack the passwords, we can choose a new dictionary, or we can test against a single word. Let's just use the word test for this demonstration. We're not likely to break anything with it, but it lets you see how the program works."

"All right," Jeremy replied. He promptly entered the password Tyler had asked for and pressed the Break button on the bottom right corner of the interface.

Stego Break Dialogue 6

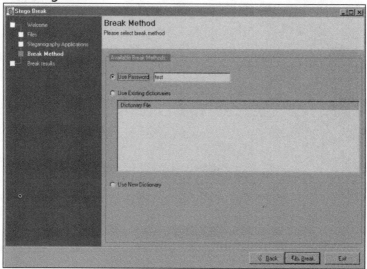

It took only a few seconds to run the check on a single file using the single password that Jeremy had entered. As they had thought, it hadn't broken the file.

Stego Break Dialogue 7

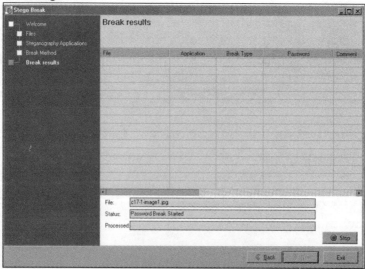

"So, that's it, eh," Jeremy said with a smile.

"Yeah, that's it. We send a lot of the files we can't break with this off to a team at the National Security Agency for cracking. It takes significantly longer, but there are some things that we just don't have the resources to do ourselves." Tyler looked at the clock on his desk. "Whoa. You've been here for a long time. You had better get back upstairs."

"You're right. Neil is probably having a cow," Jeremy replied with a smile. "We're still working on figuring out when and where the next attack is supposed to take place. It seems so surreal sometimes, almost not even real. Oh hey, can I get that DVD from you, the one with the dictionaries on it?"

"Oh yeah, hang on." Tyler turned around and faced his cabinets about his desk. He opened the one on the far left and picked through a pile of CDs. "Ah, here you go." He took one of the CDs off the shelf and closed the cabinet again. Turning around, he handed the DVD to Jeremy. "Here, use this to test the software back at your office. You have any questions about how it works, or are you okay?"

"I think I'm good to go. Our copy of the software comes in tomorrow." He stood up from the chair and walked toward the opening of the cube. "I'll play around with it. It should be good for my research. Do you mind if I come back down sometime?"

"Not at all; help yourself. We're supposed to be adding your badge to our system in the next couple of days, so keep testing it when you come down and maybe next time you won't have to knock on the door," Tyler laughed. "Besides, soon this could be a permanent arrangement."

"I hope so," said Jeremy. "I'll talk to you later. Take care. Do me a favor and let me know if anything cool pops up in the next few days." With that, he turned and walked toward the door of the office.

Chapter 18: Taking Back Control

December 8, 2004

Jimmy sat back in the hard wooden chair and waited as the web browser loaded. He had quickly become a regular at the library in this small town, using the computer several times a day, sometimes for hours at a time. His resolve and motivation had been strengthened when the perfect location for the second phase of attacks had occurred to him. The inability of the local authorities to secure the area, combined with the sheer number of Americans, made the target attractive. He had spent time wondering why this particular idea had never occurred to him or Salah before that moment. But in time, he had come to the conclusion that Allah was aware that Salah would betray the rest of the group and had saved that target for a time when it was safe to do so.

The web browser finally came up, and Jimmy typed the address to his web e-mail. There had been fewer and fewer e-mails messages sent back and forth between the team members as they grew increasingly more comfortable with the new mechanism for communicating. Jimmy had sent an e-mail message to the list of original group members, telling them all that he was changing accounts and would no longer be using the web page as a means of communication. *Reply to this e-mail if you have the motivation to continue,* he had written. *I will contact you with the new information.*

A few of the members had been lost, but the loss to his overall plan was minimal. Jimmy had believed that there were likely too many people involved anyway, too many possible weak links in the chain. Any one of them could damage this project if they were captured. This belief had grown stronger since the capture of one of the men from the first phase. But that was Salah's fault. He had condemned that man, along with himself, when he went to the American authorities.

The young man smiled when he saw that there were no new e-mail messages in his mailbox. Everyone who was going to move on to the next phase was already in line with the new means of communication. That was good. Jimmy entered a new web address and waited as the new site loaded. *It might be slow,* he thought, *but it's all I have right now.*

The web page came up quickly in the browser, obviously already having been cached somewhere on the tiny hard drive. It was a USENET portal, a web-based mechanism for accessing the USENET newsgroups. The newsgroups had been around for decades, used mostly by hobbyists who shared information, pictures, and other files on whatever the topic was in that particular group. There were literally thousands of newsgroups, hundreds of which had hundreds of new messages each day.

The use of newsgroups as a communication mechanism was something that had been mentioned very early in his initial conversations with Salah. In fact, until recently, he had never even seen a real newsgroup. Jimmy had been stuck at a decision point. He could no longer reliably use the web page for communication, plus it didn't provide much in the way of back-and-forth communication between the team members. There were some limitations on the use of newsgroups, especially from a computer as old as the one he was using.

He needed a group that was very popular, with hundreds of participants from around the world posting messages to it each day. That would allow his group's messages to blend in, go almost unseen and unnoticed. He also needed a group that would allow attachments. Two week ago, he had been experimenting with the newsgroup and posted a picture to a group only to get flamed by the group members for posting a binary file to a discussion-only group. From that point on, Jimmy had concentrated his search to only those groups that allowed binary posting and still met the other requirements.

The computer he was using had become a constant source of frustration as well. Most of the USENET newsgroup reader applications downloaded the large number of message, message headers, and attachments to the local disk. The hard drive on this particular computer wasn't large enough to accommodate that much storage. From a more practical perspective, it was likely much safer to not have the newsgroups archived on a local drive. There's no telling who might be snooping in on his activities, although he highly doubted any of that might be occurring considering the fact that the only other person he ever found in the library was the librarian.

The online newsgroup browser was a subscription service, and Jimmy had paid for an entire year, up front and in cash, to avoid any probing questions into who he might be and what his interests were at the time. All the messages were available for him to view and download. The problem he had run into was creating new covert content that could be loaded onto the library computer and sent out to the newsgroup. To solve his problem, he had purchased an older model laptop, but one still equipped with a USB port, floppy drive, and a CD burner. He could download new attachments to a few floppy disks that he would bring with him to the library each day. Those disks could then be loaded onto his laptop and the information decoded. When he wanted to send new information out to the group, he would create his content on the laptop and then burn it to a CD. The library's computer would accept normal CDs, allowing him to store a tremendous amount of data for dissemination to the rest of the group.

The laptop wasn't all that powerful, but it had been cheap and would easily get the job done. It was an old Compaq model running Windows XP Home Edition. Someone apparently had reloaded the laptop at some point in the past because the laptop was certainly older than the currently loaded operating system. The stale gray shell had a small crack near the keyboard. Other than that, the computer showed very few signs of abuse or damage. The difficult part of the entire ordeal had been finding a sufficient number of blank compact disc recordable drives. The only supplier in town had a single spindle that was already half-used. Jimmy had paid the man in advance for 200 more CDs that had come in just seven days ago. All in all, Jimmy had spent a full month's worth of his budget buying the computer supplies and the newsgroup subscription, but he had no intentions of being in this rundown town a year from now. There were other things he wanted to do in his life once this project was completed.

He twisted uncomfortably in the hard wooden chair, his frustration brimming to the surface momentarily. *I hate this chair*, he thought abruptly. As the web site finally loaded within the browser window, he readjusted himself within the chair once more, reminding himself to bring a sweatshirt to sit on next time. Jimmy logged in to the service using his new username and password. The main page came up, giving Jimmy several options of what to do next. His subscription was for a complete account on the Internet, including e-mail and the access to the newsgroups.

When he initially had purchased the account and logged into his personal page with the service, he had been inundated with the sheer number of newsgroups he would have to choose from. Hundreds of those listed had little to no recent traffic, above and beyond the standard spam messages. Other newsgroups had consistent postings, but a relatively low new message count each day.

After several days of searching through the various newsgroups, he had started watching about 15 different groups, looking for the number of messages and the number of images. Several of the groups were related specifically to pornography, whereas a smaller number were strictly hobby groups. In the end, however, Jimmy decided that the groups containing pictures of nude people would only serve as a distraction to the other team members. He had taken to monitoring only a single newsgroup now, alt.pets.dogs.binary.pictures. The dog lovers' group had the next highest volume of traffic each day and wouldn't be so much of a distraction to the others in the group. He needed them to keep their minds on their work. Salah had never wanted to micro-manage each person on the team during the first phase, which Jimmy thought was part of the reason the entire phase failed so miserably. If ensuring success on this next phase meant that he had to personally oversee everything each person did, then so be it. This phase of attacks *would* succeed.

Jimmy's new username, Skeezer, was what he would use to post new messages to the newsgroup. He had e-mailed each person who had responded back to him, in turn, so that each of the team members would know with whom they would be communicating. They were told which newsgroup he had chosen, what software they could use to view the newsgroups, and what password to use in the communication. Each team member knew that messages posted by Skeezer were ones they should read and download. He, in turn, would look for messages posted by each of their names, download the messages onto his floppy disk, and take them back to the shabby little hotel room where he would pull out the hidden information.

Generating the sheer number of dog images was easy enough, too. Each day he would search the Internet, download the various pictures of dogs that popped up in the results, and store them on the floppy disks he carried in his pocket. He then would bring the disks back to his tiny hotel room on the edge of town where he would load them on to the laptop hard drive and use them to hide his messages to the others. He was communicating with the group at least three times a day now, via the dog lovers' newsgroup. Each team member had the ability to ask questions, give input, and receive direction from Jimmy. His days were filled with walking back and forth between the hotel and the library, several times a day, and the occasional stop each day at the restaurant in town.

He never skipped his visit to the restaurant, regardless of how busy his day had been. The food was cheap, hot, and filling. He now knew the waitress by her first name, Lucinda. There was an obvious language barrier, but there was also sufficient attraction between the two to overcome such a small handicap. But he would not let himself become distracted, not yet. When this was all over, he would take her away from here. She would make a good wife.

Jimmy spent his nights alone in the hotel room. There were no distractions to detour him from his mission. There was no telephone. There was no television. No magazines or books, except for the Holy Book, were in his room. His time there was filled with planning. Each night he went back over each of the messages he had received from his team and responded to each one, hiding each message in an image. Once the messages had been hidden, he burned the images to a blank CD using his laptop. The computer at the library had no problem reading the CDs he was burning, and there was plenty of space for him to load all the images he needed, messages included.

The routine he used was set now. It was simple and worked well. He had already run plenty of test messages through the newsgroup; each team member who had survived the transition responding back to him in the same fashion. The first message he sent out to the newsgroup was hidden in the picture of a gold and white Pekingese. It was a map of the French Quarter in New Orleans, complete with street names and addresses. *I need to know where each of you works now,* he began. *Mark the address of your work on this map and send it back to me.* He needed to know where they all were, where they worked, how they could best be used.

French Quarter Grid

The French Quarter was the perfect cover for what he was trying to accomplish. The streets were all very small, and the buildings were crammed together in a cramped layout. There were sewers and drainage grates throughout the entire area. Each night, even when it's not Mardi Gras, hundreds, even thousands, of people are known to pack themselves together in those tight streets, a symbol of America's overindulgence and sinful nature.

The area in and around the French quarter is laid out in grids of nearly perfect squares. Streets and alleyways bisect each other at 90-degree angles, with very few exceptions. The celebrants would likely be in a drunken stupor, slow to respond, making it that much easier to kill them. *Like setting fire to a termite mound*, he thought with a smile on his face. The idea was appealing and reminded him of the American saying, *like shooting fish in a barrel*. There would be nowhere for them to run. Those who did run would trample innocent bystanders in their frenzied eagerness to flee and escape death.

All five of the people he had asked to gain employment in the area had already responded. This was going so much better than he had hoped. He had been able to put all fives pieces of the map together into a single map of the area. He was still planning what they would do, based on where these team members worked and what events were planned in the French Quarter. For the most part, all five had been evenly spread out across the area. *If even one of the bombs goes off that day, hundreds will likely die.*

Team Members' Locations

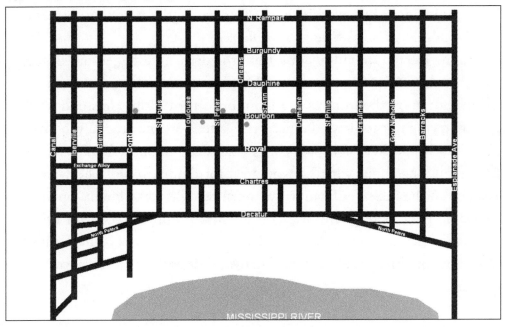

Jimmy looked back at the computer screen and the waiting home page. He had been daydreaming. That had to stop. With so much at stake, he had to stay focused on actively working on the project instead of simply thinking about it. The chair creaked loudly as he sat back up and put his right hand on the computer mouse. He glanced over at the librarian at the front desk. She had not noticed the noise. *She looks as if she's going to fall asleep in her chair*, he thought.

Moving the mouse pointer to the browser window, he clicked on the link that would take him to the newsgroup. There were 93 new messages since the last time he had checked. *Excellent!* He browsed through the messages, looking for familiar names that he knew would contain a communication back to him. He found only two this time. Jimmy pulled a floppy disk from his pocket and slid it into the old drive slot. The drive clicked as the disk was pulled down into place within the computer. He opened the messages one at a time and saved their attachments to the floppy. A slow grinding noise assured Jimmy that the messages' contents were indeed being copied to the disk in the drive. Opening the Windows Explorer window, Jimmy quickly checked to see the two new images on the disk. *Great. Now it's time for some dinner.*

Jimmy ejected the floppy disk from the drive and logged out of his session online. After closing out the browser window, he pushed the grimy button on the front of the monitor to turn it off. He stood up quietly, trying not to draw the librarian's attention and stuffed the disk back into his pocket. As he walked out the front door of the library, he began thinking about what he would eat for dinner. Tonight he would respond to the messages. Tomorrow morning, when the library opened, he would post his responses back on the newsgroup and look for other messages that needed his attention. The heavy wooden door to the library closed behind him, and he walked across the street, toward his favorite restaurant.

Tyler knocked on the door apprehensively. He had never actually come upstairs before. The entire feeling of the surrounding area was cold and businesslike. "Come in," came the response from inside. He turned the handle on his side of the door and opened it slowly. "Hi, Neil," he began, "I've got some information for you."

"Great," Neil replied. "Come on in and have a seat. I hope you're okay with Jeremy being here. You said something about it impacting our investigation into the second phase, so I thought he should be here."

"Actually, that works out great." He smiled at the two men and then took a seat across the desk from Neil in the empty chair next to Jeremy. "The information I have could make all the difference in the world for your case." He laid the white CLASSIFIED folder on the desk in front of him and removed the manila envelope from inside. Untying the red string that kept the envelope closed, he began speaking again. "We were able to confiscate the computers from the three ships attacked in the first phase. We ran some basic analysis on the computers and came across one of the computers that had some clues for your next case." He pulled the documents from the envelope and laid them on top of the folder, sliding the entire collection across the desk toward Neil.

"Are these your findings?" Neil asked as he began fingering through the documents.

"Yes they are," came the response from Tyler. "The computers from two of the ships were clean. If any one was using those, they must have cleared the cache from the browsers and defragged the hard drive every once in a while. The only computer we managed to get anything from was from the same ship that we captured one of the terrorists on."

"Did he leave information on the computer he was using?" Jeremy asked.

"Yes and no, Jeremy," Tyler replied. "He didn't really leave much in the way of actual evidence, but apparently at some point in the past he allowed the browser to store the username and password for his web e-mail. We found lots of these types of accounts on the computer from all three ships, but this one computer had a username not associated with any of the current employees on the ship."

"It says here that you have actually logged in to this e-mail account and retrieved his messages," Neil said with a smile. "Was that something that you did for all the accounts you found?"

"Absolutely, we were taking no chances that someone else who was still onboard one of the original target ships was actually a silent member of the terror group." Tyler looked over at Jeremy. "We had a little fun with that one. A lot of personal stuff goes on via e-mail. But one account signed by a person named Jimmy was sent to an account that had been stored on that one computer. The attachment is under that sheet you're looking at now, Neil. Check it out."

Neil flipped the page he had been reading over and looked at the next page. It certainly looked like an e-mail. It had been printed directly from the web e-mail interface and still had the banner ads in place. After a quick glance through the contents, he slid the page across the desk to Jeremy, who was looking at him expectantly. "It looks like they've moved on to a new means of communication," he said to Jeremy.

Jeremy also read through the e-mail. "They're not going to use the web page anymore."

"Yeah," Tyler started, "it looks like they suspect your friend has gone to the authorities, which is why the last phase didn't pan out so well for them."

"Well," Neil chimed in, "Jimmy seems to want more communication and control over the project. He doesn't sound too satisfied with the one-way communication medium. In fact, he mentions a need to hide in the shadows of a crowd of people talking. What the hell does that mean?"

"It sounds to me as if we're going to need to focus on technology via the Internet that would allow multiple people to communicate with each other without necessarily giving up their identities or e-mail addresses," replied Jeremy.

"That's pretty much the same direction we were headed," replied Tyler. "I've got our analysts watching newsgroups primarily at this point, but we're also checking out some of the online auction sites. I'm still a little concerned about the safety of our star witness, Layla."

"What's causing you so much concern about it?" Neil asked.

"If they know that Salah betrayed them, they're going to try to find her," Tyler began. "Plus, if they know, the chances that Al Qaeda knows as well are pretty high. I'm just wondering what the Al Qaeda members would do to take someone down who had done this to them."

Neil glanced across the table at Jeremy, who was quite certainly upset by the current conversation, but was holding his tongue. "Jeremy, what are your thoughts?"

"Of course, I'm concerned for her safety," he replied, running his fingers through his hair. "And it's not really just the fact that she was a good friend. If we lose her as a source of information and guidance on this, our jobs will all be that much more difficult."

"You're right about that." Neil sat back in his chair and rubbed his chin with his fingers. "We should probably put her under a 24-hour watch. We have very little information to go on at this point, but if we lose her, we're really screwed."

"Keep in mind, guys," Tyler said, "they probably aren't aware that she's even a woman. If that news comes out, she's as good as dead. They'll kill her for sure. Their honor is at stake as well."

"Oh man, I think it's hitting the press today," Neil said nervously. "Someone from the cruise lines leaked the fact that this was indeed a terrorist plot and that someone was already in custody. The State Department wanted to follow up on the story by saying they had one of the leaders of the plot in custody. Layla is about to be brought up on formal charges. Her story will likely be on the front page of every newspaper in the country."

"They what!" Jeremy was furious. "You told me you were going to try to protect her, Neil. You totally lied to me."

"No, Jeremy, I didn't lie. I tried as best I could. But the government needs a sacrifice, or the public will panic. Layla and our other capture are the best candidates." Neil sighed. "I really tried. The rug was pulled out from under me this morning."

"He's right, Jeremy," Tyler joined in. "There's really not a lot we could have done in this situation. They're raising the official Terror Alert level tonight in conjunction with the release of this news."

Jeremy sat back in his chair, angry and hurt. He knew the two men were right, but this person was not just a terrorist. She had been his friend. He sighed deeply and tried to collect his composure. Regardless of what happened in the next few months, he had to keep his nose clean and to the grindstone. He needed to avoid suspicion in relation to the case. "All right, I understand. I'm not real happy about the outcome, but I suppose there was really only one direction this could all go anyway. So where do we go from here, boss?" he finished as he looked at Neil.

"We should probably spend some time going over these documents that Tyler just gave us," Neil answered. He was happy to see Jeremy taking responsibility for his job and avoiding any potential emotional conflicts of interest in the case. "We're going to have to adjust our thinking if they're definitely not using the web anymore." He looked at Tyler and continued. "I know we have fairly strong evidence that they're going to move on, but is anyone still monitoring the web site for changes?"

"Absolutely. We've got automated scans watching the site everyday to see if any of the images change. But we've moved our primary focus off of the web entirely."

"I thought you said you were watching auction sites on the web," Jeremy said inquisitively.

"We are watching them, but that's a secondary activity," Tyler responded. "We're beginning to think they've moved into the USENET somewhere."

"What makes you think that?" Neil asked.

"A few things," he began. "Considering the fact that Jimmy wants the ability to communicate directly back and forth, we believe that web sites make a poor choice. But newsgroups provide a facility allowing multiple people to communicate back and forth in fairly quick order. They can still use attachments, which is where their messages are hidden, and there are no post limits. And finally, if they use a newsgroup that has lots of traffic, like one of the more popular porn newsgroups, they would blend in with the background noise. There are literally thousands of people talking in these groups during the course of a week. Quite honestly, what we've seen from a technology perspective so far hints that none of these people are overly technical. They're all using available tools and software to do the dirty work. If they had been more technical, I'd lean more toward a more complex solution."

"So the USENET newsgroups are easy enough to use?" Neil asked.

"Yeah, anyone can use them."

"Why wouldn't they use something more along the lines of Instant Messenger or another peer-to-peer chat program?" asked Jeremy.

"Those servers are all housed by big corporate entities and are relatively easy to tap into," Tyler answered. "We've already got taps on those lines of communication in place with the owners of the service. They understand the potential for harm here, so we're keeping it all very quiet."

"What about network tunnels or something more protocol based?" Jeremy had seen many different tools up to this point, and some of them were pretty inventive.

"Again, we're dealing with amateurs here, at least up to this point." Tyler reached across the table and took the folder from in front of Neil and swung it around so that Jeremy could see. "Here, look at this," he said. "This is a listing of all the tools and applications we know have been used up to this point. See anything in common?"

"They're all Windows based?"

"Exactly! They're all GUI-based Windows applications. Every single one of them is a point, drag, drop, and click type application. That implies very little technical knowledge on the operator's part. You've seen some of the tools that work under Linux, right?"

"Right."

"Those tools are typically much more powerful, but they're also more technical. Now don't get me wrong, I'm not saying these folks will always use simplistic tools, but I do believe they're trapped by their own technical ignorance."

Neil looked at the two young men. "I tend to agree with Tyler on this one. I think they will likely evolve past this point in the future, but for now, we should count our lucky stars that they aren't more technically capable yet. We'd never find them with our current tool set if they were using any more technical tools."

"I suppose you're both right," Jeremy acquiesced. "But it's not always going to be this way."

"I agree," said Tyler. "For now, though, we're spending more time on the newsgroups. The trouble we're having now is that there are so many groups. Thousands of them have continuous traffic every day. But we've started looking. The problem is whether we actually find anything. I'll keep you updated on what's going on downstairs. Feel free to come down anytime."

Chapter 19: Vengeance for Deceit

December 10, 2004

"Sources claim that federal officials have two of the terror suspects currently in custody in the Washington, D.C., area. One of the suspects is said to have been the mastermind of the recent failed attacks on three American cruise ships, and the other was captured while trying to escape. Officials are not saying how they learned of the attacks beforehand, except to say that intelligence sources led them to suspect the possible attacks only hours before they were carried out."

The news in this country was so littered with lies and fallacies. The American mind had grown lethargic and seemed incapable of processing simple information on its own. The woman currently speaking on the television was likely reading off a teleprompter, speaking the words of someone else who had taken the facts and congealed them into an attractive, easy to digest, yet totally inaccurate fairy tale. This evening's news was certainly no different. It was almost humorous to an outsider. The Americans were so arrogant, but at the same time they let the government and mass media lead them around by a very short leash.

The actual facts of the story were well known to the man watching the news from his living room chair. He had been in this country for 25 years, working and living as an American, but secretly maintaining his ties to his homeland. He sent money home each month to help support the family still living there. His connections with Al Qaeda had been in place since before he came to the United States, and were well established. He trusted Al Qaeda members with his life, and they trusted him with his mission. They were one in the same.

"Today," the woman continued, "our cameras managed to capture images of the individual we believe to be the suspected mastermind of the cruise ship attacks. We believe these to be the only public images of the suspect to date. The images will likely surprise our viewers as much as they surprised our news crew."

Talk, talk, talk, he thought to himself. *All these Americans do is talk. Show me my target already.* The images were obviously taken from a video camera, not a still shot model. The grainy images were blurry and difficult to see, but one of the images came clearly into view. The man stood up in his chair and shouted obscenities at the figure on the television set. *It's a woman. A woman was behind the plan. That explains why it failed so miserably.*

He replayed the images using his TiVo™, watching closely for distinguishing features that would help him locate his target. The buildings and other landmarks behind the figure in the images told him right where the picture had been taken. It was a spot downtown, near one of the federal buildings, the Department of Homeland Security building to be specific. The two guards in blue jackets with the letters DHS emblazoned across the back in bright yellow confirmed his assumption. *Good, it's right near work. Now all I have to do is find a suitable location for my ambush.*

Realizing he was still standing, he walked over to the computer that sat on a desk near the window in his suburban home in Bethesda, Maryland. *I should let them know. They probably don't even know it was a woman yet.* He turned on the monitor and brought up his e-mail. A few minutes later, halfway around the world, another person would relay the message to the ones in charge. The entire operation would know a woman had tricked them. *They will be more careful in the future. But for now,* he thought, *I'll take care of this particular problem.* He clicked Send on the e-mail he had just composed and shut off the monitor. The speakers next to the monitor would let him know if a reply came back in tonight. High-speed Internet definitely had its perks. But for now, it was time for dinner.

The man walked into the kitchen and watched as his wife and daughter prepared dinner. His son, now 9 years old, was just setting the dinner table. His daughter was pulling bread from the oven, and his wife was cutting the meat on the stove and placing the slices on a plate nearby. "What can I do to help, dear?" he asked, smiling. "I'm starving."

Jeremy sat in his living room, fuming. He was angry, but he found that he was more scared for Layla than he was angry. His anger was founded in the simple fact that her identity had just been publicly broadcast across national television. Everyone in America would know about the woman mastermind of the latest terror attacks. The press used the federal government to gain a higher percentage of viewers, which inevitably leads to better revenues from advertising.

But the feds did their own share of *using* as well. They had used the press to alter public perception about the incidents on the cruise ships. The American people just as easily could have protested the obvious inadequacies in the federal intelligence and response agencies, creating another public relations nightmare for everyone involved. Instead, the government had learned from their former mistake and pushed a scapegoat out for the public to hate. Layla had been the perfect scapegoat, and to make matters worse, she went willingly.

In her rush to relieve herself of the emotional and psychological prison her father had placed her in, years before, she had come to the United States government on her own. She had permanently lost the ability to ever live in peace again. The true mastermind of the entire terrorist project was still out there somewhere, free. Jimmy was working as hard as he could to bring the country to the brink of chaos, while the American people were under the impression that the government had everything under control. The truth was that the government didn't have anything under control, not yet.

He picked up the bottle of beer sitting on the coffee table next to his chair and took a long swig. It was getting stressful at work. Everyone he worked with was now running around like mad trying to tie all the loose ends together. At times, the explanations and scenarios they concocted sounded more like something from a B-rate movie than from real life. But no one was taking chances these days. Phase two could be tomorrow for all they knew. Every single theory deserved at least a few moments of consideration.

Jeremy was doing a good job at separating his personal life and his work, although he found himself working 50 to 60 hours every week now. He loved his job, but he hated this particular case. The irony of the entire situation never escaped him. It was his first case; he was expected to prove himself in front of the entire agency. She was his friend and had come to him for help. The story was so convoluted that it could almost be funny, if it weren't so damned personal.

But despite all the hurdles and emotional debris laid out in front of him at the moment, he never let his connection with Layla change the way he should be reacting at work. The truth was simple—innocent people could die any day if they didn't learn the answers. He spent hours upon hours each day looking through newsgroups, reexamining the evidence, and going over the notes from interviews with Layla. Like a chicken running around the farm yard in circles after having its head cut off, Jeremy spent his days trying as hard as he could to find something new, something meaningful, but still coming back to the same place he had started.

Leaning back in his recliner, he took another deep swig from the beer bottle, emptying it, and placed it back on the coffee table. Jeremy was never one to drink more than one beer per night, but he had surprised himself how quickly that one had gone down. The bottle hadn't even had time to draw condensation. He ran his fingers through his hair and let his mind drift, hoping to catch some mental breeze that could carry him to some conclusion they had failed to reach up until this point.

What would I do if I were in Jimmy's place right now? The use of the newsgroups made sense to Jimmy as well. He had thought long and hard about the various methods that would be available to someone like Jimmy, a fugitive on the run. Access to the Internet was fairly easy in most parts of the world. The tricky part would be to pick a medium that would allow person-to-person communication, not just the broadcast style that Layla originally had used.

Online auctions provided a great means for disseminating information to a group of individuals, but provided very little in the way of feedback. The tone of Jimmy's e-mail indicated that he wanted direct communication and contact with each team member. In order to carry out something as in depth as this on an online auction site, all the participants would need to have their own auctions running. And since auctions expire, they constantly would have to start new auctions and communicate those back to the remaining team members. It simply wasn't an efficient option for someone trying to keep the lines of communication open and near real time.

Web pages had a very similar issue, in that it would be most useful for a broadcast situation. Unless each team member had access to the web site, they couldn't post responses. They would all need their own web sites, which, again, would require a tremendous amount of logistical overhead that eventually would impact operations. Jimmy didn't sound like a stupid man. He was trying, as best he could, to enable the success of his plans. But what was he doing?

E-mails had too many issues associated with them. Spam blockers could stop participants from receiving a vital message. There was a virtual paper trail that could eventually trace back to each person in the group. They needed to remain anonymous to the remainder of the world. E-mails also gave direct evidence of person-to-person contact. The header information in most e-mails could be traced back to both the sender and the receiver. Sure, there were ways to change those headers, but you can always trace back to the originating e-mail server, and *that* was the issue with e-mail. It was simply too unsafe.

Taking a deep breath, Jeremy tried to relax and clear his mind. The stress level at work had reached such a peak that he had gone to the bookstore and purchased a book on relaxation. At the end of each day, Jeremy had hundreds of details swirling around in his head, impossible to put together. Most of the ideas in the book hadn't helped much at all, but he found that the simple breathing techniques it taught could clear his mind of some of the noise.

So let's just follow the path of least resistance, he thought to himself as he sat there. *What if he really is using the USENET to communicate? What type of group would he use?* Tyler's group was already researching roughly 120 groups that might be suspects. They had already eliminated any groups that frowned on the use of attachments, such as digital images or audio files. Jimmy had grown accustomed to using steganography as a covert channel, and according to the interviews with Layla, he wasn't nearly educated enough on the topic or technical enough to move to something else this quickly. So that likely ruled out any of the more advanced network-capable channels. *Thank God,* he sighed. *There would have been no way to catch them then.*

Out of the120 groups they were looking at now, there were dozens of different topics for discussion and file sharing. Tyler had gone to Neil and asked if he could use Jeremy for some research. Neil had agreed reluctantly. Everyone knew they were in a bind. Every technical person working on the case in one way or another was being pulled into the analysis.

Jeremy was given the list of suspect groups and asked to narrow down the list to ones he thought would most likely be used by the terrorist. Tyler had done the same thing with everyone else as well. *Go through the list,* he had told Jeremy, *and think about what makes sense in your mind. Which one would you use?* Tyler was trying as hard as he could to get the creative brain cells in the entire team pumping again. *Don't just tell me which ones you like. I want to know* why *you would use those groups.*

The list was long, but not painfully so. Jeremy reached back over to the coffee table beside his chair and took the four-page list and set it in his lap. It contained the name of the group, the topic of discussion, average number of daily participants, and average number of daily messages. As he looked down at the first page again, he ran his fingers through his hair out of nervous habit. Almost the entire first page was dedicated to a variety of pornographic groups specializing in everything from women, men, midgets, animals, toys, gay, lesbian, amateur, and circus acts. The array was astounding, and the sheer number of messages that were posted each day shocked even Jeremy.

Any one of these might be a decent group for Jimmy to set up shop. The number of people in the groups would certainly hide the identity of the individuals on Jimmy's team. But aside from the fact that the topics were definitely outside the realm of what a good Muslim would be willing to look at each day, there was always the simple fact that men are men. Looking at naked bodies is an easy way to lose track of what you're doing. He wasn't sure how he felt about those sites.

The remaining three pages covered various topics from hacking computers, swapping commercial software illegally, comic collecting, role-playing games, music swapping, fan groups for movies and television shows, and other hobbies. *It's crazy what people will spend their days talking about.* Jeremy grabbed a pen from the coffee table and started reading through the list once more, from the top, marking the groups that made the most sense. As he considered each group in turn, he realized that it likely was going to be a very long night. *It's Friday,* he thought. *Maybe I will have another beer.*

Chapter 20: Eliminating False Positives

December 17, 2004

Jeremy flicked his pencil into the air again with his left hand and caught it rather precariously with the two middle fingers on his right hand. His documents were strewn across his desk haphazardly, unorganized piles of information. He had been going over the information repeatedly for what seemed like weeks now. Regardless of how much time he looked at the evidence, it never changed. Neil was pushing him to find as many variants of the terrorists' plans as he could. To be fair, Neil was slaving mindlessly away over the same task, apparently according to orders sent down from ranks higher than his. But the facts don't change, no matter how long you stare at the words.

"I think I've developed tunnel vision," he said quietly to no one in particular. His voice was barely audible over the heater vents blasting air into the office space. He flicked the pencil into the air again, but missed it as it came back down. The phone on his desk rang loudly and broke his concentration. The pencil would have to wait. He reached across the desk toward the phone and picked up the headset.

"This is Jeremy," he said as the receiver reached his ear.

"I've got to tell ya, Jeremy," Tyler began, "out of all the lists I got back, your list had the most interesting observations."

"Really," Jeremy replied uncertainly. "What do you mean?"

"Well, most of the team went immediately for the pornography-based newsgroups, including a lot of gay porn," Tyler answered. "It seems that many of them are under the impression that gay porn would make a perfect cover medium since most nosey folks wouldn't really want to look there. The content would be too extreme." There was a slight pause on the phone before Tyler continued. "But they never really justified their line of thinking beyond that."

"I guess I don't follow what you're trying to tell me, Tyler." Jeremy was confused. "What did I do differently?"

Tyler laughed. "In your mind you tried to be the terrorist. You aligned your thought processes to those required to plan, organize, and carry out an attack like this. In a nutshell, you asked the simple question, *What would I do if this were me?* That's extremely helpful."

"Oh, cool. Thanks."

"No, thank you," Tyler replied. "I think it's probably because you're still so new to this type of work. Your thinking hasn't been tainted." Tyler laughed again. "I guess you haven't been issued your standard pair of federal blinders, yet."

Jeremy laughed. "It's not that bad, is it?"

"You'd be surprised," came the response. "The majority of the results I got back said pretty much the same thing. We've all been trained to think about terrorist a certain way. But the truth of the matter is that we're all just as likely to be wrong as you are."

"So now that you've looked at all the results, what do you think?" Jeremy asked.

"I think you're probably right on target," Tyler said. "I've already realigned some of the newsgroups we were looking at so that we can focus on a few of your suggestions."

"Wow, thanks. Any chance I can come down and watch? Neil left after lunch for a medical appointment, and I'm really tired of running these same pieces of evidence through my head. I'm honestly not certain it's making much of a difference."

"Yeah, come on down. You're welcome to hang out. A few of us are planning on working late tonight just so we can see where this research is going. We'll be ordering pizza, and there will be plenty of soda. You're welcome to stay with us, if you want."

"Cool. I'll be down in a few," Jeremy replied. "I want to see which of my groups you liked."

"All right, see you in a few."

Jeremy hung up the phone and sat up in his computer chair. *Wow,* he thought, *he actually liked some of my observations. That's so cool.* He put his laptop in hibernation mode and pulled it out of its docking station. After packing it up in his backpack, he grabbed a notepad and pen and shoved them alongside the laptop in the small black bag. A quick check of the area told him he was ready, so he grabbed his coat and walked out of the cubical toward the door to the office.

Jeremy turned down the short hallway toward the door to the analyst's work area. The heavy gray metal door was nondescript and looked more like a door to the maintenance room than a real work area. But then again, all the doors down there looked that way. As he approached the door, he took his badge in hand and swiped it in the access device mounted next to the door. There was an audible click and Jeremy pulled the door handle and walked inside.

When he reached Tyler's cubical, he realized that no one was in there. Several voices on the other side of the office were talking, and Jeremy thought he heard them talking about the newsgroups. He left Tyler's area and walked toward the voices he was hearing. As he turned the corner around the last row of cubicles, he saw several people sitting around a large table laden with six different computers; one of them was Tyler. "Hi, folks," he said as he approached.

"That was quick," Tyler replied. "You must have been in quite a hurry."

"Yeah, as I said on the phone, things are getting pretty repetitive up there." He took a chair on the other side of the table, looking across at Tyler. "Besides, you get to do all the cool stuff down here."

The others around the table laughed. "Eh, it can be frustrating and repetitive down here as well," Tyler began. "Remember what I said about having blinders on." Tyler stood up and faced Jeremy across the table. "Let me introduce you to the team." He began to point around the table, counterclockwise, as he introduced each person in turn. "This is Lydia.

Next to her, to your left is Herschel. On my left is Parviz. And over here is Kylie. Everyone, this is Jeremy."

After everyone had said his or her mutual greetings to one another, Jeremy asked Tyler a question. "What are you all doing over here, working in a group?"

"We decided it made more sense, considering how unknown our timeline is and how important this case is, that we all work in the same area for a while. We even set up a computer for you, just in case," he smirked.

"Oh, sweet," Jeremy replied. "This is mine to work on?"

"That's why it's there. Have at it. We've loaded all the tools that we use for this type of research, including the ones I showed you before. The one you're on right now boots strictly to Windows, but we've loaded up a Linux-based virtual machine in case you need any of those tools, too." Tyler took a notebook off of the table and grabbed several sheets of paper from inside. "These are the groups we're focusing on for now. We just started this morning, and I've assigned certain groups to each person at the table. You have the groups that are circled on the last page." Tyler handed the documents across the table to Jeremy.

"Okay, so where do we start?" Jeremy flushed slightly and ran his fingers through his hair. "Sorry, everyone, I'm totally new at this."

"Oh, don't apologize," Parviz chimed in. "Everyone starts at the same place."

"That's the truth," Kylie responded. "But from what Tyler says, you've got a natural knack for this type of work. And to be honest, we could use some new input on this one. So far we're not making as much headway as any of us might like."

"They're right, Jeremy," Tyler said with a smile. "Don't apologize. It takes only a few minutes to learn the methodology we are using, and you've already got a strong technical foundation." Tyler pointed to one corner of the office and said, "We've built USENET servers that are subscribed to the full array of newsgroups available. The RAID drives sitting in the rack next to the server house all the information the server downloads each day."

"Okay, I'm with you so far."

"Each computer on this network is connected to that USENET server as well as to the Internet. We're using a secure in-house chat application to chat from computer to computer while we work."

"Wouldn't it be easier to just talk across the table?" Jeremy laughed.

"It would be easier if we didn't have to share files or send links back and forth," Lydia replied. "It might seem like the geek factor on this setup is relatively high, but it serves a purpose."

"Ah, that makes sense," Jeremy responded. "So this network is completely isolated from your actual day-to-day network?"

"That's correct," Tyler answered. "We use the applications you see on your desktop to scan the newsgroups with the software I showed you previously. Then the suspicious files get manual checks as well. The files that really raise eyebrows are sent off to our partner group at NSA for decryption. We'll show you how to do that when it pops up." Tyler sat back down in front of his own computer and reached for his notebook again. "Do you mind if we spend a few minutes asking you about why you picked certain newsgroups?"

"Not at all. I hope I didn't sound too ignorant in my responses."

"Actually," Herschel piped up, "your answers were so different from our own that we realized that either you were out in space somewhere or that we might be missing something in our thinking. They're not bad comments at all. They're just ideas I guess we missed somewhere along the way."

"Why don't we just toss a few groups out there and see what you think, Jeremy," Tyler started again.

"Sure."

Tyler looked at the first sheet of paper he had picked up. "The first thing we noticed was the lack of pornographic choices on your submission. What were you thinking along these lines?"

"Well, honestly, I think the entire pornographic thing is overplayed," Jeremy answered. "It's really an obvious choice. If I were trying to get something by someone else, I certainly wouldn't use something that obvious." Jeremy adjusted in his chair, sitting up straight. "If you put yourself in the shoes of someone who isn't a complete slug, you might choose to avoid those groups simply because they already draw so much suspicion. I don't completely dismiss them, but they just seem so obvious."

"I can understand that," replied Parviz.

"Are there any other reasons you didn't lean toward them?" Tyler asked curiously.

"Ha," Jeremy laughed. "To be honest, I was thinking that if I were the one trying to run an operation like this, I certainly wouldn't want the distraction of a bunch of nude people. I would imagine it's difficult enough to get men to all work together like this without throwing in pictures or videos of naked women." He laughed again.

"Good point, actually," Tyler responded.

"I see where I missed the mark on this one," said Kylie. "I just wasn't putting myself in the shoes of the terrorist leader. The adult-oriented groups would be great because they offer so much cover, but they're also the obvious choice, as Jeremy said. Now that I think about it," she said as she adjusted her shirt, "we'd be much better served as terrorists if we picked a benign newsgroup that still generates a large number of messages each day."

"That's where I was headed with all this," Jeremy responded proudly. "In my mind, it made more sense to use one of the more popular hobby- or fan-based newsgroups. Imagine trying to find a hidden message in that Star Wars™ fan newsgroup," he said as he pointed at the list Tyler was holding in his hands. "I didn't know there were so many people still hyped up on that movie. There is are a huge number of new messages posted to that group each day." Absently, Jeremy ran his fingers through his thick hair and continued speaking. "That's why most of the groups you see on my list are ones like that."

"I'm still not sure we should discount the adult newsgroups," Lydia replied.

"Oh, neither do I," Jeremy answered back. "I just filled it out as if I were the one trying to make this terrorist plot work. My thought processes have always been a little different from others around me. I'm not sure there is a right or wrong answer."

"There's not, Jeremy," Tyler said with a smile. "We were just wondering how you came up with what you did. But it makes sense. I think everyone agrees, at least on some level, that your ideas are worth looking into a bit further. So we're going to work on those groups more intensely than we have been. In fact, if you look at your list, a few of those groups are yours to research."

Herschel laughed out loud. "I hope you don't mind, but I stole the Star Wars group. I'm one of those people who still really likes that story."

Jeremy laughed, too. "Not at all. Have at it. I like the movies and all, but I was never a huge fan."

"Just don't let it distract you, Hersch," Tyler replied, laughing. "I'd hate to think that we're getting bogged down by our own interest in the newsgroups we're researching."

"Not a problem, boss man," Herschel replied smiling wide.

"Well, why don't we get back to work," Tyler asked. "Any of us can help you with issues you run into, Jeremy. You're familiar enough with the tools at this point, right?"

"I think so," he answered. "But I'll certainly ask if I'm confused or lost. Some of the tools on the desktop are ones that I haven't played with before, but I should be okay."

"Just ask if you need anything," said Herschel. "It's easy since we're sitting right here next to each other. And I'll be sure to let you know if I find anything cool in the Star Wars group."

Jeremy smiled at Herschel and responded, "That sounds great."

"Good," Tyler began again. "It sounds like we're all good to go now."

"Oh, Jeremy," Kylie started, "what kind of pizza do you like? I'll be ordering in about a half-hour so that we have stuff to munch on tonight."

"I like the hot kind, Kylie," he answered with a smile. "Seriously, I'm not picky at all. If it's pizza, we're good."

"Great."

"Herschel, can you help him get on chat so he can participate as well?" Tyler asked from across the table.

"Not a problem, boss man," came the reply.

Jeremy looked back at the monitor as everyone else started focusing back on his or her work. He recognized some of the icons on the desktop as applications that Tyler had shown him or that he had researched on his own in the past.

"Here," Herschel said, leaning over toward Jeremy. "Let's get you online so that you're part of the action."

Jimmy sat down in front of the rundown computer at the small library and turned on the monitor. The computer was left on continuously, and he wasn't quite sure how the thing managed to stay running. Today, there was a raspy grinding noise coming from the rear of the tower case. *This thing is on its last legs*, he thought irritably. From across the room, the librarian smiled at him. Jimmy shot back a fake smile knowing that she considered him to be her one consistent visitor. *There must not be a single person in this town who reads.* It surprised him, but he understood that it actually made his job that much easier. There was no one else in town to compete with for Internet time.

He opened the web browser, as he always did when he got there. But this time he wasn't there to check on the newsgroups. The library would be closing in less than 20 minutes, but that left him plenty of time to check his e-mail and ensure that everything was still running smoothly.

The default web page came up, and Jimmy typed in the address to his new web mail. Logging in, he saw that he had 13 new messages since he had last checked just before dinner. It seemed like a lot of e-mail in such a short period of time, but it had become increasingly normal. Jimmy knew that it was likely all spam, but he had the time, so he might as well see for sure.

All but one of the e-mails turned out to be spam. That single e-mail was from his Al Qaeda contact.

```
Jimmy,
We have located Salah. Our contacts in the Washington, D.C., area had
confirmed that Salah is actually a woman in American custody. The
situation will be resolved shortly. Continue your hard work in the name
of Allah. You will be celebrated in the afterlife.
Allah bless you.
```

Jimmy stared at the screen for several minutes, unable to believe his eyes. Salah was a woman? He could feel the temperature of his blood rise as his anger began to boil over inside. *How could I let myself be misled by a woman?* he asked himself angrily. *Now it all makes sense.*

Jimmy hit the Forward button on the web interface and typed the e-mail alias he had created for all the group members. *They will know what happened now. It will strengthen their resolve. We cannot fail.* After removing the original sender information from the header, he added just one more line of text to the forwarded e-mail:

"Our reason for failure in the first attacks, but not for the next one."

Chapter 21: Gaining a Finger Hold

January 5, 2005

"So how many target images have we actually passed off to the agency now?" Jeremy asked Tyler. The two men were sitting with Neil at a small sandwich shop around the corner from their office. They had been working on finding suspect images for weeks, and he was beginning to feel as if there was simply no way they were going to stop this attack. He fought back the urge to say that the attack was likely not even going to happen, considering how long it had been now since Layla had first come to them.

"We've passed off about 1,500 images, total," Tyler answered. "But that doesn't include any of the analysts who are still looking at the other Internet services, like the web. They've passed off a large number of suspect files as well and aren't having any better luck."

"The agency is probably inundated at this point," Neil countered, stuffing a potato chip in his mouth. "We've given them so much stuff to look at now. It might take a while for them to dig themselves back out."

"We've gotten some feedback on what we've sent them so far," Tyler responded. "Most of it is either child pornography or just trash. We're still getting a bunch of false positives. If someone would just create a good tool for detecting covert channels, they could make this a whole lot easier."

"The worse part about all of this," Jeremy started, "is that we just don't know when it's supposed to happen. It's not just a where issue. We don't have any information."

"I'm beginning to wonder if there is really even going to be an attack at all," Tyler replied with a sigh. "What if they've called it off, and we're just spinning our wheels out here, wasting time?" He picked up his tuna melt and took a healthy bite from one side.

Jeremy laughed anxiously. "I was thinking the same thing, but didn't want to be the one to say something." He took the cup of hot coffee and took a sip from the dark liquid. It was cold outside in D.C. this time of year, and he had taken to drinking mostly hot drinks to keep his blood from freezing solid.

Neil sighed and placed his sandwich back on the wax paper wrapper it had come in. Wiping his mouth with his napkin, he looked at the other two men. "I'm frustrated, too, guys. But we can't ignore the possibility, not yet. Let's give it just a little more time. My biggest concern is that the Terror Alert level has been elevated for so long now that people will start to ignore it. We've created a new acceptable watermark for the public. They could be totally ignoring possible signs of an attack even as we sit here eating lunch."

Jeremy finished chewing and looked at Neil. "How many analysts, counting you and me, are there working on this now? There must be a ton now."

Neil's brow furrowed slightly. "That's part of our problem, guys. We were woefully unprepared for something like this. We've got 44 people working on this project doing various bits of research and analysis." He rubbed his fingers above his eyes and continued. "With that many people dedicated to most projects, we'd be ahead of the game, but not in this one."

"If it makes you feel any better," Tyler explained, "I know the agency has had to create some dedicated tools for this type of work. So we've spanned that knowledge gap somewhat. Sure, we still have a ways to go yet, but we've made some progress." He took a quick drink of his iced tea and set the cup back on the table. "There are American lives at stake. We need to nail this thing down."

The sound of a shrill ring cut the conversation short. Each man reached to his waist, checking to see whether it was his cell phone causing the racket. Tyler brought his phone to his ear and answered. "This is Tyler." Neil and Jeremy watched patiently, wondering what the call was about. Jeremy continued to eat the rest of his sandwich, while Tyler listened to the voice on the other end.

"Really," Tyler said excitedly. "I was beginning to think we were beating on empty bushes. That's great news." The other two men put down their food and began listening to Tyler.

"Okay, great. We'll head back to the office now. Thanks for letting me know, Herschel." Tyler closed the phone and clicked it back into place in the belt clip at his side. "The agency found something. We need to get back to the office."

"Woohooo," Jeremy said with a smile. He stuffed the remainder of his lunch, along with all the wrappers back in the bag and stood up. "Let's get going," he said as he walked to the trash can.

Together, all three men walked from the sandwich shop back toward the office. As he looked at the other two men, Jeremy could see the slightest hint of optimism in Neil's eyes. *Maybe we're finally on to something*, he thought.

Tyler's office area was afire with activity as the three men walked in the door less than 10 minutes after receiving the phone call. They could hear voices in the back of the office near the computers that were set up specifically for this investigation. "Tyler, is that you?" a woman's voice called.

"Yeah, it's me. We're back," he answered as the three men sped up their pace slightly.

"NSA was able to pull the information out of one of the images we pulled down from a newsgroup," Kylie began. "Apparently, the message was encrypted with a decent password, and it took them longer than they had expected to get the contents back out. But it's the only image so far that has yielded a message that appears to relate to our case."

"What newsgroup was the message from?" Neil asked.

"It was from alt.pets.dogs.binaries.pictures," Herschel responded. "Jeremy was right. They went for the less obvious choice in topics." He smiled as he patted Jeremy on the back.

"Don't congratulate me, yet," Jeremy responded. "Let's see what we have now. Do you all know what the password was the terrorists used?"

"They didn't give us that information, yet," Kylie said. "But they did say that they're going to go through every submission from that group and run the same password. They had just started on the images from that group when this message popped up."

"So where's the message?" Tyler said impatiently as he moved to sit in front of the computer he had been using for the last few weeks.

"Here it is," Herschel said as he handed a printed sheet of paper to Tyler.

```
Jimmy,
Had to find a new job, but I'm settled in again. I'll still be ready on
the 15th.
Allah bless you.
Adnan
```

"The 15th?" Tyler asked. "This month?" He handed the sheet of paper to Neil and Jeremy and sat back in his chair.

"Nobody knows, boss man."

"If it's this month, we don't have much time," Neil responded after looking at the message. "But we can't be sure when it really is. And there's no clue as to where the attack will be either."

"Well, I suppose it's a start," Tyler replied. "Let's hope that they used the same password for the rest of the images as well. You said they were going to go back through all the images we submitted for this newsgroup, right?" he asked Herschel.

"That's what they said," came the reply, "but they're not sure how many they have yet specifically from this group. They have to go through all the images we sent and sort them out. Apparently, they haven't done that yet."

Neil sighed and looked at Tyler. "Is there anything we can do to help? It honestly looked as if we're in a holding pattern until we get more information, so maybe we can help look for more images?"

"You two are welcome to hang around and look through the images with us. We should keep up with all the new messages that have been posted. So why don't we keep on doing what we've been doing. I don't see any reason to change that until we get enough information from NSA to move on, do you, Neil?"

"I agree with you."

Jeremy smiled. He enjoyed doing this type of work. Moving around the table to his computer, he sat down in his chair and turned on the monitor. "Well, what are we waiting for?"

Chapter 22: Compressing Timelines

January 10, 2005

The days were getting cooler, even in this small, dry Mexican town. Jimmy stared out the cracked window of his small hotel room at the night sky. His appearance had changed drastically over the last two months. He had let his black hair grow longer, and it now hung down just above his shoulders. A dark beard now covered his young face. He kept it trim and clean, but it made him look more like the locals. The fact that all the residents of the small hotel had to share a shower room meant that Jimmy was much less clean than he preferred now, but he forgave the small inconveniences in life because he was able to work on his plan in peace and safety.

The local population took no notice of Jimmy now as he walked down the dirty streets. He had become one of them. It reminded him of the way he had become a part of the American culture, but he held no hatred toward these poor people. They were all doomed to hell unless they found the truth, but they meant him no harm, and he respected that. His reflection in the thin glass of the window stared back at him. He barely recognized the man who looked back at him.

The cold winter sky was clear tonight. Bright pinholes of light glowed brightly against the pitch-black background. He knew that Allah was up there somewhere, watching his every movement, measuring his worth based on his actions. My goal is pure, Allah, he whispered into the night air. I only want to end hundreds of years' worth of occupation, interference, and deceit by the West. But there came no answer; the night was silent. His god was leaving him to his own devices. There was little choice but to continue on and prove his value. When he had started this project he hadn't been so religious. The change in his character had come about based on the events of the last year. He was depending more heavily on his relationship with Allah. Many of his core decisions about this project and his life in general were now made in accordance with the Islamic religion. Jimmy smiled to himself. *I've certainly changed, haven't I?*

Jimmy looked down at the dim streets below. There were very few lights in this town. Most of the light at night came from the moon, but that moon was hiding tonight. The resulting light from the stars was barely enough to penetrate the shadows between the old brick and mud buildings. But something else was lighting the streets below—a car. He hadn't seen many cars in this old town and he watched curiously as a dark sedan drove slowly down the street in front of the hotel. It continued to the other end of the small town, where it turned around and came back to the hotel, parking alongside the front of the hotel.

A cold chill took hold of Jimmy as he watched three men get out of the car and unload small suitcases from the trunk of the sedan. He couldn't tell what color the car was, just that it was dark. The men, however, were Caucasian. Each one wore simple clothes: blue denim pants, and T-shirts. They weren't speaking among each other, so Jimmy couldn't tell immediately what nationality they might be. But whoever they were, they were checking into the same hotel as Jimmy. He would need to watch these men closely. Overreacting could affect the success of the plan. They were only a week away. If he fled because of unsubstantiated fear, the remainder of the group would have no one to lead them. Besides, Allah had tested his resolve in the past. What was to say this wasn't just another test?

The three men walked inside the hotel, and Jimmy lost sight of them. He took a deep breath and looked back at the stars above his head. *Please give me strength and wisdom, Allah. I'm trying to do what you've asked me to do.* He sighed to himself and stepped away from the window, closing it tightly as he moved away. It was getting late, and he still wanted to go back over everything once more. Everything had to be perfect this time around. With five different individuals placed around the French Quarter, Jimmy knew that all he had to do was stay focused and keep his team strong and informed.

He walked over to the small bed. The room he was staying in wasn't much larger than his room on the cruise ship had been, but at least it was private and quiet. The walls were painted a dirty pale white color, and the comforter on the bed was a dark mustard yellow. A small rickety wooden nightstand occupied the space next to the bed, and a wrought iron lamp sat precariously on its surface. And although Jimmy had already had to change the lightbulb in the lamp several times since he had been here, the lamp still flickered. He assumed it had more to do with the quality of the power at the hotel versus the lamp itself.

On the nightstand was a small folder. It was worn from months of use. He had carried it back and forth between the hotel, restaurant, and library for months now. The contents of that folder had evolved during that time period, and Jimmy's plans came closer to fruition. He took the folder, laid it on the bed, and climbed onto the surface of the bed. Quietly, he opened the manila folder and stared at the documents inside.

The majority of the documents inside the folder had been handwritten by Jimmy. The one printer in town was located at the library, along with the computers he had been using for Internet access. It seldom worked at all, and Jimmy was forced to write down the information he wanted in hard copy. The constant staring of monitors, both at the library and here at the hotel on his own laptop, had started giving him headaches. The written word was a needed break at times, and it allowed him to continue his planning.

In the hallway, Jimmy heard mumbled voices talking as they moved passed his door toward the opposite end of the hall. The deep voices carried through the thin door to Jimmy's room, but the men were speaking so quietly that he still could not tell what language they were speaking. There is nothing I can do about it tonight, he told himself reassuringly. Tomorrow, I'll find out what I can about them.

He looked back down at the collection of documents now sitting in front of him on the bed. There was very little time left, and he knew he needed to focus on the task at hand. He took the top piece of paper in his hand and brought it closer to his face, where the light from the small lamp shone on it. It was the map he had created of the French Quarter. The digital map he had created on his laptop, but this one he had drawn out by hand, with more detail. It was still easier for him to draw by hand than to use software, but he had created this one because of a different need. Since he could not print out the image he had created on the computer, he had drawn the map by hand on a piece of paper so that he could plan the day of the attacks.

The map had a series of green dots on it, indicating where each person on his team currently was placed. A collection of other hand-drawn icons were scattered around the map, each one indicating a certain Mardi Gras event that was going to take place between now and January 15, the date the group chose for the attack. Jimmy had done his research on the six-week celebration that culminated on Fat Tuesday, so he understood the activities nearly as well as someone intimately involved in them.

Many of his initial options for the attacks centered on the dozens of parades that occurred during that six-week period and across the entire city of New Orleans. But there were notable drawbacks to attacking during the parades. First, the parades' routes were cleared of people, except outside the parade barriers. The spectators stood alongside the roadways as the parades passed by. He figured that strategic placement of explosives within those crowds would kill, at most, about 50 people, not nearly the number he had in mind.

The other negative aspect of parade attacks would be the possibility that someone would notice the suspicious box or package lying on the ground near the parade route. Dozens of police officers were on duty and in the area during each parade, and the space beyond the spectators was wide open, making suspicious devices all that more noticeable. One thing Salah had said still made sense, even though he hated to admit it to himself. There really was no reason for any of the men on this project to die, and Jimmy had decided that he wasn't about to ask any of those men to carry an armed device into a crowd of people and set it off.

The reasonable alternative was to simply wait until the parades were over each day. The crowds would flood to the French Quarter after each event and began their partying. They flocked there by the thousands, filling Bourbon Street and the surrounding area with a sea of intoxicated humans. Trash littered the streets there. Trashcans were filled past their brims, and their contents would spill out on to the sidewalks and streets. A small device would never be noticed in that mess. His team members would never even be seen as they mingled with the crowd, carrying their small backpacks. Every other person in the French Quarter had a back-pack or a bag. They belonged there. They would have beads on and would sing along with the crowd.

Delivery would be simple; placement would be even easier. Small bat-tery-operated timers, available at most corner drug stores, would provide a timing mechanism for the devices. His men would carry the explosives in small backpacks, similar to the ones many other people carried during Mardi Gras. Those backpacks would be left among the piles of debris in the French Quarter, the timers set for a mere 15 minutes. The men could slip away in the crowd and out of the French Quarter; their cars would be parked nearby. They would each drive away to a distant location and watch their e-mail for further information from Jimmy.

Creating the explosives was the easy part. All the materials were avail-able. Instructions and guidance for building the devices were available in mass doses on the Internet. Batteries, timers, metal pipes, nails, razor blades, bits of glass, and the core combination of chemicals that would trigger the explosion were already acquired. They had been assembled, and test versions had been set off in remote swamps surrounding the city. The team was nearly ready. In just five more days, the United States would be shaken to its core, once more, by terrorists.

All Jimmy was doing anymore was answering last-minute questions and providing guidance. They knew what they had to do. The date and time had been set. Everything was ready. Each person on the team had received the cash they would need to find sufficient safety and seclusion.

His heart pounded as he reconsidered every detail. Finally, finding no flaws in his plan, he folded the papers back into their folder and placed it on the nightstand. It was time for a prayer of thanks to Allah and then sleep. Soon he would leave this town and find his way back home.

Jeremy thumbed through each piece of paper in turn, reading the messages in the order they were originally sent across the newsgroup. The messages spanned a period of the past three weeks. And although they confirmed the date of the attacks as January, 15, 2005, they gave no clue as to where the attacks were to take place. The team consisted of five people plus their leader, the infamous character known as Jimmy. The messages gave more details, but none was the one they really needed.

Jeremy turned in his chair to look at Herschel. "You said these came in last night?"

"Yes," came the reply. "The agency sent them over and said those are all the messages they were able to pull information from. Apparently, there were a few that are still suspicious, but they haven't been able to retrieve any information."

"I wonder if those images are just corrupt or something," Jeremy said partly to himself and partly aloud to Herschel.

"You may be right. Regardless, we don't have any of the messages prior to that point that could give us a clue about where the attacks may be," Herschel replied grimly.

Jeremy grimaced. He was well aware of the problem that now confronted them all. There was now a confirmed terror attack scheduled against the United States of America and no one knew where it was going to occur. The federal government had already raised the terror level once more, telling the American people that there was validated intelligence that an attack on U.S. interests was going to happen in the next week.

All the standard warnings had been passed out to the public. Keep your eyes open. Look for anything suspicious. Report odd vehicles, people, objects, anything. But Jeremy couldn't help wondering whether anyone would heed those warnings, whether anyone had actually been paying attention. It was a depressing thought.

To top everything else off, Layla was going to be transported to a federal holding facility this afternoon. He would likely never hear from or see the young woman again. In his mind, he felt guilty that he hadn't been able to help her more. She was his friend, but he had led her into the lion's den, where she was now being sacrificed to satisfy American curiosity.

"What are our plans now, Herschel?" he asked, trying to bring his mind back to the task at hand.

"Tyler is trying like hell to find a local Internet service provider that may have archives of the newsgroups that are older than three to four weeks. If we can locate an archive of the newsgroup, we can go through our normal routine and pull out all the images and test them."

"I wonder what the chances are that they'll actually find what we need." Jeremy sat back in his chair, feeling deflated by the past week's events. The others had to be emotionally exhausted as well at this point, not to mention physically exhausted.

"You've seen how many messages were in just that one newsgroup, right?"

"Sure, we all have."

"Oh yeah, I know, but the point I'm trying to make is that there are literally thousands of newsgroups and a full one-third have active messages every day."

Jeremy smiled, finally understanding. "That's a lot of traffic. It would likely take a lot of drive space."

"Exactly," Herschel replied with a grin. "But that's not all, right? What is it that we're pulling from these messages?"

"Image files."

Herschel smiled again. "Yep. And those take up a heck of a lot more space on a hard drive than a simple text message does."

"Okay, so that's the reason the service providers don't keep more than a few weeks' worth of the newsgroup archives on file."

"That's been our problem so far." Herschel sighed this time. He was as concerned about this as Jeremy and the rest were.

"And the federal government doesn't have an archive of this stuff hidden away somewhere?" Jeremy asked.

"You would think," came the response from the other man. "But as it turns out, we have the same issue that the ISPs do; it would take up too much drive space to archive all the groups. There are various agencies or divisions within the federal government that keep archives of some groups, but normally only those that pertain to the work they do every day."

Herschel put his hand back on the computer mouse and moved it to a list of the newsgroups. "Look at this, Jeremy. Some groups like this are known vehicles for child pornography. So some departments archive these groups knowing what's there."

"But who's going to archive a group on pet dogs?" Jeremy asked rhetorically. He took a deep breath as he had learned from the book he had been reading. "I feel like we're trapped in this now, Herschel."

"I know how you feel, buddy. It's hard to keep your chin up when you feel like you keep getting knocked back down. But we have to hang in there. We're doing the right thing. Innocent lives are at stake and depend on how quickly we figure this out." He patted Jeremy on the shoulder and smiled. "This was a really rough first case for you to get broken in on."

Jeremy laughed through his frustration. "That's what I hear."

"Does it make it more difficult knowing that Layla started all of this?" Herschel asked sympathetically. "I can't imagine how I'd react to a situation like that. Honestly, I keep wondering why they let you stay on this case."

"It is difficult sometimes because she is a friend. You care about your friends, you know." Jeremy sat back in his chair again and sighed. "But the

Layla I knew didn't have the personality for this type of thing. I know for sure it's not her but her father living through her that has caused all of this. It took a lot of guts for her to come and ask for help to stop this. But I still have a job to do, and I have a country to serve."

"I suppose I can understand that mix of feelings," Herschel responded. "Just so you know, I think you're doing a bang-up job. Keep it up."

"Thanks, man," Jeremy replied. "Why don't we get back to these messages? There might be another clue in a new message."

"Sounds good to me."

Layla's tears had run out long ago. All that was left were two swollen red eyes, dry and sore in their sockets. She had given up everything to try and stop this insane plan from succeeding. The rest of her life resting precariously on the hope that nothing bad would come of all this. The likelihood that she would ever walk the streets of the world as a free woman again was slim, and she knew it. *Better to live in a stone cell for the rest of my life, knowing I did the right thing in the end, than to let this happen and live free.*

She stared out of the darkened windows in the government car. From her vantage point in the back seat, she could see all sorts of people moving through the crowded sidewalks toward their destination. They were free. Better yet, she thought, they're alive. She released the breath she had been holding and relaxed as a fresh gust of oxygen entered her lungs.

Today was her first meeting with anyone from the American judicial system. She had been assigned an attorney by the courts to protect her interests. His name was Peterson, and he sat next to her in the back seat of the car, droning away about American law and how he intended on fighting her case for her. But she was disinterested, knowing instead that no court in this country was likely to ever let her walk free again. She watched as a group of Catholic school children walked down the side-walk beside the car. The laughter of those small children made her smile, if only briefly. I did the right thing, she said to herself.

The car drove only another block before stopping in front of a large stone building with massive steps leading to its entrance. The stone had been white at some point in the past, but as she looked at it now, it was dirty and tinged with age. The steps leading up to the front doors were divided at intervals by brass handrails. Layla watched as an elderly man used those same handrails to ascend the long flight of granite steps.

"Oh," said Peterson suddenly. "It looks like we're here. Now remember, don't worry. It's all under control. This is just the first step in a very long process, and I'd hate to see you become exhausted so soon."

Layla nodded silently. She hadn't said very much since coming to America, and she spoke even less with those she wasn't sure she could trust. She wished Jeremy could be here, but she understood how compli-cated the situation was right now. He had helped her unload a terrible burden, and she loved him for that. Surely, he would come visit her when this all settled down.

Her daydreaming was interrupted as Peterson opened the door on his side of the car and climbed out; stepping into the street. He closed the door behind him and spoke momentarily with the agents before coming around to open her door.

"Shall we go?" he said with a smile as he opened the door for Layla.

"Okay," she said, trying not to look as grim as she felt.

"Would you stop looking so glum," he said with a smile. "Everything is going to be fine. You've been helping the federal government by sup-plying information they never had before. You have a reliable track record of trying to help. Things will work out just fine."

"I wish I was as confident as you are," she replied, stepping from the car. "But we both know that I also have a track record of planning the original attack on innocent Americans. They're not going to simply look past that, and you know it."

Peterson winced noticeably. Try as he might, he had not been able to convert her negative attitude about this case. It was reasonable for her to be as concerned as she was, but he did have a game plan. It wouldn't be as bad as she imagined. Conveying that optimism to Layla was an art that he hadn't quite mastered yet. "No, you're right. But those actions will be weighed against your attempts to stop the attacks, Layla. Believe it or not, those actions do count for something in the United States of America." He smiled again and closed the door behind her. "Come now, let's go."

"All right," she said with a sigh. Standing up straight, she took a deep breath of fresh air and relaxed her tired mind. "We'll never win this case if we don't go inside," she answered with a small smile. *Maybe there is hope after all*, she told herself.

The two of them walked toward the steps of the courthouse, followed closely by the two agents. There were no reporters, no crowds of people. Layla was thankful for that much, to be sure. The American government might be using her as a pawn in its war on terror, but at least it had kept the details about her case relatively quiet.

A fire suddenly broke out inside her, and she fell to the ground panting for air, the pain ripping through her delicate insides. She never noticed the granite steps as they collided with her head. Layla fought to keep her eyes open, but they would not cooperate with her. It seemed to her as if the sun were setting; the air around her was getting increasingly darker. She moved her hand slowly to her side and felt her sweater, now moist and warm. An alkaline odor filled her nose, a smell she remembered from when she was a small girl. Images of her brother being pulled from a pile of rubble swept through her head. *Allah*, she wept inside, *help me. I understand. I'm trying to fix all of the things I started. Please.*

"Layla," she heard Peterson yell. "Jesus, guys. Someone call an ambulance." He knelt beside her, whispering in her ear. "Hang in there, girl. We're still going to win this one."

Somewhere in the distance, she could hear the explosive sounds of gunfire as the two agents went to work, protecting her. She could feel the life seeping from her even as countless hands rolled her over onto her back and started working on the wound in her side. The pain was gone. The light had disappeared. All sounds of life around her were drifting into a quiet muffle. She needed to let go and rest. The last words she heard seemed like they were from miles away, "We're losing her!"

January 11, 2005

He walked from the dark hotel into the bright sun. It was late morning and he had slept in, much to his own chagrin. He had intentions of getting up early and watching for the three men who had checked into the hotel late last night, but his physical exhaustion was at a peak, and his body had chosen to sleep. It was too late to worry about that now; he had things to do.

He had his small backpack in his hand and had packed it that morning with all the things he would need when he arrived at the library. Jimmy walked down the dirty street toward the center of town. The library would already be opened, and he wanted to log on to the Internet and check on the remaining team members.

It took only a couple of minutes to reach the center of town, where the majority of shops, restaurants, and the library were located. As he passed the restaurant on the opposite side of the road, he saw the young waitress serving two local men at a table near the window. She didn't notice him as he continued walking. *All the better*, he thought. *I have other things to focus on.*

Jimmy walked up the steps to the small library and pushed the heavy doors open. The librarian was standing behind the front desk looking annoyed about something. She never even looked up at him as he walked past the front counter toward the area that contained the computers. As he neared the area, he heard men's voices near the computers, speaking quietly. He walked slowly and quietly along the aisles of books nearest the computers. As he got closer he realized the men were speaking English.

"Someone has definitely used this computer recently, Adam," said the first man. "The file markers on the drive have been modified recently, showing activity on the computer. Someone has been here."

"Do you see any signs of tools or applications that could have been used?" asked one of the other two men. They spoke perfect English. Jimmy felt a cold chill run through his blood. They had found him. Somehow they had found him. That meant they knew about the second phase. *But how?* he cried out inside his head.

"No, all the software on this computer is older. I don't think anyone has loaded anything on these computers in a couple of years," the first man responded again.

"What about cached files from the Internet, Adam?" the third man asked. "We need evidence. All we have at this point is speculation that this computer was used. Surely, there are signs left in the browser or registry somewhere."

"No, I've already looked, Ted," the first man replied with a frown. "The browser cache is totally clean, the address cache has been cleared, and there are no stored files on this box. Every file on this box is at least two years old. It just doesn't make any sense to me."

"Should we just hang out and wait for whoever had been using this computer to come back?" asked the second man again. "He's bound to come back at some point, right?"

"All right, but let's get off the computer and check out the selection of reading materials; just make sure you're within eyesight of the computer.

As the men started logging off the computer, Jimmy moved quickly toward the front door of the library, his mind struggling to keep up with what was happening. He reached the front door and pushed through impatiently. *I have to get out of here*, he heard his mind say. *I've failed again. Forgive me, Allah.*

He moved back toward the hotel, never glancing back at the library and not sparing a moment to look across the street into the restaurant windows. When he reached the hotel, he climbed the dingy stairs to the second floor and walked to his room door. A quick check confirmed that the door was still shut and locked. *Not that it matters anyway,* he thought. *The men who are after me have been at the library, and I had all my materials with me.*

Jimmy opened the door and walked into the room. There were really only a few of his things left in his room. It wouldn't take long for him to pack up. Suddenly, a thought struck him. *They don't know who I am.* Relief flooded through him. They had no clue what he looked like or where he was. They had managed to trace the traffic back to the computer at the library, no further. And in all the time he had been in town, he had never seen the librarian outside of the library. She didn't know who he was either. *For now, I'm safe.*

Jimmy fought the urge to pack up his bags and leave right now. He sat on the corner of his bed considering what to do next. The men would likely be in the library for hours, waiting for him to come in and use the computers. It was all they had. He had been lucky, stumbling upon them when they weren't expecting him. Allah was definitely looking out for him. Then it occurred to him what he should do.

I'll go out now and find a map and a car. I have plenty of cash to buy what I need. I'll take the car and park it just outside town. This evening, once the sun has gone down, I'll take my stuff and leave this town. Then it occurred to him that he hadn't taken the young waitress into account. *There's no time,* he chided himself. *She's not your lover anyway. Get over it.*

With a plan in mind now, he packed up his belongings. There were only a couple of places in town that had vehicles for sale. It would take only a few minutes to get to there. Cash could buy plenty in this small town. He grabbed his backpack and placed it on his shoulder. Opening the door to his room, he walked down the hallway and back out of the hotel toward the other end of town. Tonight, he'd be gone, and they would lose his scent. But this entire thing had angered him. He might have failed this time, but they would never catch him. He had Allah on his side and a lifetime to carry out his plans.

Chapter 23: A Plan Comes Together

January 13, 2005

The old junker ground to a halt in front of a small petrol station roughly 150 miles from where Jimmy had started. He had bought the only vehicle available in town, an old pickup truck whose rust-covered surfaced hinted that blue had been the original color. It had been just after midnight when he actually left the small town for good, following the small road out of town for 15 miles until he met with the main highway that ran south.

The roads here were littered with potholes and cracks. The sun had beaten the life from the highways and roads, making it difficult for Jimmy to drive much more than 40 kilometers per hour. It had slowed him down, but it hadn't stopped him. There hadn't been time to warn the others in the group of what had happened. For all he knew, they had all been busted. Jimmy wiped his forehead with a shirt from his backpack and stepped from the truck into the dusty parking lot.

He pulled the backpack from the front seat of the truck and fumbled through it for the small map he had purchased in town. It had been that same map that had told Jimmy where to go. This particular town had a bus station where he hoped he could buy a ticket further south, eventually hoping to catch a flight or ship that would take him back across the ocean toward his home. He walked over to a bench that had been set off to one side of the station and unfolded the map, looking carefully at his options.

This was, by far, the largest town in the surrounding area. His choices limited, he decided to walk over to the bus station and see when the next bus left town and where it was going. In the back of his mind, a torrential storm of angry emotions churned. *She* was the reason they knew. He *would* right this wrong. He *would* ensure the Americans paid for their foreign policies. But for now, he had to relocate and reorganize. As he walked across the street toward the bus station, he prayed silently to Allah for the safety of the other team members. *This all would have worked if it weren't for that woman!*

January 13, 2005: 7:56 P.M.

The young man blended in perfectly with the crowd. He had taken to walking the streets of the French Quarter each night, watching carefully to see how the others in the area acted. It had been several days since he had last heard from Jimmy and was growing concerned. But the plan was already laid; he had prepared everything according to what he had been told. This was all a very noble act. Allah would reward them for these sacrifices. Now all he had to do was wait two more nights, then he could escape this hell on earth. How could human beings act like this? Were they not afraid of going to hell?

The crowd was unbearable. Bodies were crushing against him, invading his personal space. At one point a young woman with yellow hair had grabbed his crotch and kissed his face. That had made his blood run both hot and cold at the same time; lust blazed in his heart while disgust threatened to empty the contents of his stomach onto the cold cement sidewalks. *Aren't you a doll?* she had said to him. He smiled as best he could, trying hard to hide the revulsion and show her only the lust he felt. You must fit in. The words echoed through his head. Jimmy had been right to remind them of that. The task was going to be difficult, but it was needed.

He had gone into one of the small side shops and purchased about 50 dollars' worth of beads, tossing them at women baring themselves in the street. The meaning of it all totally escaped his mind, and he was finding it increasingly more difficult to continue in the charade. Only two more nights, he reminded himself again. He moved back through the crowd, finding it easier to move alongside the buildings and homes on Bourbon Street than to walk straight down the center of the street.

There were plenty of police officers on duty here, but most watched with only passing interest as the events in the French Quarter unfolded. They were used to this form of revelry and never appeared shocked to see any of it occur. They stopped only the most heinous activities and let the rest go without so much as a second glance.

As he wandered through the streets back to his small apartment several blocks away, he understood completely why Jimmy chose this place as his target. The people were caught up in the celebration and would never notice one person setting down a backpack. Those not killed by the explosions would be trampled by the remaining crowd fleeing the area as they tried as best they could to escape the violence. Humans act much like cattle when frightened. He smiled to himself and turned the corner toward his home. *Only two more nights*, he thought with a grin.

January 13, 2005: 8:43 P.M.

"Tyler," a voice yelled above the din of the office area. "They've found an archive!"

Tyler, Neil, and Jeremy all turned toward the voice to see Herschel standing up straight in his cubical. "They're going to forward us all the information so that we can pull the images."

"That's awesome," Jeremy said with a smile. It was the first time in a while that he had actually felt like smiling. "We're still in the game."

"When are we going to see the archives, Herschel?" Tyler asked without a smile. "We're going to have a lot of work to do in a very short period of time."

"We'll have everything we need within the hour. They're bringing an entire backup system, RAID drive included, over from their department so that we can plug it directly into our research network."

"Well, Tyler," Neil said as he patted the young man on the back, "It sounds as if we're all back in business." Neil was genuinely happy, and Jeremy watched the two men speak back and forth. Tyler looked worn out and irritated.

"Why the glum look, Tyler?" he asked.

"It just occurred to me, Jeremy, that we're all likely to be working nonstop for the next two days, maybe longer." He sighed and sat down in the chair nearest him. "We have no idea how many messages are in those archives or how long it will take the agency to pull the messages back out. This is going to be a lot of work, and our chances of success by our deadline are not guaranteed."

"Hey, Herschel," Neil shouted across the room. "How far back do the archives span, anyway?"

Herschel walked out from around his cubical and walked their way. "They say they've got at least another three weeks, maybe a little more. There was a local animal rescue that sponsors access to animal-related newsgroups for school kids. They were hosting the archive in a library over in Arundel County."

Jeremy smiled wide at the answer. "See, Tyler. We can get through those fairly quickly." He pointed at the others watching the exchange from their respective chairs. "We have all these people to help get this done, and three weeks' worth of data could make all the difference in the world."

"He's right, you know," Neil said with a smile as well. "There's a good chance we'll be done with this before morning. Lydia, is everything ready with this network to accept the new system? What can we do to help?"

Herschel walked over to Lydia and handed her a piece of paper. "Here are the specs for the system they're bringing over. It shouldn't be a big deal to connect it to the rest of the boxes. The network card is installed and operational, so we should just need to change the network settings and export all the messages."

"You're probably right," she replied with a smile. "According to this diagram it should be quick work. Why don't you three run out for drinks for everyone, and I'll order some more pizza. It sounds like we'll be here for a while."

"Sounds good to me, Lydia," Tyler answered. "Hey, Parviz, you still have that iPod here?"

"Sure do," Parviz responded.

"Well, plug it into our intercom system, and let's get to work," Tyler said with a small smile. "Jeremy, would you mind taking everyone's drink order? I'm going to run to the restroom before we go."

"Will do, boss man," Jeremy responded with a small laugh. This is all going to work out, he thought to himself happily as he pulled a piece of paper from his notepad.

January 14, 2005: 6:00 P.M.

Tyler sat back in his chair and rubbed the back of his neck with his fingers. It had been a long night at work. They had exported all the images from the newsgroup archive and examined each of them using all the tools they had at hand. All in all they ended up sending another 21 messages to the agency for final examination and extraction. That had been at 7:00 this morning. Once the images had been sent off, they had all gone home to get some needed rest.

He was the first back to the office, and it was already 6:00 P.M. Even though he was already sleep deprived from the last few weeks of work, Tyler had found it difficult to actually rest during his time at home. The few hours he had managed to get helped a little, but he wasn't back to normal, not yet. He was too worried about the impending attack to rest. His mind wouldn't let him. Hundreds of people, perhaps even thousands, could die and his team had been key in trying to stop it. Failure was unacceptable.

The frustration was stewing inside him and he sat in his cubical watching silently as the screensaver spewed colorful patterns on his monitor. There was no logical reason he could conjure up for these people attacking innocent citizens, and it angered him. His complete lack of control over the situation was stressing him out. No matter how hard he worked to put a stop to the attack, there were still certain things he had no impact on whatsoever. The time it took for NSA to dump the messages back was out of his control. Detecting the hidden messages in the first place was also sketchy at best. Everything seemed to be conspiring against him.

Tyler set his elbows on his desk and put his head in his hands, leaning on the desktop and relaxing his neck. *I've got to relax*, he told himself. But the strain was eating him alive. He ran his fingers through his hair and let his head rest totally in his hands. The blood in his veins felt as though it were barely moving. His eyes closed involuntarily.

He could hear a distant but insistent ringing in his ears. *What is that?* he could hear his own mind ask. His eyes opened slowly, and Tyler realized he had fallen asleep in his cubical at work. The clock on his desk read 6:43. Reaching across the desk, he grabbed the phone receiver, thankful to hear the ringing stop.

"This is Tyler," he answered. The voice on the other end was frantic. "You did what?" he asked. "Really? Oh gawd. Have you told anyone else? Okay. Yes, we'll get agents on the ground as well. I just need about two hours to get everything arranged." He sat back in his chair. "No, sir. I totally understand. Sure, I can contact the local authorities. Will you be in charge of this operation on the ground? Yes, sir. Okay, I'll take care of it right away."

Tyler hung up the phone and realized suddenly that he was holding his breath. He let the old air out of his lungs and set the receiver back on the phone. Dozens of things were running through his head; there was so much to get done in such a short period of time. People needed to be sent on-site, and it needed to be done now. He picked the receiver back up and dialed Neil's extension.

Neil's voice mail answered automatically, apparently set on the Out of Office setting while he was working downstairs. Tyler jotted down the cell phone number provided on the greeting and decided to leave a message in case Neil came into the office soon.

"Neil," he began, "this is Tyler. I just got word back from the National Security Agency. The attack is going to be in New Orleans. I'm trying to get people on the ground in the next four hours. Call me." He hung up the phone; adrenaline was now pumping through his veins. *Mardi Gras*, he whispered. *This is going to be bad.* Picking up his cell phone, he began dialing the numbers to his own team members. There wasn't much time left. They had to move *now*.

January 15, 2005: 12:02 A.M.

The man moved within the throng of people in the French Quarter, barely able to breathe from all the people pressing against him. With crushing force the revelers pushed against one another, with small gaps forming where women were pulling their shirts up. There had to be thousands of people crammed into this tiny little area, most of them in a drunken stupor.

The part that concerned him the most was the sheer numbers of law enforcement officials in the area. He had never seen so many in such a small area, even in the time he had spent in the French Quarter over the last few months. Something was definitely suspicious, but then again, why were they not clearing the area if they suspected something? A man bumped up against his left side and a well-endowed woman squeezed by on his right, her body pushed tightly against his. Immediately his blood ran hot. Aroused, he tried desperately to focus his mind back on the task at hand. *Please, Allah*, he whispered, *give me strength in my hour of greatest trial.*

The backpack sitting against his back seemed much heavier than it normally did; maybe it was just his nerves. The contents didn't weigh much more than his normal cargo, but the weight of the task associated with those contents pulled him toward the ground. He continued moving with the crowd, trying to smile and laugh. At one point, he gave some beads to a woman who had pulled her shirt above her shoulders. He wanted to look as though he belonged there, as if he were enjoying himself. Finally, he reached a spot near a sidewalk where a large red trashcan had been stationed. Even with one trashcan every 20 feet down the street, there were still piles of garbage littering the area. Trash poured unto the sidewalk from trashcans that had been stuffed past their rims. The smell was nauseous, and he held his breath.

The young man avoided a puddle against the curb; one smelled suspiciously like urine. *Oh God*, he thought. Reaching his hand behind his back, he pulled the soft green bag from his shoulder and pulled it around in front where he could better see the contents. He stuck his hand inside the backpack and set the timer mechanism. *Fifteen minutes should give me plenty of time*, he thought with a smile. Once the timer was set, he connected the last wire to the device and zipped the bag back up.

Looking around, he saw no one in the crowd who seemed to take particular notice of him. He took the opportunity to give his remaining beads to another young woman. She kissed him on the cheek, the strong smell of rum permeating his nostrils as she walked away from him. When the crowd filled in again, he laid the bag gently next to the pile of trash sitting on the curb. *It is done*, he said with conviction. Turning around, he walked away from the garbage heap, making his way slowly down the sidewalk. As he moved, a hand grabbed him by the shoulder. He turned to face a man in a blue uniform staring at him.

"Isn't this yours?" the man asked with a look of distrust. The young man prayed one last time. Within moments, Bourbon Street was clear, and the man watched from within a guarded patrol car as the backpack was detonated within a large bomb disposal unit. A single thought ran through his head: *I have failed.*

Chapter 24: Turning Fiction into Reality

The story you've just finished reading was completely fictional. Well, at least the story itself was fictional. The technology was very real and accessible today on the Internet. The unfortunate, and very scary part about all this is that the story fails to touch on the reality of the situation. For years, the Western world has ignored the threat of destructive activities over the Internet. Our perception has been that the technology is neither known nor prevalent in the parts of the world we consider to be dangerous.

I left the conclusion of the story hanging, intentionally. It mirrors real life. The good guys manage to catch one of the terrorists in this book, but what about the other four? It was difficult for Tyler and Jeremy to find the messages hidden in all the garbage on the Internet. Without a little creative maneuvering on the government's part, they might have missed the mark entirely. The threat is *real*. We live in a time period that parallels the end of the story.

Government entities aren't the only potential victims of covert channels, either. If you perform a keyword search on the Internet, you can find a plethora of news articles that present both evidence and speculation on the use of these mechanisms in the real world. Commercial entities can just as easily become victims to covert channels, losing customer information, affecting competitive advantage, and disrupting the finances of the organization.

The truth of the matter is that we've fallen well behind the curve on detecting these types of covert channels. Sure, we're getting better at detecting steganography and breaking the simple encryption utilized in some of the older tools and applications, but we're not gaining any ground on the newer technologies that are coming to the forefront.

This chapter highlights some of the possible paths that the future of covert channels can take. Each one of the options described in this chapter is realistic and plausible. If you ask any wartime military commander, he or she will tell you that when a form of communication is compromised, it is rarely used again. Let's take a few minutes and address the potential future of covert channels so that we can better understand what areas we may need to focus on in the coming years.

The Future of Steganography

Steganography can most easily be described as hiding data, information, or a message within another object in such a way that it will not be noticed. The history of steganography dates backs to when man first began to publish books. Ancient Greeks would melt the wax from their wax message tablets and scratch their covert communication on to the wood of the tablet itself, replacing the wax on the surface when they were done. This effectively hid the message from prying eyes, allowing vital military and political information to slip past nosey guards. If we take this concept and place it in current technology, we're talking primarily about hiding data within other binary objects, such as images, audio files, and executables.

Modern forms of steganography have several limitations. We can expect more robust forms of steganography to be released in the near future. Already, the older forms have been rewritten with more robust encryption algorithms, like the AES algorithm already being used in some tools. But this is really just the first step in an escalating war. All the possibilities presented to you in this chapter are possible today, with current technology. The programming libraries already exist to make development of these tools easier. Only by creatively attempting to predict the future of covert channels, can we begin to protect ourselves from their effects.

Carrier Groups

Steganography, historically, has been a one-payload-to-one-carrier proposition. It was simpler this way. Bob has a data file he wants to hide, so he chooses an appropriate carrier file. He then combines the two files using a specific application and, voilà, his information is now hidden.

This type of covert channel, although easily performed using methods like the LSB modification discussed earlier in the book, are limited by the size of the carrier file. Large amounts of information are difficult to hide within a single image without causing noticeable distortion to the carrier file that might draw unwanted attention. Audio files offer space for a larger payload, but again, as technology continues to evolve at an enormous rate, there will inevitably be a need for more storage within these covert channels.

At the beginning of 2004, I coined the term *carrier group* to refer to a collection of carrier files for each payload. So instead of the traditional 1 to 1 ratio we had before, we can now select the appropriate number of carrier files based on the size of our payload. This gives us flexibility to designate specifically how much of the payload is hidden within each carrier file. Smaller amounts of hidden information within each carrier file are more difficult to detect utilizing current technology.

For example, Figure 24.1 shows the traditional single-carrier-per-payload structure. The carrier is 400 kilobytes (KB) in size. Research shows that in order to maintain the integrity of the carrier and avoid distortion, the payload should never be much more than 25 percent to 30 percent the size of its carrier. For example, we've used a 100KB document as the payload. This should not create any noticeable distortion in the carrier file, which in this case is a digital image. Modern detection tools *do* have the ability to detect hidden data from 15 percent and higher in many cases, even if there is no noticeable distortion in the carrier file.

This process would be the same regardless of whether we're using an image file or audio file. The distortion would just be expressed differently depending on the carrier. Distortion in a digital image could come in the form of grainy patterns in the image, whereas distortion in a music file might come as elevated volume, white noise, or grainy sound distortion.

Figure 24.1 One-to-One Carrier/Payload Ratio

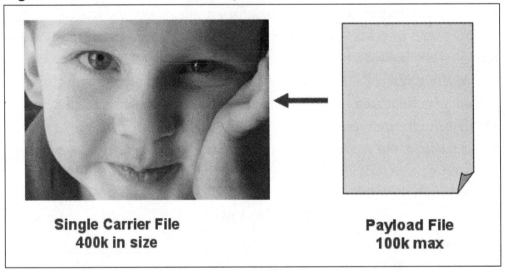

Single Carrier File
400k in size

Payload File
100k max

As time passes, technology inevitably evolves. Taking this concept into account, we see that at some point in the near future, the storage capacity of these mechanisms will increase to accommodate the increasing size of file in nearly every platform. The carrier group concept addresses this by allowing users to select as many files as they need in order to ensure adequate, and protected, storage of their data. For example, in Figure 24.2, Bob has taken the same payload and spread it across five carrier files. Instead of using a single 400KB carrier, which might be detectable using today's analysis software, Bob now uses five different 400KB carrier files.

The software would take the 100KB payload, divide it into five equal parts of 20KB each, and store each part into a different carrier file. This process provides two separate benefits to individuals creating the covert channel. On one hand, they now have the ability to store significantly higher rates of data. The channel has become more effective since there are virtually no files of normal size that could not be transmitted in this manner.

The second benefit is that the carrier file will be undetectable in most cases using modern detection tools and applications. By hiding a single 20KB chunk of our payload in each 400KB carrier file, we've shrunk the payload size to 5 percent of the size of each carrier in our group.

Figure 24.2 Example Carrier Group

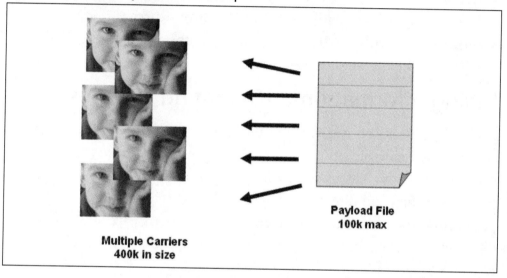

Payload File
100k max

Multiple Carriers
400k in size

This concept would work equally well with any digital image or audio file format available on the Internet. Someone using this type of concept in reality might decide to post 10 completely separate images on a public web site. Only five of these images might be part of the carrier group, and since the modern arsenal of detection tools would never detect steganography within the images, the information could be deemed reliably safe from prying eyes.

The last issue with utilizing the carrier group concept is that the images must be put back in the correct order before the data can be pulled from the carrier and reassembled back into a meaningful message. It provides one last level of protection for individuals communicating via channels similar to this and another hurdle for analysts to overcome before they're able to access the hidden information within this format of covert channel.

Applying this technology to MP3 music format files, which are abundant across the Internet and via peer-to-peer file-sharing networks, we afford ourselves even greater storage capacity without sacrificing the secrecy of the data. Music files like this can easily be 5 megabytes (MB) in size. Using the same scenario we used earlier with the digital images, we take five audio files with a size of 5MB as our carrier group, which, in turn, gives us a full 1 MB of data storage without telling the world that we have hidden information there.

Hiding Information in Operating Systems

Back when Microsoft was creating the Windows NT operating system, it also created a new file system called New Technology File System (NTFS), which was designed to allow users and administrators to better secure their files and directories by assigning user rights and protective permissions to each object they created or owned. As part of this new architecture, Microsoft provided backward compatibility with Apple's Macintosh operating system and its file system.

The older Macintosh OS versions stored their files and directories as a single object with two distinct parts. One part was the resource fork, and the other was the data fork. The resource fork provided the information to the Apple operating system about the *type* of file being accessed by a user. The data fork provided the actual data for that file. Whereas the Microsoft Windows OS relies on the extension of each file to determine the format of the data inside and what application to load, the older Macintosh OS versions relied on this resource fork.

To maintain compatibility with the older versions of Apple's operating system, Microsoft created Alternate Data Streams (ADS) within its NTFS architecture. Now when users copied files between the two differing operating systems, both information streams would be carried over, allowing Windows to read files created on an Apple computer.

By doing this, Microsoft has created a double-edged sword. An ADS provides increased security through powerful permission settings, but also creates a mechanism for hiding tremendous amounts of information on a hard drive that is not detectable with the default tools shipped with Microsoft's operating system. Users have the ability to create as many of these ADSes on a computer, using tools supplied with the operating system and regardless of the permission settings on the parent file.

The really scary part of all this is that administrators cannot, by default, check for these ADSes. Commands like *dir,* that work under the Windows Command Prompt, and the Windows Explorer interface will not display information for ADS, nor will they display any change in file size. Bob could hide a 5MB music file under the explorer.exe file, and none of the default tools that ship with the operating system would tell a user the ADS existed. The only sign a user would have would be the drastic loss of hard drive space with no apparent reason. This vulnerability has been around for years now and was even the target of the W2k.stream virus that struck various Windows operating systems starting as early as September 2000.

Fortunately for administrators, there are third-party companies that have created tools for scanning, detecting, and removing ADS from computer systems. There are still no tools shipped with the Windows operating system that will provide this function as part of the default installation.

The Future of ADS

An ADS is an interesting form of covert channel in that currently it cannot be transmitted across a TCP/IP network unless it's being moving from one shared NTFS drive to another. Third-party applications, such as File Transfer Protocol (FTP) applications or compression applications, do not pick up the streams when they deal with files on the file system.

These applications utilize only the data stream of the original file. Although currently there is research being done by a group in Salt Lake City to try and encapsulate ADS information for transmission across the Internet, it doesn't exist yet. This limits the effects of this type of covert channel to strictly NTFS networks.

Taking a look at the ADS problem and how we could turn this into a more secure tool for covert communication and file storage, we look back at the architecture that we used in the previous section on steganography. Bob is now a child pornographer and wants to hide a 5MB compressed file on his hard drive that authorities will not be able to put back together in case he ever gets busted. Without that evidence, the cops have nothing to hold him on, and he's released back on to the streets of Normalville, USA.

So Bob writes a piece of software that takes his payload and splits it into pieces, hiding each piece in a random ADS hidden within a system file somewhere on his computer. As we see in Figure 24.3, the software takes Bob's compressed file, prompts Bob for an encryption password, splits it into four pieces, and then stores each one of these pieces as an ADS on his computer. When Bob wants to access his file later, he loads the software and enters his password. The software pulls the various pieces back together and decrypts the contents back on to Bob's desktop.

Figure 24.3 Secure ADS Usage

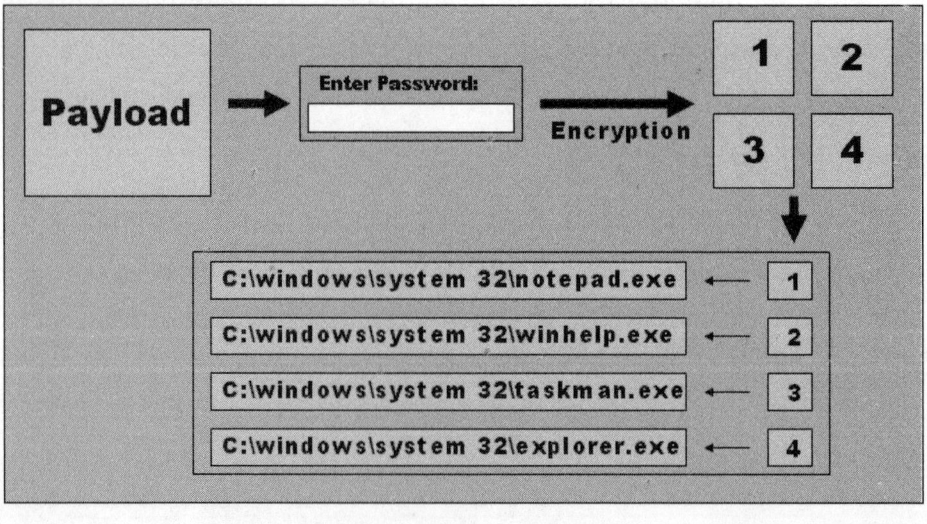

Bob's ingenuity has enabled him to create a more secure method for storing information on his computer. And since Microsoft Windows allows a user to create as many ADSes under any file as he or she wants, Bob now has as much secure storage as his hard drive has space.

Covert Network Channels

The field of network-based covert channels has been expanding at an alarming rate. Over the last two years, new tools have been released that provide on-command network-based covert channels. Some of these tools create covert channels via secure TCP/IP tunnels. Others provide a simple message-based channel where the information being hidden is transmitted in a manner acceptable by the operating system and core networking technology. We'll concentrate solely on the latter example to illustrate where these mechanisms could be headed.

One of the first forms of this type of network channel was called Covert_TCP. Tools like these use the headers within the Transmission Control Protocol (TCP) and Internet Protocol Version 4 (IPv4) to hide simple text messages, passing one character per second to a receiver on the other end. In Figure 24.4, a standard IPv4 header is shown with the identification field highlighted for our example.

The identification header of the IPv4 protocol is used to identify fragments of a single datagram. When a user sends data across the network, that data is broken into datagrams, which are then fragmented and sent across the network. Each of the fragments that belong to the same datagram will have the same identification number in the identification header of the IPv4 protocol.

Figure 24.4 Standard IPv4 Header

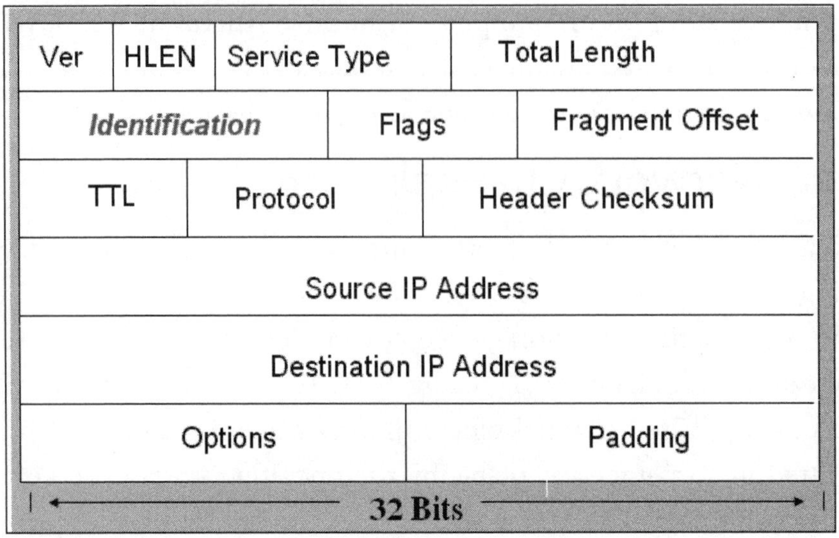

Each character in the English character set on computers has a number associated with it. As an example, the letter *H* has a numeric representation of 72. Suppose Bob wanted to send the message *hello* to a friend. The number 72 is too short to look legitimate as an identification header value within IPv4, so he must do something to create a larger and more realistic number. The solution he comes up with is to multiply the numeric value of each character times 256.

Using this schema, Bob's computer now sends five different packets of information across the network, one at a time. Each one contains a different value in its identification field, based on the English character from Bob's message that it contains. The word hello would equate to 18432 in the first header, 17664 in the second, 19456 in the third and fourth, and 20224 in the fifth header. The receiver on the other end would simply pull out the identification header information, divide by 256, and read Bob's message.

The Future of Network Covert Channels

This concept has been around for some time as a means for communicating covertly across the Internet. It tends to be slow because of reliability issues. There are no error-checking mechanisms when information is sent this way because data is transmitted outside the realm of the normal TCP/IP error checking. This means that we may never know if all the information made it across the network to our receiver.

The future of the Internet will rely on a new version of the Internet Protocol (IP) known as IP Version 6 (IPv6). Most new networking equipment is now IPv6 compatible, and governments around the world are now requiring new networking hardware to be IPv6 compliant when purchased for use on their networks. As the new technology begins to take its place in the world, so does the potential for newer forms of covert channels.

In fact, we can build similar channels to what is currently being used in IPv4 by selecting new target headers for modification. In Figure 24.5, we see a standard IPv6 header structure that would be used on any IPv6 network. The specific header we'll concentrate on is the Next Header option.

Figure 24.5 Standard IPv6 Header

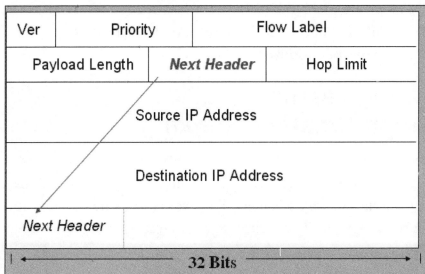

IPv6 was built to be more robust and simpler to use. At the same time, however, the architects of the new standard had to build in the potential for growth within the protocol. They did this in the form of the Extension Headers using the *Next Header* option. As of the writing of this book, this header has no real use or function, except to save space for later use. But it's considered a mandatory header within IPv6 and will not be discarded by routers like some other superfluous headers will be.

The *Next Header* header option allows users to chain together extension headers, passing further information to routers based on their need. Customized headers can be inserted into an IPv6 transmission by applications or users. Routers are told what header to read next by looking at each *Next Header* option in the chain. Using this to our advantage, we could easily use the *Next Header* function to hide information in much the same way we did earlier.

The *Next Header* is actually a pointer to a new IPv6 header that exists just after the destination IP address and just before the actual data of the transmission. Network devices read each header in an IPv6 transmission, in turn, until they reach the *Next Header*. At this point, the router will redirect to the header indicated in the *Next Header*. When there are no more extension headers to add to the transmission, the *Next Header* field will point to the parent header; for example, the TCP header. This functionality gives us a great hiding place for information. The router won't remove the information stored in those extra headers, thus allowing us to hide numeric messages similarly to IPv4.

Learning Lessons through Creative Thinking

The goal of this book is to help readers understand the impact that covert channels easily could have on their lives. Covert channels are easy to create and not so easy to detect. They come in many different forms, not just steganography. The technology for creating these types of covert communication channels is evolving much quicker than the technology to detect them and remove them.

The examples provided in this book are just that, examples. They are possible paths that the evolution of these technologies could take in the very near future. No one can read the future and tell us where the threats will come from later in life. But we *can* take action by understanding that these forms of communication already exist and that they will continue to evolve, just as the rest of the Internet evolves.

Covert channels work because of weaknesses in the human body and mind. They send messages outside the logical construct of everyday computer applications. Data can be hidden anywhere and in many different ways. To protect ourselves, we must be willing to admit that the threat exists and that the technology is there, growing more complex with each passing year. Security experts around the world need to think outside the box and beyond the design. Creative solutions may be our best defense against a silent and invisible threat that easily could affect every single facet of our professional and personal lives.

Glossary

Access Control List (ACL) a list or database on a server that contains permissions for specific users to access specific services or files

Algorithm any set of instructions or rules for solving problems

Alternate Data Streams a feature specific to Windows® operating systems in which hidden files containing attribute information are attached to standard files. This feature was developed for cross-platform support of Macintosh® files, which have a data "fork" and resource "fork" associated with any particular file.

American Registry for Internet Numbers (ARIN) a web site run by a nonprofit organization that registers *IP* numbers and allows one to determine what organizations own specific IP address ranges (www.arin.net)

Binary the base two numeral system in which numbers are represented strictly by 1's and 0's

Bitmap (BMP) the standardized digital image file format that consists of grids of pixels. Each pixel stores a numerical value that represents a color, and these pixels are combined to render the picture. Examples of types of BMP files are GIF and JPEG.

Carrier the vessel in which a payload, or secret message, is hidden. In the case of steganography, it is described in electronic format; namely, digital image and audio files. However, it can actually be anything that can hold information.

Checksum A mathematical value that typically serves as a way to detect errors in data through a redundancy check (see cyclic redundancy check)

Cipher a coded message

Color Buddies in digital image *steganography*, a term used to describe the close color matches created by tools that employ least significant bit (LSB) modification as a method to hide information. Because each pixel's color is represented by a number, LSB modification creates colors that look close to identical but differ slightly in numerical value. It is in these slight value differences that hidden information is stored.

Compile the process that transforms a computer application from the programming language it is written in to an executable form

Covert Channels for the purpose of this book, a broad term used to describe information-hiding mechanisms; these channels include anything that may be exploited for secret communication.

Covert Channel Tunnel Testing (CCTT) a UNIX-based covert channel tool that embeds information in network traffic to include HTTP packets

Covert TCP a UNIX-based covert channel tool that hides information in the unused areas of TCP packets

Cyclic Redundancy Check (CRC)-32 a type of hash function used to create a checksum. The CRC-32 differs from SHA-1 and MD5 as it is not a cryptographic hash function; it can detect errors and changes, but provides no security against them.

Database any collection of information; modern usage refers to electronic databases stored on computer systems.

Dataset for the purpose of this book, categories of software types, such as steganography software or keystroke logging software

Defense Advanced Research Projects Agency (DARPA) the central research and development organization for the Department of Defense

Denial of Service (DoS) a type of malicious network attack in which a system is overwhelmed with traffic and is unable to respond to legitimate requests

Department of Homeland Security (DHS) a federal agency created by consolidating existing functions with the express purpose of protecting the United States from terrorism

DCT Coefficient Within JPEG files, the color values of the compressed image are represented numerically by the discrete cosine transform coefficients. The quality of a JPEG can be varied by adjusting how accurately the coefficients are stored. It is these coefficients that are modified when steganography is applied.

Discrete Cosine Transform (DCT) a mathematical technique used to compress digital image files, particularly JPEGs. It allows one to achieve a balance between file size and image quality.

Dots per Inch (DPI) the spatial frequency at which a digital image is sampled; a higher number often indicates higher resolution. Also known as pixels per inch.

EFNet an IRC network (www.efnet.org)

File Transfer Protocol (FTP) a format that allows the transfer of large amounts of information from one point to another over the Internet

Gargoyle™ a commercial tool designed to scan for malware on target systems

GNU Image Manipulation Program (GIMP) free software that allows image manipulation tasks such as photo retouching, image composition, and authoring

GNU Network Object Model Environment (GNOME) free software that provides a Windows®-like environment for a user interface

Graphics Interchange Format (GIF) a proprietary digital image file format. GIF images contain eight bits per pixel, meaning they use a 256-color palette to represent the image.

Hash a unique value calculated from electronic files, much like a fingerprint. Any type of electronic file can be hashed (e.g., image files, text files, or even network traffic). Also known as a message digest, it is often used to confirm the integrity of files since any change to a file will result in a different hash.

Hijab the headscarf worn by Muslim women, which typically conceals the hair and neck

Histogram a bar graph representation of values; in digital image analysis, viewing an image's histogram allows you to see the frequency of individual colors

Hydan a UNIX-based steganography tool that hides information within executable files without impacting their operation

Hyper Text Markup Language (HTML) a type of programming language used to create web sites

Hyper Text Transfer Protocol (HTTP) the format used to transfer information from web site servers to end users so that they may be viewed in a browser

Internet Protocol (IP) Address a unique number that identifies a particular machine on a computer network

Internet Relay Chat (IRC) a service that allows users to communicate online in real time in a public forum

Internet Service Provider (ISP) a company that provides users access to the Internet

Joint Photographic Experts Group (JPEG) most accurately, a compression scheme for true color images, but most commonly known as a digital image file format. It is arguably the most common found on the Internet today and uses discrete cosine transform technique to produce a sliding scale of graphics compression.

JP Hide and Seek (JPHS) a free steganography software tool that hides files in JPEGs

Keystroke Logger hardware or software that records all keys pressed on a target computer keyboard

Kufi a type of round, brimless hat worn by many Middle Eastern and African men

Least Significant Bit (LSB) the digit to the far right in numbers that are represented in binary. Changing this digit changes the value of the number by one.

Linux a nonproprietary UNIX-based operating system for computers

List Alternate Data Streams (LADS) freeware that allows the listing of all alternate data streams associated with an electronic file

Lossless Compression a method for decreasing the size of digital files for storage, processing, or transmission without losing any information in the file. When uncompressed, the file is bit for bit identical to the original.

Lossy Compression a method for decreasing the size of digital files for storage, processing, or transmission in which information considered redundant or expendable is discarded. When uncompressed, the file will have permanently lost this information.

ls a UNIX command that provides a listing of the unhidden files in the current directory

Malware malicious software, or software created for the purpose of exploiting systems in a manner that is harmful or disruptive

Message Digest (MD)5 a type of mathematical function used to create a *hash*. The MD5 is considered a cryptographic hash function as it is (1) mathematically improbable to recreate the original file from the hash and (2) mathematically improbable that two dissimilar files would result in the same hash. It should be noted that significant security flaws in MD5 were reported in 2004.

.mdb the file extension for Microsoft® Access database

National Institute of Standards and Technology (NIST) a federal agency within the U.S. Commerce Department's Technology Administration whose mission is to develop and promote measurement, standards, and technology

National Security Agency (NSA) a federal agency whose mission is to protect U.S. information systems and produce foreign intelligence information

National Software Reference Library (NSRL) a library of known file hashes created and maintained by NIST and supported by the U.S. Department of Justice's National Institute of Justice. Often used in computer system investigations in order to filter out files associated with known and/or standard software, saving time and effort. It uses CRC-32, SHA-1, and MD5 file hashes.

Null Cipher a method of covert communication in which a secret message may be hidden within the text of an inconspicuous message

Octet eight binary digits (1's and 0's). In decimal form, this is represented in a range from 0 to 255.

Palette also known as a color lookup table (CLUT). It is a predefined table of colors used to render 8-bit digital images (e.g., GIF).

Payload the secret message; this is what is hidden in the carrier.

Pixels picture elements; the smallest visual component of a digital image. Digital images are sampled and mapped as a grid using pixels. Each pixel's color is represented as binary code (1's and 0's).

Pixels per Inch (PPI) the spatial frequency at which a digital image is sampled; a higher number often indicates higher *resolution*. Also known as dots per inch.

Port the physical or logical point through which information enters and leaves a computer

Port Scan an activity in which a computer's *ports* are examined, often to determine vulnerabilities

Proxy Server an intermediary Internet server that filters and fulfills applicable incoming requests in order to improve efficiency of the real server. Proxy servers also function to relay information.

Redundant Array of Independent Disks (RAID) a type of disk drive that actually stores information on more than one drive to ensure backup capability, higher performance, and/or fault tolerance

Resolution the ability to distinguish fine spatial details

Root User the administrative account on any UNIX machine; it has access to all files.

Sam's Big G Play Maker a covert channel tool that creates text from a secret message that appears to be a script

Secure Hash Algorithm (SHA)-1 a type of mathematical function used to create a hash. The SHA-1 is considered a cryptographic hash function as it is (1) mathematically improbable to recreate the original file from the hash and (2) mathematically improbable that two dissimilar files would result in the same hash.

Shell a user interface; a way for the user to interact with a computer application

Spam Mimic a web-based covert channel tool that creates text from a secret message that appears to be spam e-mail content (www.spammimic.com)

Spyware a type of application, usually installed without a user's knowledge or consent, that secretly logs information about the user and/or the user's computer and sends it to the originator

Steganography for the purpose of this book, the hiding of information in a binary medium such as a digital audio or image file

Stego Suite™ a commercial steganography detection and analysis tool

S-Tools a free steganography software tool that hides files in GIFs, BMPs, and WAV files

Substitute User (su) a UNIX command that allows you to become other existing users in a particular system

Tape Archive (.tar) a UNIX-based application that groups files together

Telnet an application used to connect computers to servers

Transmission Control Protocol (TCP) one of the formats used for information sent and received on the Internet

Trojan a type of malware that appears to be a legitimate application, but actually contains something harmful or disruptive to the computer system

True Color any image that is rendered using 24 bits per pixel to represent the red, green, and blue values. Mathematically, this means that any pixel can be one of more than 16.7 million possible colors, resulting in near photographic-quality images.

Universal Serial Bus (USB) a standardized *port* used to transfer information in and out of a computer

USB Key Drive small, portable computer storage devices that use the *USB* port. Owing to their storage capacity and size (about the size of a key), they are rapidly gaining popularity over floppy disks.

USENET an Internet-based news distribution system consisting of a wide variety of interest groups. Members are able to post public e-mails as well as upload attachments such as image files.

WAV a digital audio file format

GNU GENERAL PUBLIC LICENSE

Version 2, June 1991

Copyright (C) 1989, 1991 Free Software Foundation, Inc.

59 Temple Place - Suite 330, Boston, MA 02111-1307, USA

Preamble

The licenses for most software are designed to take away your freedom to share and change it. By contrast, the GNU General Public License is intended to guarantee your freedom to share and change free software—to make sure the software is free for all its users. This General Public License applies to most of the Free Software Foundation's software and to any other program whose authors commit to using it. (Some other Free Software Foundation software is covered by the GNU Library General Public License instead.) You can apply it to your programs, too.

When we speak of free software, we are referring to freedom, not price. Our General Public Licenses are designed to make sure that you have the freedom to distribute copies of free software (and charge for this service if you wish), that you receive source code or can get it if you want it, that you can change the software or use pieces of it in new free programs; and that you know you can do these things.

To protect your rights, we need to make restrictions that forbid anyone to deny you these rights or to ask you to surrender the rights. These restrictions translate to certain responsibilities for you if you distribute copies of the software, or if you modify it.

For example, if you distribute copies of such a program, whether gratis or for a fee, you must give the recipients all the rights that you have. You must make sure that they, too, receive or can get the source code. And you must show them these terms so they know their rights.

We protect your rights with two steps: (1) copyright the software, and (2) offer you this license which gives you legal permission to copy, distribute and/or modify the software.

Also, for each author's protection and ours, we want to make certain that everyone understands that there is no warranty for this free software. If the software is modified by someone else and passed on, we want its recipients to know that what they have is not the original, so that any problems introduced by others will not reflect on the original authors' reputations.

Finally, any free program is threatened constantly by software patents. We wish to avoid the danger that redistributors of a free program will individually obtain patent licenses, in effect making the program proprietary. To prevent this, we have made it clear that any patent must be licensed for everyone's free use or not licensed at all.

The precise terms and conditions for copying, distribution and modification follow.

TERMS AND CONDITIONS FOR COPYING, DISTRIBUTION AND MODIFICATION

0. This License applies to any program or other work which contains a notice placed by the copyright holder saying it may be distributed under the terms of this General Public License. The "Program", below, refers to any such program or work, and a "work based on the Program" means either the Program or any derivative work under copyright law: that is to say, a work containing the Program or a portion of it, either verbatim or with modifications and/or translated into another language. (Hereinafter, translation is included without limitation in the term "modification".) Each licensee is addressed as "you".

Activities other than copying, distribution and modification are not covered by this License; they are outside its scope. The act of running the Program is not restricted, and the output from the Program is covered only if its contents constitute a work based on the Program (independent of having been made by running the Program). Whether that is true depends on what the Program does.

1. You may copy and distribute verbatim copies of the Program's source code as you receive it, in any medium, provided that you conspicuously and appropriately publish on each copy an appropriate copyright notice and disclaimer of warranty; keep intact all the notices that refer to this License and to the absence of any warranty; and give any other recipients of the Program a copy of this License along with the Program.

You may charge a fee for the physical act of transferring a copy, and you may at your option offer warranty protection in exchange for a fee.

2. You may modify your copy or copies of the Program or any portion of it, thus forming a work based on the Program, and copy and distribute such modifications or work under the terms of Section 1 above, provided that you also meet all of these conditions:

a) You must cause the modified files to carry prominent notices stating that you changed the files and the date of any change.

b) You must cause any work that you distribute or publish, that in whole or in part contains or is derived from the Program or any part thereof, to be licensed as a whole at no charge to all third parties under the terms of this License.

c) If the modified program normally reads commands interactively when run, you must cause it, when started running for such interactive use in the most ordinary way, to print or display an announcement including an appropriate copyright notice and a notice that there is no warranty (or else, saying that you provide a warranty) and that users may redistribute the program under these conditions, and telling the user how to view a copy of this License. (Exception: if the Program itself is interactive but does not normally print such an announcement, your work based on the Program is not required to print an announcement.)

These requirements apply to the modified work as a whole. If identifiable sections of that work are not derived from the Program, and can be reasonably considered independent and separate works in themselves, then this License, and its terms, do not apply to those sections when you distribute them as separate works. But when you distribute the same sections as part of a whole which is a work based on the Program, the distribution of the whole must be on the terms of this License, whose permissions for other licensees extend to the entire whole, and thus to each and every part regardless of who wrote it.

Thus, it is not the intent of this section to claim rights or contest your rights to work written entirely by you; rather, the intent is to exercise the right to control the distribution of derivative or collective works based on the Program.

In addition, mere aggregation of another work not based on the Program with the Program (or with a work based on the Program) on a volume of a storage or distribution medium does not bring the other work under the scope of this License.

3. You may copy and distribute the Program (or a work based on it, under Section 2) in object code or executable form under the terms of Sections 1 and 2 above provided that you also do one of the following:

a) Accompany it with the complete corresponding machine-readable source code, which must be distributed under the terms of Sections 1 and 2 above on a medium customarily used for software interchange; or,

b) Accompany it with a written offer, valid for at least three years, to give any third party, for a charge no more than your cost of physically performing source distribution, a complete machine-readable copy of the corresponding source code, to be distributed under the terms of Sections 1 and 2 above on a medium customarily used for software interchange; or,

c) Accompany it with the information you received as to the offer to distribute corresponding source code. (This alternative is allowed only for noncommercial distribution and only if you received the program in object code or executable form with such an offer, in accord with Subsection b above.)

The source code for a work means the preferred form of the work for making modifications to it. For an executable work, complete source code means all the source code for all modules it contains, plus any associated interface definition files, plus the scripts used to control compilation and installation of the executable. However, as a special exception, the source code distributed need not include anything that is normally distributed (in either source or binary form) with the major components (compiler, kernel, and so on) of the operating system on which the executable runs, unless that component itself accompanies the executable.

If distribution of executable or object code is made by offering access to copy from a designated place, then offering equivalent access to copy the source code from the same place counts as distribution of the source code, even though third parties are not compelled to copy the source along with the object code.

4. You may not copy, modify, sublicense, or distribute the Program except as expressly provided under this License. Any attempt otherwise to copy, modify, sublicense or distribute the Program is void, and will automatically terminate your rights under this License. However, parties who have received copies, or rights, from you under this License will not have their licenses terminated so long as such parties remain in full compliance.

5. You are not required to accept this License, since you have not signed it. However, nothing else grants you permission to modify or distribute the Program or its derivative works. These actions are prohibited by law if you do not accept this License. Therefore, by modifying or distributing the Program (or any work based on the Program), you indicate your acceptance of this License to do so, and all its terms and conditions for copying, distributing or modifying the Program or works based on it.

6. Each time you redistribute the Program (or any work based on the Program), the recipient automatically receives a license from the original licensor to copy, distribute or modify the Program subject to these terms and conditions. You may not impose any further restrictions on the recipients' exercise of the rights granted herein. You are not responsible for enforcing compliance by third parties to this License.

7. If, as a consequence of a court judgment or allegation of patent infringement or for any other reason (not limited to patent issues), conditions are imposed on you (whether by court order, agreement or otherwise) that contradict the conditions of this License, they do not excuse you from the conditions of this License. If you cannot distribute so as to satisfy simultaneously your obligations under this License and any other pertinent obligations, then as a consequence you may not distribute the Program at all. For example, if a patent license would not permit royalty-free redistribution of the Program by all those who receive copies directly or indirectly through you, then the only way you could satisfy both it and this

License would be to refrain entirely from distribution of the Program.

If any portion of this section is held invalid or unenforceable under any particular circumstance, the balance of the section is intended to apply and the section as a whole is intended to apply in other circumstances.

It is not the purpose of this section to induce you to infringe any patents or other property right claims or to contest validity of any such claims; this section has the sole purpose of protecting the integrity of the free software distribution system, which is implemented by public license practices. Many people have made generous contributions to the wide range of software distributed through that system in reliance on consistent application of that system; it is up to the author/donor to decide if he or she is willing to distribute software through any other system and a licensee cannot impose that choice.

This section is intended to make thoroughly clear what is believed to be a consequence of the rest of this License.

8. If the distribution and/or use of the Program is restricted in certain countries either by patents or by copyrighted interfaces, the original copyright holder who places the Program under this License may add an explicit geographical distribution limitation excluding those countries, so that distribution is permitted only in or among countries not thus excluded. In such case, this License incorporates the limitation as if written in the body of this License.

9. The Free Software Foundation may publish revised and/or new versions of the General Public License from time to time. Such new versions will be similar in spirit to the present version, but may differ in detail to address new problems or concerns.

Each version is given a distinguishing version number. If the Program specifies a version number of this License which applies to it and "any later version", you have the option of following the terms and conditions either of that version or of any later version published by the Free Software Foundation. If the Program does not specify a version number of this License, you may choose any version ever published by the Free Software Foundation.

10. If you wish to incorporate parts of the Program into other free programs whose distribution conditions are different, write to the author to ask for permission. For software which is copyrighted by the Free Software Foundation, write to the Free Software Foundation; we sometimes make exceptions for this. Our decision will be guided by the two goals of preserving the free status of all derivatives of our free software and of promoting the sharing and reuse of software generally.

NO WARRANTY

11. BECAUSE THE PROGRAM IS LICENSED FREE OF CHARGE, THERE IS NO WARRANTY FOR THE PROGRAM, TO THE EXTENT PERMITTED BY APPLICABLE LAW. EXCEPT WHEN OTHERWISE STATED IN WRITING THE COPYRIGHT HOLDERS AND/OR OTHER PARTIES PROVIDE THE PRO-

GRAM "AS IS" WITHOUT WARRANTY OF ANY KIND, EITHER EXPRESSED OR IMPLIED, INCLUDING, BUT NOT LIMITED TO, THE IMPLIED WARRANTIES OF MERCHANTABILITY AND FITNESS FOR A PARTICULAR PURPOSE. THE ENTIRE RISK AS TO THE QUALITY AND PERFORMANCE OF THE PROGRAM IS WITH YOU. SHOULD THE PROGRAM PROVE DEFECTIVE, YOU ASSUME THE COST OF ALL NECESSARY SERVICING, REPAIR OR CORRECTION.

12. IN NO EVENT UNLESS REQUIRED BY APPLICABLE LAW OR AGREED TO IN WRITING WILL ANY COPYRIGHT HOLDER, OR ANY OTHER PARTY WHO MAY MODIFY AND/OR REDISTRIBUTE THE PROGRAM AS PERMITTED ABOVE, BE LIABLE TO YOU FOR DAMAGES, INCLUDING ANY GENERAL, SPECIAL, INCIDENTAL OR CONSEQUENTIAL DAMAGES ARISING OUT OF THE USE OR INABILITY TO USE THE PROGRAM (INCLUDING BUT NOT LIMITED TO LOSS OF DATA OR DATA BEING RENDERED INACCURATE OR LOSSES SUSTAINED BY YOU OR THIRD PARTIES OR A FAILURE OF THE PROGRAM TO OPERATE WITH ANY OTHER PROGRAMS), EVEN IF SUCH HOLDER OR OTHER PARTY HAS BEEN ADVISED OF THE POSSIBILITY OF SUCH DAMAGES.

END OF TERMS AND CONDITIONS

How to Apply These Terms to Your New Programs

If you develop a new program, and you want it to be of the greatest possible use to the public, the best way to achieve this is to make it free software which everyone can redistribute and change under these terms.

To do so, attach the following notices to the program. It is safest to attach them to the start of each source file to most effectively convey the exclusion of warranty; and each file should have at least the "copyright" line and a pointer to where the full notice is found.

one line to give the program's name and an idea of what it does.

Copyright (C) *yyyy name of author*

This program is free software; you can redistribute it and/or

modify it under the terms of the GNU General Public License

as published by the Free Software Foundation; either version 2

of the License, or (at your option) any later version.

This program is distributed in the hope that it will be useful,

but WITHOUT ANY WARRANTY; without even the implied warranty of

MERCHANTABILITY or FITNESS FOR A PARTICULAR PURPOSE. See the

GNU General Public License for more details.

You should have received a copy of the GNU General Public License
along with this program; if not, write to the Free Software
Foundation, Inc., 59 Temple Place - Suite 330, Boston, MA 02111-1307, USA.

Also add information on how to contact you by electronic and paper mail.

If the program is interactive, make it output a short notice like this when it starts in an interactive mode:

Gnomovision version 69, Copyright (C) *year name of author*
Gnomovision comes with ABSOLUTELY NO WARRANTY; for details
type `show w'. This is free software, and you are welcome
to redistribute it under certain conditions; type `show c'
for details.

The hypothetical commands 'show w' and 'show c' should show the appropriate parts of the General Public License. Of course, the commands you use may be called something other than 'show w' and 'show c'; they could even be mouse-clicks or menu items—whatever suits your program.

You should also get your employer (if you work as a programmer) or your school, if any, to sign a "copyright disclaimer" for the program, if necessary. Here is a sample; alter the names:

Yoyodyne, Inc., hereby disclaims all copyright
interest in the program `Gnomovision'
(which makes passes at compilers) written
by James Hacker.

signature of Ty Coon, 1 April 1989
Ty Coon, President of Vice

This General Public License does not permit incorporating your program into proprietary programs. If your program is a subroutine library, you may consider it more useful to permit linking proprietary applications with the library. If this is what you want to do, use the GNU Library General Public License instead of this License.

SYNGRESS PUBLISHING LICENSE AGREEMENT

THIS PRODUCT (THE "PRODUCT") CONTAINS PROPRIETARY SOFTWARE, DATA AND INFORMATION (INCLUDING DOCUMENTATION) OWNED BY SYNGRESS PUBLISHING, INC. ("SYNGRESS") AND ITS LICENSORS. YOUR RIGHT TO USE THE PRODUCT IS GOVERNED BY THE TERMS AND CONDITIONS OF THIS AGREEMENT.

LICENSE: Throughout this License Agreement, "you" shall mean either the individual or the entity whose agent opens this package. You are granted a limited, non-exclusive and non-transferable license to use the Product subject to the following terms:

(i) If you have licensed a single user version of the Product, the Product may only be used on a single computer (i.e., a single CPU). If you licensed and paid the fee applicable to a local area network or wide area network version of the Product, you are subject to the terms of the following subparagraph (ii).

(ii) If you have licensed a local area network version, you may use the Product on unlimited workstations located in one single building selected by you that is served by such local area network. If you have licensed a wide area network version, you may use the Product on unlimited workstations located in multiple buildings on the same site selected by you that is served by such wide area network; provided, however, that any building will not be considered located in the same site if it is more than five (5) miles away from any building included in such site. In addition, you may only use a local area or wide area network version of the Product on one single server. If you wish to use the Product on more than one server, you must obtain written authorization from Syngress and pay additional fees.

(iii) You may make one copy of the Product for back-up purposes only and you must maintain an accurate record as to the location of the back-up at all times.

PROPRIETARY RIGHTS; RESTRICTIONS ON USE AND TRANSFER: All rights (including patent and copyright) in and to the Product are owned by Syngress and its licensors. You are the owner of the enclosed disc on which the Product is recorded. You may not use, copy, decompile, disassemble, reverse engineer, modify, reproduce, create derivative works, transmit, distribute, sublicense, store in a database or retrieval system of any kind, rent or transfer the Product, or any portion thereof, in any form or by any means (including electronically or otherwise) except as expressly provided for in this License Agreement. You must reproduce the copyright notices, trademark notices, legends and logos of Syngress and its licensors that appear on the Product on the back-up copy of the Product which you are permitted to make hereunder. All rights in the Product not expressly granted herein are reserved by Syngress and its licensors.

TERM: This License Agreement is effective until terminated. It will terminate if you fail to comply with any term or condition of this License Agreement. Upon termination, you are obligated to return to Syngress the Product together with all copies thereof and to purge and destroy all copies of the Product included in any and all systems, servers and facilities.

DISCLAIMER OF WARRANTY: THE PRODUCT AND THE BACK-UP COPY OF THE PRODUCT ARE LICENSED "AS IS". SYNGRESS, ITS LICENSORS AND THE AUTHORS MAKE NO WARRANTIES, EXPRESS OR IMPLIED, AS TO RESULTS TO BE OBTAINED BY ANY PERSON OR ENTITY FROM USE OF THE PRODUCT AND/OR ANY INFORMATION OR DATA INCLUDED THEREIN. SYNGRESS, ITS LICENSORS AND THE AUTHORS MAKE NO EXPRESS OR IMPLIED WARRANTIES OF MERCHANTABILITY OR FITNESS FOR A PARTICULAR PURPOSE OR USE WITH RESPECT TO THE PRODUCT AND/OR ANY INFORMATION OR DATA INCLUDED THEREIN. IN ADDITION, SYNGRESS, ITS LICENSORS AND THE AUTHORS MAKE NO WARRANTY REGARDING THE ACCURACY, ADEQUACY OR COMPLETENESS OF THE PRODUCT AND/OR ANY INFORMATION OR DATA INCLUDED THEREIN. NEITHER SYNGRESS, ANY OF ITS LICENSORS, NOR THE AUTHORS WARRANT THAT THE FUNCTIONS CONTAINED IN THE PRODUCT WILL MEET YOUR REQUIREMENTS OR THAT THE OPERATION OF THE PRODUCT WILL BE UNINTERRUPTED OR ERROR FREE. YOU ASSUME THE ENTIRE RISK WITH RESPECT TO THE QUALITY AND PERFORMANCE OF THE PRODUCT.

LIMITED WARRANTY FOR DISC: To the original licensee only, Syngress warrants that the enclosed disc on which the Product is recorded is free from defects in materials and workmanship under normal use and service for a period of ninety (90) days from the date of purchase. In the event of a defect in the disc covered by the foregoing warranty, Syngress will replace the disc.

LIMITATION OF LIABILITY: NEITHER SYNGRESS, ITS LICENSORS NOR THE AUTHORS SHALL BE LIABLE FOR ANY INDIRECT, INCIDENTAL, SPECIAL, PUNITIVE, CONSEQUENTIAL OR SIMILAR DAMAGES, SUCH AS BUT NOT LIMITED TO, LOSS OF ANTICIPATED PROFITS OR BENEFITS, RESULTING FROM THE USE OR INABILITY TO USE THE PRODUCT EVEN IF ANY OF THEM HAS BEEN ADVISED OF THE POSSIBILITY OF SUCH DAMAGES. THIS LIMITATION OF LIABILITY SHALL APPLY TO ANY CLAIM OR CAUSE WHATSOEVER WHETHER SUCH CLAIM OR CAUSE ARISES IN

CONTRACT, TORT, OR OTHERWISE. Some states do not allow the exclusion or limitation of indirect, special or consequential damages, so the above limitation may not apply to you.

U.S. GOVERNMENT RESTRICTED RIGHTS. If the Product is acquired by or for the U.S. Government then it is provided with Restricted Rights. Use, duplication or disclosure by the U.S. Government is subject to the restrictions set forth in FAR 52.227-19. The contractor/manufacturer is Syngress Publishing, Inc. at 800 Hingham Street, Rockland, MA 02370.

GENERAL: This License Agreement constitutes the entire agreement between the parties relating to the Product. The terms of any Purchase Order shall have no effect on the terms of this License Agreement. Failure of Syngress to insist at any time on strict compliance with this License Agreement shall not constitute a waiver of any rights under this License Agreement. This License Agreement shall be construed and governed in accordance with the laws of the Commonwealth of Massachusetts. If any provision of this License Agreement is held to be contrary to law, that provision will be enforced to the maximum extent permissible and the remaining provisions will remain in full force and effect.

*If you do not agree, please return this product to the place of purchase for a refund.

Other books from Russ Rogers and Security Horizon, Inc....

Other books from Russ Rogers and Security Horizon, Inc....

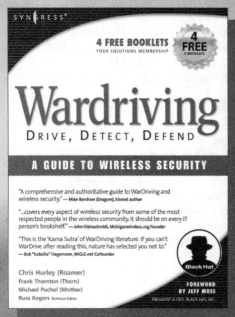

WarDriving: Drive, Detect, Defend
A Guide to Wireless Security

Chris Hurley, Russ Rogers, Frank Thornton, Michael Puchol

Wireless networks have become a way of life in the past two years. As more wireless networks are deployed the need to secure them increases. This book educates users of wireless networks as well as those who run the networks about the insecurities associated with wireless networking. This effort is called WarDriving. In order to successfully WarDrive there are hardware and software tool required. This book covers those tools, along with cost estimates and recommendations. Since there are hundreds of possible configurations that can be used for WarDriving, some of the most popular are presented to help readers decide what to buy for their own WarDriving setup.

ISBN: 1-931836-03-5

Price: $49.95 U.S. $69.95 CAN

SSCP Study Guide and DVD Training System

By Russ Rogers, et. al.

A one-of-a-kind integration of text, DVD-quality instructor led training, and Web-based exam simulation and remediation. This system gives you 100% coverage of the official International Information Systems Security Certification Consortium, Inc. (ISC)2 SSCP security domains plus test preparation software for the edge you need to pass the exam on your first try.

All seven SSCP domains are covered in full: Access Controls; Administration; Audit and Monitoring; Risk, Response and Recovery; Cryptography; Data Communications; and Malicious Code/Malware. This package includes a Study Guide, a DVD containing instructor led training, and Web-based exam simulation and remediation.

ISBN: 1-931836-80-9

Price: $59.95 US $92.95 CAN

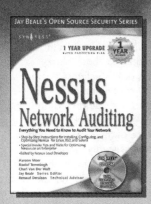
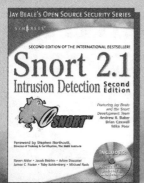

Game Console Hacking: Xbox, PlayStation, Nintendo, Atari, & Gamepark 32

Joe Grand and Albert Yarusso

In November of 1977, Atari shipped its first 400,000 Video Computer Systems. Since that time, over 1.2 billion consoles have been sold worldwide, and a large percentage of those are still hanging around as "classic systems." An avid (some would say rabid) community of video game hackers and hard-core gamers has developed around a common passion to push their consoles, and the games themselves, beyond the functionality originally intended by the manufacturers. This book is the first on the market to cover the entire range of consoles produced over the last 25 years. It provides detailed instructions on how to customize and reconfigure consoles to a wide variety of ends—from the cosmetic case modifications to the ambitious porting of Linux to the Nintendo GameCube. Platforms covered in this book include Atari, Sega, Nintendo, PlayStation, Xbox, and Game Boy.

ISBN: 1-931836-31-0
Price: $39.95 US $57.95 CAN

Wireless Hacking: Projects for Wi-Fi Enthusiasts

Lee Barken, with Matt Fanady, Debi Jones, Alan Koebrick, and Michael Mee

As the cost of wireless technology drops, the number of Wi-Fi users continues to grow. Millions of people have discovered the joy and delight of "cutting the cord." Many of those people are looking for ways to take the next step and try out some of the cutting edge techniques for building and deploying "homebrew" Wi-Fi networks, both large and small. This book shows Wi-Fi enthusiasts and consumers of Wi-Fi LANs who want to modify their Wi-Fi hardware how to build and deploy "homebrew" Wi-Fi networks, both large and small.

ISBN: 1-931836-37-X
Price: $39.95 US $57.95 CAN

SYNGRESS®